£1.50

GW01464178

Inside the Grey Box
Choosing, building and upgrading a PC

by

P D Coker

PRESS

I/O Press

First Published 1992

©I/O Press

Illustrations ©David Conrad

ISBN 1 871962 14-5

British Library Cataloguing in Publication Data
Coker,PD
    Inside the grey box : upgrading and building your PC
    I. Title
    004.16

ISBN 1-871962-14-5

All Rights Reserved. No part of this publication may be reproduced, stored in a
retrieval system, or transmitted in any form or by any means, electronic,
mechanical, photocopying, recording or
otherwise, without prior written permission.

Products mentioned within this text may be protected by trade marks, in which
case full acknowledgement is hereby given.

Although every effort has been made to ensure the correctness of the information
contained herein neither the publisher nor the author accept liability for any
omissions or errors that may remain.

Typeset by I/O Press
Printed and bound in Great Britain by Billing &Sons Ltd, Worcester

Preface

A few years ago, the idea that someone interested in computers could actually build one for him or herself without too much trouble, appeared to be a little far-fetched. I built my first computer (a Nascom 1) in 1978 and was amazed that dozens of resistors, capacitors and integrated circuits all fitted onto a board and actually produced a machine which worked. The TV and a cassette recorder were pressed into use, and I wrote some really awful programs which ran in the 1KB of usable memory which was all I could get on the board. It cost a bit over £200, took three evenings to build, and I was proud of it - every soldered joint, burnt finger and all.

I must admit to being slightly biased in favour of building my own electronic equipment where possible, and since 1978, I've built more than 50 computers of one sort or another (mostly for other people!). Until comparatively recently, most of these had to be constructed from individual components - quite a delicate and time-consuming task - and not every computer worked first time either.

The first kit for home construction of a PC-XT look- and work-alike (clone) was produced in the USA during 1984-5. It was featured as a project in the June 1985 issue of Elektor, the electronics magazine, and was available from a few sources in the U.K. either partly assembled or as a bare motherboard, into which a large number of components had to be soldered. The complete, home-built computer, with a monochrome screen, 256KB of memory and single floppy disk drive cost about £1000 to put together - considerably cheaper than a genuine IBM XT.

Since that time, both the difficulty of building a PC that works and the cost of doing so have declined dramatically. The choice of components is enormous, and a machine can be built to suit both your requirements and what you are prepared to spend. The motherboard now comes completely assembled, apart from the memory chips, and construction usually consists of assembling a series of circuit boards into a case. The only tools you need are a couple of screwdrivers, and a pair of pliers; the job has never been easier!

People build their own computers for a variety of reasons - they may need a machine with particular facilities which are not available as standard features; they might want to save money or they may just enjoy a modest challenge. Some may even want to find out just what does go on inside the anonymous-looking boxes one sees in magazines or High Street shops. The reasons for pursuing the upgrade path are equally diverse. Usually, an upgrade is called for when the existing computer cannot carry out a new task or if the breakneck speed of accessory development enables you to purchase a new peripheral or adapter that will extend your existing facilities at a price which will not cripple your bank balance.

What are you waiting for? You don't need a lot of technical expertise, merely a certain amount of manual dexterity and common sense. With the aid of this book you will be able, with the minimum of problems, to assemble a computer which should work first time. Ugrading is pretty easy, too!

Many people have, whether they like it or not, contributed at one time or another to the sum of knowledge in the following pages or to the way in which it has been treated. At one time or another, I've bothered Steve Birch, Ian Cullen, Graeme Duncan and John Parker and I'd like to thank them for their advice and, on occasion, commiserations. In particular, I should like to thank John Kilcline, of Just Computer Books, who gave me the necessary swift kick to get it done and continued to do so, as well as my wife, Rosemary and daughter, Bryony who have put up with my interest in computers for so long, without **too** many complaints.

Thanks are also due to the many colleagues and friends (who are still colleagues and friends) who unknowingly allowed me to learn while building their machines - the truth can now be told!

PD Coker   Farnborough, Kent
                                                                    March 1992

Contents

Chapter 1
Outside the grey box

This chapter discusses the way that a knowledge of the modules that make up a modern PC can help you buy, build or upgrade the machine that you need. It also introduces some of the basic distinctions between different types of PC.

The modern PC is quite unlike any other item of electronics that you will encounter. In one sense it is very complex, indeed perhaps the most complex piece of electronics you will ever buy or use, but because it is built from modules that have a very clear and understandable function, it is also simple. As long as you only want to understand and work with the PC at the module level and not down at the level of the individual chips then you can quite easily upgrade and even build an entire machine. You certainly don't need to delve into electronics at the chips and transistors level to understand the way in which a PC works enough to build one from modules. Knowing what the individual modules do, and a little of how they do it, also helps in making intelligent decisions when buying new machines, facing upgrade choices and in diagnosing and repairing a broken machine. In short it can save you money, time and frustration.

Before you start to worry about the possibility of having to buy and use a soldering iron I should say that it is very rarely that you need anything more than a screwdriver when working inside the grey box. (Not all PC boxes are actually grey but I've yet to come across a red or an orange one!) Once inside the case, nearly everything is just a matter of plugging the correct plug into the correct socket and tightening fixing screws. The only difficulties are in knowing what to do rather than in actually doing it and supplying this knowledge is exactly what this book is about!

Another worry that is worth putting to rest right at the start is the idea that opening the grey box leads you into a world that might be dangerous in some way. While it is true that many machines have warning notices about opening the case, these are more to do with invalidating warranties than anything else. The power supply inside most PCs is fully enclosed and only low voltages (5V and 12V) are present on the circuit boards. This of course isn't an excuse for or an encouragement of reckless behaviour - you do need to take precautions against damaging the machine or yourself but this basically comes down to two simple rules that are worth stating as early as possible:

» **don't** work on or inside the machine while it is switched on

» **don't** open the inner case of the power supply

It isn't likely that you would open the inner case of the power supply because to do so is a major task and there are always very visible warning notices stuck to it.

There are one or two other rules, but these can be summarised as 'know what you are doing'. Before you do anything read the relevant chapters of this book and work out exactly what you have to do - then actually doing it will be a safe and simple procedure.

A collection of modules

If you currently see a PC as a single indivisible entity then what you can do with it will be very limited. Essentially you will be restricted to buying it as a whole and selling it as a whole. If, on the other hand, you see it for what it is - a collection of modules - then your courses of action are much more flexible. You can now buy exactly the PC you want by picking the modules that make it up. If budget is a problem then you can make economies in buying modules that you can later replace with something more suitable. You can also tailor the machine to be more specialised than anything available on the market. By the same token you no longer have to dispose of a machine as a single unit. If some part of your machine is letting it down then replace just that module. Seeing the PC as a modular machine means that you are always free to upgrade without having to endure the trauma of scrapping what you have and buying new. Instead of a PC upgrade being an upheaval it becomes a process of evolution.

Repair

The same knowledge that allows you to select modules for upgrading also allows you to debug a machine that isn't working properly. By knowing what the modules do you can track down the fault to a single module and then simply replace it. This may sound like an expensive way of going about a repair but given the cost of maintenance contracts and workshop repair time it is usually the lowest cost option. We are rapidly approaching the day where the PC is, at the module level at least, a disposable commodity. In most cases the time and expertise needed to repair a malfunctioning module makes it more cost effective to buy new. There are of course exceptions to this rule, a colour monitor is usually worth having repaired rather than replacing for example, but they are rarer than you might think!

Buying, building, upgrading

It always helps to know the way in which a book is organised before you delve very deep into it. This book starts by looking at the PC as a whole. Next we take a look at each module in some detail with a chapter devoted to each one. These chapters form the core of the 'how-do-it' part of the book. If you have an existing machine that you want to upgrade then this is where you will find the information that you need. The final part of the book looks at the slightly larger problem of building your own machine from scratch. Of course this is really only a matter of putting all of the information in the earlier chapters together but there are new issues that arise in tackling the biggest upgrade possible - from nothing to a working machine!

The PC family

Before looking in detail inside the grey box you do need to know something of the types of PC that are currently available. PCs divide into two distinct groups - XT and AT designs. You could also include a third type - the PS/2 - but this is more or less exclusively an IBM model and not generally available or popular. The XT (eXtended Technology) corresponds closely to the original PC (1981) design and by today's standards it lacks power and expandability. Although it was introduced in 1984, the AT (Advanced Technology) design has been developed over the years so that it still offers the best performance available.

The other main distinction between PCs is the type of processor that they use. The processor is the chip that actually does the work of running a program and so it determines the power of the machine. To complicate matters, each type of processor also comes in a range of clock speeds - and the faster the clock speed the faster the processor will run a program. This means that it is possible to find a more powerful processor outperformed by a theoretically less powerful processor simply because its clock speed is higher. In short, processor power depends on type and clock speed.

Currently processors fall into three general families:

» the 8088 group - the 8088, 8086, NEC V20 and NEC V30 which are used only in XT class machines

» the 80286 which was the original processor used in the AT design

» the 80386 group - the 80386DX, 80386SX, 80486DX and the 80486SX - which are used in high performance AT designs.

These processors are listed in order of processing power. The 8088/86 group is the least powerful and there is a growing body of software and applications that simply will not run on XT machines. The 80826, just referred to as the 286, isn't quite in the same poor position as the 8088/86 but it already has the status of a second choice. Finally the 386 and the 486 are currently the best processors available, although the 586 is on the horizon! The important point to bear in mind is that the 386/486 family of processors is compatible in the sense that any software that runs on any 386 will run on any 486 - the only significant issue is how fast. This isn't the case, however, with the 8088/86 and the 286. The 286 has facilities that the 8088/86 doesn't have and the 386 family has even more sophisticated features, that neither the 8088/86 nor the 286 have. What this means in practice is that a program written to work on a basic 8088/86 XT will work on any other PC, but there are programs that will work **only** on a 286 or 386 AT machine and even some that demand at least a 386.

This is an admittedly complicated situation but its practical consequences are fairly straightforward:

» you should aim for at least a 386 based PC/AT because currently it is the only type of machine that can run all of the available software.

Processor details

If you are happy with the broad outline of the PC processor family then it is time to look a little closer at some of the differences. One of the most important is the size of the data bus that the processor uses. This sounds very technical but all it concerns is the size of the largest chunk of data that a processor can work with in one go. A single character of text corresponds to 8 bits and the earliest processors used in personal computers were 8-bit processors and so could deal with a single character at one time. The first processor used in the PC, the 8088, was slightly more advanced than this in that it could work internally with 16 bits at a time but still dealt with the outside world 8 bits at a time. The later 8086 worked both internally and externally with 16 bits at a time and it formed the basis for many improved or so-called Turbo XT designs. It isn't strictly true that a 16-bit processor will be twice as fast as an 8-bit processor because there are other factors to consider - for example, a program may only require the processor to manipulate data one character at a time! However, it is clear that a 16-bit processor will be potentially more powerful than an 8-bit processor.

The 286 is a 16-bit processor and so this could handle two characters at the same time. It may sound as though the 286 was little better than the 8086 but it could work with much more memory 16MegaBytes (MB) compared to the 8088/6's limit of 1MB, and it had a more sophisticated design.

The 386 was originally designed to be a 32-bit i.e. four-character, processor but the situation here is a little bit more complicated. The 386DX is a full 32-bit processor but the 386SX is a cut down version of the processor, identical to the DX except that it only works with the outside world in 16-bit chunks. This makes machines based on the 386SX processor slightly cheaper and slightly less powerful.

Now we come to the 486, which introduces yet another difference between processors - their ability to do arithmetic. Processors are generally very poor at performing arithmetic - they do it but not very quickly. To speed up arithmetic it is possible to fit an arithmetic co-processor which is specially designed to do nothing else but arithmetic, but to do it very fast. Each processor has its corresponding arithmetic co-processor designated by changing the final digit in the serial number to a 7. Thus the 8086 has the 8087, the 286 has the 287 and the 386 has the 387 in both DX and SX versions. The only exception to this rule is the 486 because it has its numeric co-processor built into it on the same chip. In other words the 486 is much like a 386 plus a 387 all bundled together in one package. In addition to this the 486 is also faster than the equivalent 386+387 combination - especially when it comes to arithmetic.

If you are following the pattern you might expect the 486SX to be a cut down version of the 486 so that it works in 16-bit chunks with the outside world - a sort of 386SX plus 387SX in one package. It isn't. It is a cut down version of the 486 but what has been left out is the numeric co-processor and it is still a full 32-bit processor in every respect. (You can add a numeric co-processor to the 486SX by adding a 487SX but this is just a full 486DX chip in disguise.)

It can be difficult to follow the descriptions of the processor types when you first encounter them because of the range of serial numbers that are used. The following table should help summarise the position - (1GB =1GigaByte =1000 MB)

	Bits internal/ external	Max Memory	Co-processor	Type of machine
8088	16/8	1MB	8087	XT
8086	16/16	1MB	8087	XT
80286	16/16	16MB	80287	AT
80386DX	32/32	4GB	80387DX	AT
80386SX	32/16	16MB	80387SX	AT
80486DX	32/32	4GB	built in	AT
80486SX	32/32	4GB	80487SX	AT

XT or ISA bus

As already mentioned, the main difference between the XT and AT designs is the type of processor used in each - the 8088/86 in the XT and the 286/386/486 used in the AT. As well as this important difference there is also a difference in the type of add-on boards used. The XT design makes use of a connector that accepts 8-bit (XT) add-on cards. The AT design uses a connector that accepts 16-bit ISA (Industry Standard Adapter) cards and the original 8-bit cards. This is another reason to prefer the AT design because it is not only faster but in most cases it can make use of the older 8-bit XT cards as well. (Notice that the one major exception to this compatibility rule are XT disk controller cards which generally only work in XT machines - see Chapter 7 for more details.) The difference between the XT and ISA adapter cards and their associated bus - i.e. the connectors into which they are plugged is discussed more fully in Chapter 4.

Clock speeds

The hierarchy of processor types is fairly clear and roughly corresponds to 'the bigger the number the more powerful the processor'. There is one complicating factor in the way that the processor clock speed governs actual performance. Each processor is available at a range of clock speeds and at the time of writing these are:

```
                          MHz
8088/86      4.77<------>12
80286            8 <--------->16
80386SX              16 <--------------->33
80386DX                20<--------------->40
80486DX                  25<----------------->50
80486SX              20<-------->33
```
Of course higher speed processors are becoming available all the time and this situation is likely to change.

When you take into account the comparative powers of the processors and the clock speeds that are available you arrive at a hierarchy something like that shown in Figure 1.1

Buying advice

The 486DX is likely to be an expensive item for some time since motherboards currently retail (January 1992) for about £600 - £1000, compared with £250 - £350 for a fast 80386 - or even £50 for an 8088 XT-Turbo! The ranking in terms of power and price is very definitely - 8088/86, 80286, 80386SX, 80386DX, 80486SX and 80486DX. The only confusing factor is the introduction of the 486SX which could challenge the 386DX's position in the hierarchy because it could offer the same or better performance for a lower price. At the time of writing 486SX motherboards were available for for about £450 - £550.

It is also clear that the XT design is being phased out very rapidly as is the AT/286. The reason for this is that there is simply too much software that the XT class of machine cannot run and the 286 is so close in price to the 386SX that there is hardly any reason not to buy the more versatile 386SX. Of course this phasing-out also means that there is plenty of scope for bargains as people upgrade to the 386 family.

If you are considering building your own machine then it is advisable to regard the 386SX as the minimum desirable. If you are absolutely convinced that you will never want to run any of the other advanced software that is appearing daily, in particular Windows, then you can get almost the same performance from a 286. Basic XT machines have only one advantage and that's their price! If you are considering upgrading an existing machine then it is possible in many cases to change the motherboard, so altering the class of the machine from an XT to an AT or from a 286/AT to a 386/AT.

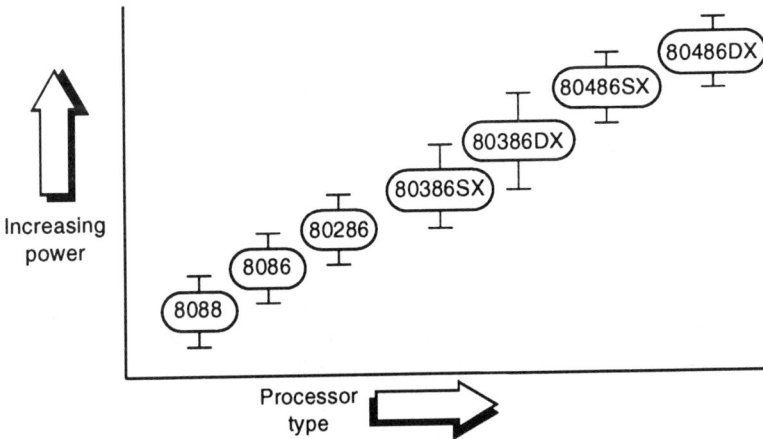

Figure 1.1
The hierarchy of machines

Key points

» The modern PC is a modular machine and there are many advantages to understanding how it works at this level.

» There is a hierarchy of price and performance in today's PC family.

» Machines fall into two general classes XT and AT. The XT machines are less powerful but very cheap.

» XTs can be based on the 8088 processor or the slightly faster 8086.

» ATs can be based on the 286, 386SX, 386DX, or the 486DX - listed in order of power. The new 486SX is intermediate in power between a 386DX and the 486DX.

» If possible, you should consider a 386SX as the minimum requirement for a new machine or upgrade. If cost doesn't permit this then a 286 can be almost as good in many applications. The only advantage of a basic XT is its low price.

» Many XTs can be upgraded to the AT standard and AT/286s can be upgraded to be AT/386 machines by changing the motherboard, but the possibility and economics of doing this deserve further study.

Chapter 2
The anatomy of a machine

It is the fact that all PCs have a modular design that means that it is possible to contemplate upgrading a system or building one from scratch. In this chapter the basic modules that make up a machine are described.

Although there are great differences between PCs they are all made up of the same basic modules. It is this modularity that makes it possible for you to build, upgrade and even repair your own machine without having to worry about the detailed electronics. Before moving on to look at each of the modules in detail, it is worth gaining an overall idea of the way that they fit together to make up a complete machine.

The general layout

If you already have a PC then it might be helpful if you remove its outer cover and see if you can identify each of the modules described in the following sections. (If you find that you need help in opening the case then see *Getting inside* in Chapter 6.)

The inside of a machine can look very intimidating at first but you can quickly learn to recognise the major components. After a while it even begins to look familiar and friendly. Inside the box you will find a motherboard containing the 'fixed' components of the system and plugged into the motherboard you will find a number of adapter boards

Adapter cards - video, disk controller,
printer port, serial port, etc..

Power supply

Motherboard

Memory

Disk drives

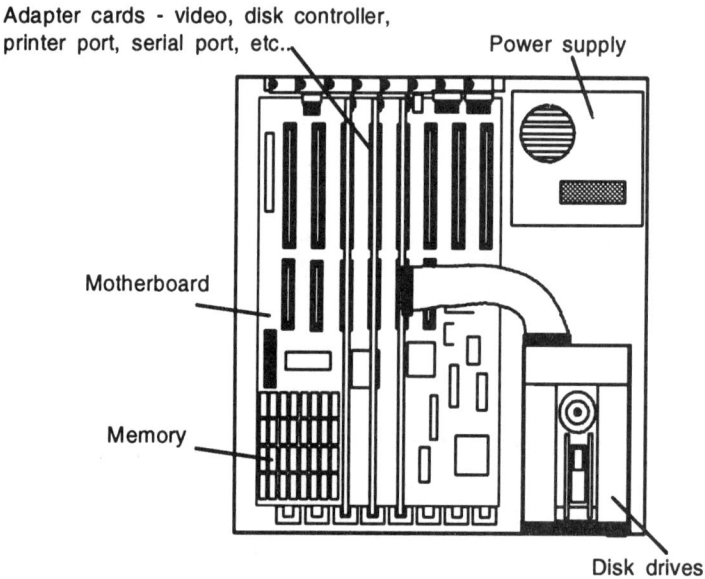

Figure 2.1
The parts of a system

which represent the configurable elements of the system. A typical system will have, in addition to the motherboard, memory, a video display and a range of other interface cards, a power supply and disk drives - see Figure 2.1. The most confusing part of any system is likely to be the number of different cables running to all parts of the machine. You may also find that the inside of the case is so cramped that you cannot see all of the modules.

The motherboard

A basic PC consists of a large circuit board, the motherboard or mainboard, containing the microprocessor and its associated integrated circuits, as well as some memory, with a number of connectors, sockets and slots to take other cards, keyboard and power supply. Depending upon the type of board, there may be a series of small switches or pins which can be connected together using a special plug, in order to change

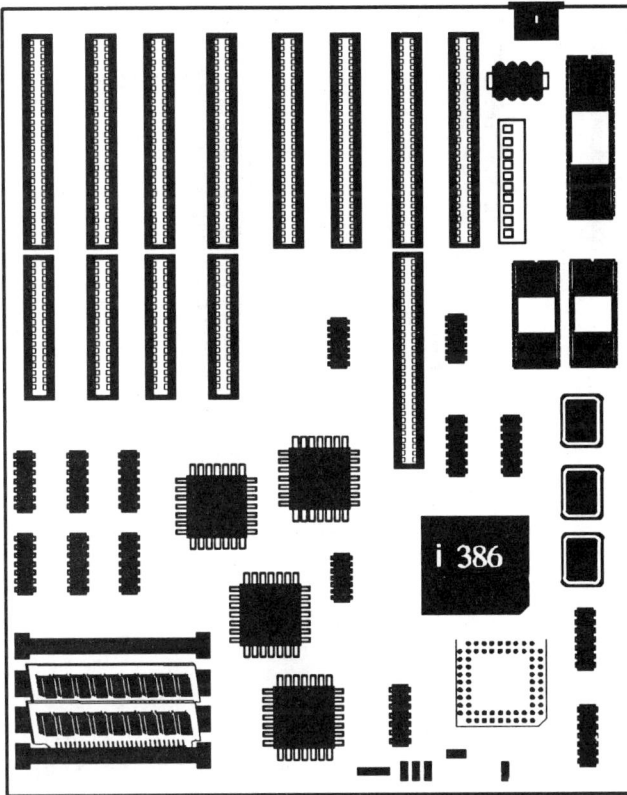

Figure 2.2
Typical motherboard

the machine's configuration. There is always a series of small 2, 4 and 5-pin connectors to which various indicator lights, a small loudspeaker and sundry other switches are attached. Clearly the motherboard is the most important module in the PC, determining the type and ultimate power of the machine.

The most prominent feature of any motherboard is the row of expansion connectors along the rear of the board. In the case of XT motherboards this takes the form of a singe row of connectors. AT motherboards have an extra smaller connector which is used to increase the size of the data bus from 8 to 16 bits. Adapter cards come in either 8-bit XT or 16-bit

Original XT
connector

AT extension
connector

Non-standard 386/486
extension

8 bit XT

16 bit AT

32 bit 386 memory expansion

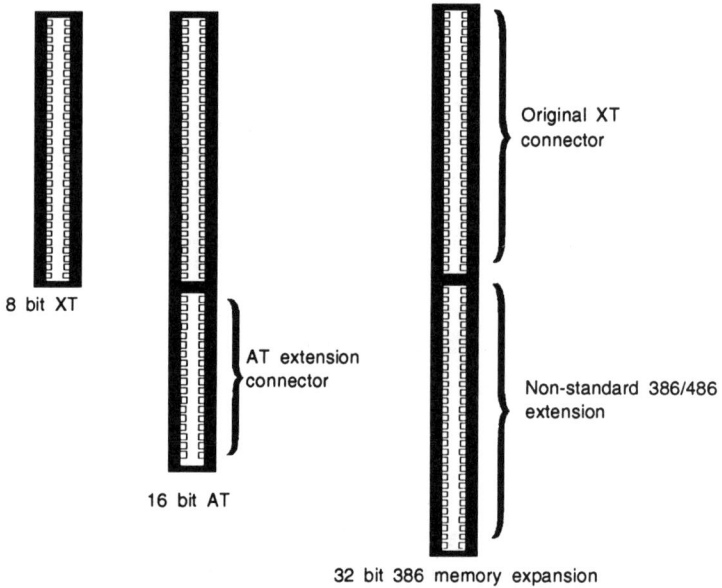

Figure 2.3
Expansion connectors

AT forms. The rear connector on an AT motherboard is functionally the same as the single connector on an XT design. In nearly all cases, the notable exception being hard disk controllers, you can plug an 8-bit adapter card into the large socket of an AT expansion connector. Notice that a 16-bit adapter should be faster than an equivalent 8-bit version.

Some 386/486 machines have a special longer slot in one position and this is usually dedicated for the attachment of an additional fast-access memory card, see Figure 2.3.

Some older AT motherboards are quite a lot larger and need a big case to accommodate them. Newer AT motherboards are the same size as the older XT and some are even smaller - there are some that are less than two-thirds the size of the standard XT. Some manufacturers call their AT type boards 'Baby AT size' to distinguish them from the older, larger types.

The case

The whole system is contained in a case (preferably made of steel to reduce interference with radio and TV) together with a power supply which will convert the mains voltage to several different voltages which are required by the computer. The case has a series of openings at the rear and these are used to allow adapter cards to present connectors to the outside world - the card plugs into the slot on the motherboard and the metal mounting plate is screwed onto the back support. On the same side of the case, you will find a circular hole, through which a 5-pin round (DIN) plug can be poked - this connects the keyboard to the motherboard.

There are a number of different types of case, for example the up-market tower and mini-tower varieties and conventional desktop boxes whose lids either slide off or hinge up. Which type is best for you depends on a variety of factors. Floor standing cases have the advantage of freeing desk space and are generally more roomy. Of the desktop models I prefer the hinged top type since it is easier to get into if something needs changing. One of the most important differences is the number of disk drive mounting bays. Tower cases usually provide space for six or more disk drive sized units to be mounted internally whereas desktop cases are limited to around four.

Figure 2.4
The three types of case

Power supplies

PCs need a lot of high quality power, particularly if they contain a lot of memory, adapter cards and a hard disk. The early PC had an only just adequate 65 watt power supply, upgraded to a 135 watt supply in the later XT. PC-ATs tend to need even more power, so a 200 or even 230 watt power supply is needed to allow for any additional expansion.

Modern power supplies tend to be small and efficient and are always equipped with a cooling fan. Their purpose is to convert the mains voltage to much lower voltages used by the motherboard and disk drives, as well as the adapter cards. The monitor usually plugs into its own mains power socket on the power supply and is controlled by the main power switch on the computer.

Although there is no standard for power supplies most will fit into any normal sized case and they generally use the same fitting. In most situations is it easier and cheaper to replace a damaged power supply with a new one.

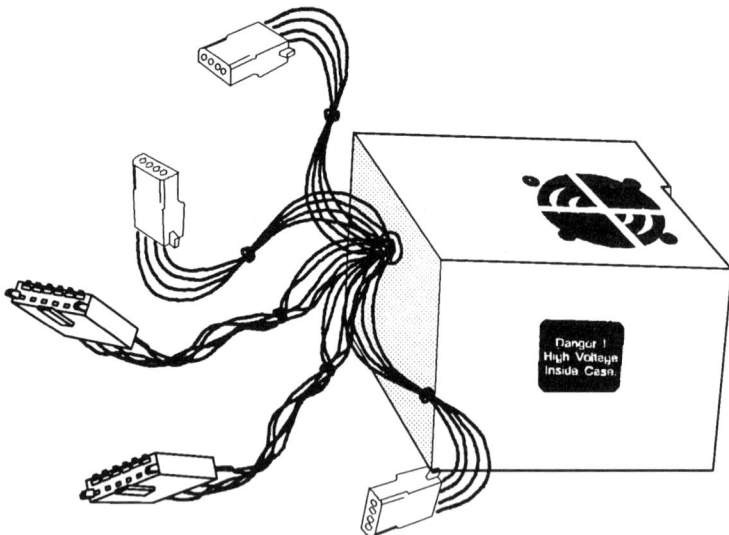

Figure 2.5
A typical power supply

Keyboards

Early PCs used a keyboard with 84 keys, including a series of ten special function keys and a set of dual purpose number/cursor control keys. More modern keyboards have 102 keys, a separate set of cursor control keys and a row of 12 function keys above the main keyboard area. Which type of keyboard you need depends on how well you type and what you spend most of your time working on. The 102 key keyboard has the advantage of a separate numeric keypad but many users claim that the function keys at the left-hand side of the keyboard is the best layout.

It is important to realise that XT and AT motherboards use a different method of connecting the keyboard. This means that a keyboard designed to work exclusively with an XT will not work with an AT. There are switchable AT/XT keyboards that can be used with either type of machine and there are even auto sensing keyboards that will automatically set themselves to work with whichever type of motherboard they are connected to. On no account should you ever attempt to use a non-switchable XT keyboard with an AT machine or vice versa.

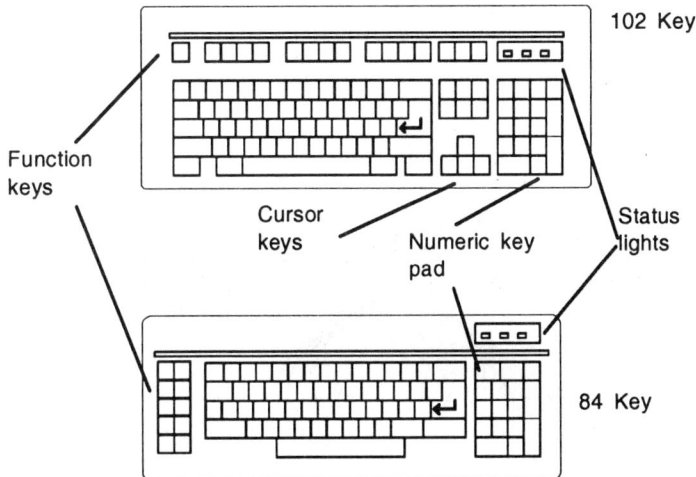

Figure 2.6
Keyboards

Memory

All machines have memory or RAM (Random Access Memory) but it can be difficult to spot. Nearly all motherboards have at least some memory fitted directly. Usually one area of the motherboard is dedicated to holding the RAM chips. This can usually be identified from the large number of other chips and electronics on the board by its regularity - there are rows of the same type of device.

Memory comes in two types of packaging. The older types are generally black plastic packages called DILs (Dual In-Line), looking like the archetypal integrated circuit. They have 16, 18 or 20 pins arranged on each side and are plugged into sockets.

More recently, several small versions of these memory chips have been mounted onto miniature circuit boards and these fit into special slots or rows of sockets. These come in two forms - SIPs - which have lots of small pins along one edge, and SIMMs, which don't - instead, they have an edge connector, similar to the sort of connectors on the lower sides of adapter cards. SIP is an acronym for Single In-line Package and SIMM means Single In-line Memory Module - see Figure 2.7 for details of their appearance.

DIL chip and socket

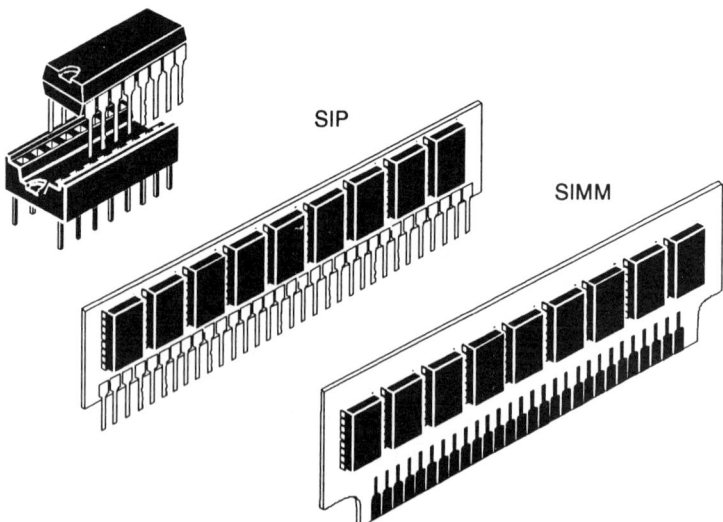

Figure 2.7
Memory devices

As well as memory on the motherboard you will also find machines that have extra memory fitted using adapter cards. As in the case of motherboard memory the actual devices used on the adapter card can be DIL, SIP or SIMM.

The fastest machines also use a small quantity of memory as a cache to speed up the rate at which data can be transferred from the main memory to the processor. This is usually installed on the motherboard and is such a small amount that it often only involves the use of four or so chips.

Data storage

As well as RAM memory all machines have some form of permanent data storage in the form of disk drives. Many beginners are confused by the difference between RAM and disk storage. The difference is quite simple, you can only run a program when it is in RAM but it has to be stored on disk when you are not running it because there isn't space to hold everything with which you want to work in RAM. You can also add the fact that RAM memory forgets everything it contains when you switch the machine off but a disk does not.

Most machines need at least one floppy disk drive - if only as a means of installing programs. Currently there are two standard types in use - the 5.25" and the 3.5". Apart from the difference in overall size there is little difference in the maximum amount of data that you can store on each. However, the 3.5" drive is the preferred type because it is more robust and reliable. The only problem is that the older 5.25" standard is still often used to distribute software and many existing computers only possess this size of drive. This makes it necessary to have both types of drive on a machine if you want to read every diskette that might come your way!

The most important point to understand about disk systems is that they are generally composed of two parts - the disk drive and the disk controller. The drive is the physical mechanism and electronics that reads and writes the disk. The controller is usually an adapter card that allows the PC to work with the drive. Some motherboards have a floppy

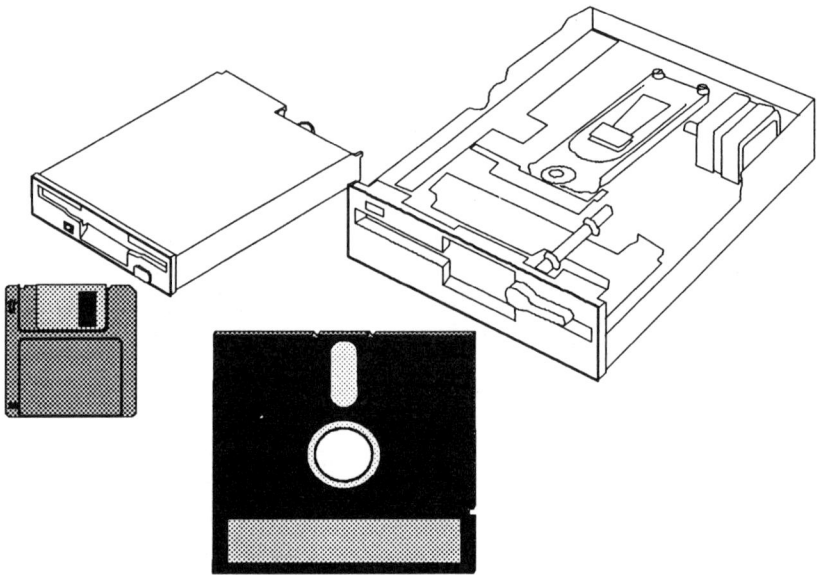

Figure 2.8
3.5" and 5.25" drives and their diskettes

disk controller built in and in this case it looks as if there isn't a controller - but it's still there!

The second form of disk drive is the hard disk or Winchester. This is much faster than a floppy, stores a much larger quantity of data but you cannot remove the magnetic disk that the data is stored on. The data is actually stored on rigid disks of magnetic material - hence 'hard disk'. The disks are enclosed in a dust free atmosphere (a small box) and rotate very fast; the information is written to and read from the disks by means of very small magnetic heads which move very precisely across the surface of the rotating disk, but do not touch it. Instead they fly a very tiny distance above the surface in the wind caused by the rapidly spinning disks.

The hard disk is connected to another controller card by two (or occasionally just one) ribbon cables. In some machines, the hard and floppy disk controllers are combined into one card. Both floppy and hard disk drives require power and this is supplied by the power unit

Controller card
and cables

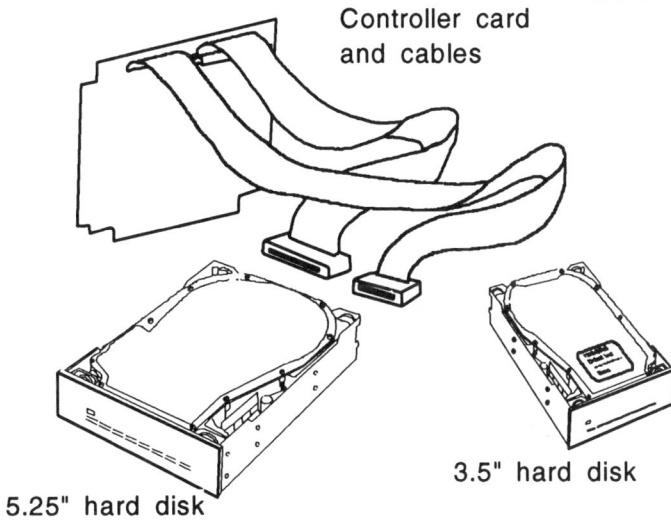

Figure 2.9
Hard disk drives

via special cables. Hard disks, despite their name, are quite delicate and don't like being bumped or banged - this can cause the magnetic pickup heads to scrape the surface of the disks and permanent damage may result.

Hard disks come in two standard sizes, 5.25" and 3.5". The main reason for this is so that hard disks can be fitted into the same space used by a floppy disk. Disks can also vary in their height. Today full height drives are rare and most are half height models.

Some hard disks are small enough to be mounted on their own controller card and these are referred to as hard cards. Opinions on hard cards vary. They can be unreliable due to overheating if they are mounted away from the cooling fan but they are undeniably easy to fit as an upgrade. Until comparatively recently, it wasn't possible to put a typical hard card in an AT machine and obtain a good performance from it, but now you can obtain genuine 16-bit hard cards with very good performance. Although they are known as 1.5 slot types, most will need space equivalent to 2 slots on your expansion bus but it is often possible to use a short card in the 0.5 slot). One particular model only takes up one slot by using an exceptionally thin disk drive but still provides 105 MB!

The display

Most machines make use of a colour or monochrome display. The complete display system is composed of two parts - the video adapter card and the monitor. In general you have to match the monitor to the display adapter or in some cases settle for a lower performance. The range of choices for an adapter/monitor combination is the widest of all the modules that make up a PC.

Display systems differ in their resolution - i.e. the number of dots or pixels that can display horizontally and vertically and the maximum number of colours that they can display at one time. To confuse matters even more each display adapter is generally capable of working in any of a number of different display modes each of which offers a particular resolution and number of colours. Which of these display modes can actually be used depends on the type of monitor to which the display adapter is connected.

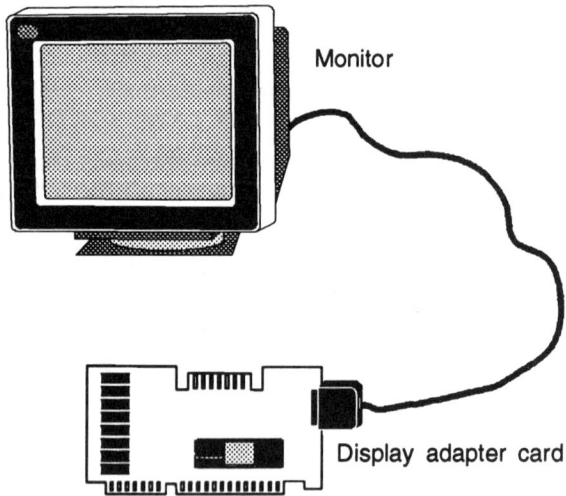

Monitor

Display adapter card

Figure 2.10
Display adapter and monitor

A minor difference is whether or not the monitor's power lead is connected to the auxiliary mains socket on the back of the machine or plugged into a separate socket. In most cases it is better to have the monitor connected to the machine because then it is switched on and off with the main machine. Notice that this arrangement doesn't make any demands on the power supply as the auxiliary mains socket is simply connected directly to the mains via the power switch. The only reason for having the monitor connected separately is to be able to switch it on first so that it is ready when the main part of the machine is switched on and can display any messages given by the POST (Power-On Self Test) routine.

Parallel and serial ports

To enable a printer to be connected, most PCs have at least one parallel port. This is often included as part of another adapter card for example, the display adapter. This can make it difficult to ensure that a machine retains a parallel port during an upgrade.

Many PCs contain a card which is often described as a serial port. This enables data to be sent to or received from another computer or similar piece of machinery which has a serial interface. The card converts data from the computer into a form where it is sent sequentially, rather than in parallel as happens with the printer port. In fact, some printers can only accept data from serial ports which have to be set up so that they will recognise each other. A serial port is also used to connect a mouse (a pointing device used instead of the cursor keys in many programs) and sometimes with a modem - a communications device which enables computers to communicate via the telephone system.

Other adapters

A number of cards are available for special purposes, such as one which allows a mouse to be run from the system bus rather than the serial port, or another which will enable an optical scanner to access the data bus directly. Electrical and electronic data acquisition may be carried out using devices which attach to cards which have an IEEE interface, while others can take a voltage and convert it from its analogue form to a digital equivalent which the computer can deal with. Additional memory for use by programs which recognise it can be added using appropriate memory expansion cards and there are even special cards which plug into a PC which add a faster and more sophisticated processor and improve the performance of the original machine by a significant amount. These accelerator cards can be purchased for almost all XT and AT/286 machines but they tend to be expensive - it's often almost as cheap to buy a new motherboard.

Multi-function cards

These are becoming more popular since they combine the abilities of two or more cards into one, with a saving in expansion slots. Examples dealt with earlier include certain types of video card and the combined floppy and hard disk controllers used in AT machines. The commonest are those in which a parallel printer port and two serial ports are combined, sometimes with a games port into which you can plug a pair of joysticks. The problem with multi-function card upgrades is finding one that doesn't supply more than you need or duplicates existing adapter boards.

Motherboards with built-in facilities

Some manufacturers are producing what are known as planar motherboards which, in order to save costs on a complete system, include such items as serial ports, printer port, a built-in floppy disk controller or specific video facilities as part of the circuitry. My personal view is that they are undesirable since you cannot choose to use a different type of controller without disabling the 'on-board' facility and this is sometimes easier said than done. In other words, it reduces the modularity of the overall machine that we are using to such good effect.

A good example of this approach is that of the Amstrad PC1512 whose on-board floppy controller and video circuitry could not readily be disabled in order to use higher performance cards. Another snag is that if one of these additional facilities goes wrong, the entire motherboard has to be replaced or repaired. What you might gain in terms of initial cost, and the ultimate size of your system, may be more than outweighed by the cost of replacement or repair and the time you will be without your system. The advantage of the less sophisticated standard motherboards or interface cards is that they are widely available at reasonable prices, if you need to replace them.

Key points

» The PC is a modular machine with the motherboard providing the base into which other adapter cards can be added.

» The facilities that the motherboard provides vary according to the type of machine and the exact design, but at a minimum it holds the processor, a large chunk of the system memory and slots for the adapter cards.

» The type of case that you choose governs the ease of access and the number of devices, such as disk drives, that can be installed.

» Memory can be fitted to a machine in a number of different ways including directly on the motherboard or by using a separate adapter card.

» A disk storage system is composed of two parts - the drive and a controller card. Floppy disk drives come in two main types 3.5" and 5.25". Hard disks are faster than floppy drives and can store larger amounts of data. These also come in 3.5" and 5.25" types to enable them to fit into the same mounting bays as the standard floppy drives.

» The video system is composed of a monitor and a graphics or display adapter card. The overall capabilities of the display depends on both.

» Other adapter cards include serial and parallel ports, mouse interfaces etc.

» The trend is towards including more functions on a single adapter card or even integrated onto the motherboard.

Chapter 3
What machine do I need?

Following a brief look at the type of machines and components that are available, this chapter examines the factors that govern the type of machine that you need.

If money is no object then the selection of a suitable machine or configuration is easy. There is very rarely any penalty other than financial from choosing a more powerful machine than you really need. In reality, there is a need to match the machine to its proposed task.

The most important questions to answer are:

» Do I want a fast machine or will a slower machine be adequate for all my foreseeable needs?

» Do I need a hard disk and, if so, of what capacity and performance?

» Do I need colour or will monochrome do?

Let's look at each of these in turn. Many of the issues discussed involve some forward reference to later chapters to understand the fine detail but at this stage you should only be concerned with making broad choices about the type of machine that you need.

Fast or slow machine?

This can be a difficult choice but it must be made. If you just want a machine for word processing or hobby use, then a not quite bottom of the range XT-Turbo might be the type to go for. This would be fast enough for everything except graphics-intensive applications such as games.

The average XT - Turbo motherboard and 1 MB of RAM would cost about £75, and a 12 MHz AT (286) motherboard with the same amount of memory would be about £10 - £20 more expensive; the additional cost of the AT hard/floppy disk controller means that an AT need cost you only £50 - £60 more than an XT at current (March 1992) prices. This is certainly worth thinking about if there is any chance that you could use the extra facilities of the AT. As time goes on there is a very good chance that XT machines will be more or less completely phased out. This suggests that there might be opportunities for even lower prices as manufacturers attempt to clear their old stock.

In most cases it is reasonable to consider a 286/AT system the starting point for deciding which machine you need. The reason is that the 286 is much more powerful than the XT and the cost differential is very slight. As with the XT class of machines, the 286/AT is likely to be phased out in favour of the 386SX, again providing the possibility of one-off bargains.

As long as funds allow, you should try to buy at least a 386SX machine. If you plan to run Windows or any multi-tasking system then not only is a 386 machine desirable, it is essential. Desktop Publishing (DTP) or Computer-aided Design (CAD), with one of the more sophisticated packages, need at least the power of an 80286, or better still the 80386, to work at a reasonable rate on all but the most trivial tasks. When it comes to choosing between the various machines based on the 80386/486 chip, then the only differences are the speed at which the software runs with the hierarchy (from lowest to highest) being 386SX, 386DX, 486SX and 486DX both in relation to speed and price.

Buying a 386/486 machine will ensure that you can at least run all of the advanced software that is available today and that which will be produced in the near future. You can never guard against obsolescence when buying a computer but there is already software that will not run on XT or AT 286 systems and so a 386/486 system is sure to have a longer life span. Of course this isn't to say that an XT machine cannot be successfully used with software that was originally developed for them. You don't need a 386 system to run WordStar 4 or 5 for example, and as long as you are sure of the application for which the machine will be used and the application software with which it will be used, then you don't necessarily need a state-of-the-art machine.

Once you have decided upon the general class of machine that you need the next step is to select among the different offerings in that class. For example, you may have decided on a full 386DX but there are a large number of different design factors that affect a 386DX's performance and these also affect the total cost. However, these are minor influences compared with the choice of the general class of the machine both in terms of performance and price and so they can be treated as "fine tuning" your selection, and will be discussed in the next chapter.

Hard disks

The best answer to "Do I need a hard disk?" is "Yes"! A machine with only floppy drives may have the speed to run advanced programs but the constant swapping of diskettes will slow you down to the point where you don't want to run anything but the simplest. A hard disk speeds up access to programs and data. It is so useful that once you have used a system with one you can never contemplate going back to a floppy-only machine. Fortunately, prices of hard disks are falling all the time as larger and larger capacity drives are introduced at the top end of the market.

The size of drive that you need depends on the type and number of applications programs you are planning to run, and to some extent on the type of machine. The size of applications packages varies greatly, with older programs designed to work on XT machines taking 1 to

2MB, and newer packages needing anything from 4 to 16MB. This makes it quite difficult to estimate the size of drive that you need. The simplest rule is always to buy the biggest drive that you can afford! The other side of this rule is that no matter how big a drive you buy you will run out of space at some time in the near future! The reason why you always run out of space on a hard disk is simply that users tend not to delete files unless they are forced to and so the drive slowly but surely fills up. The most that can be said is that the size of hard disk you need is one that only requires you to clear space at reasonable intervals.

It is possible to give some guidelines on disk capacities. If you are running MS-DOS, a word processor and a spreadsheet then the range of capacities that you should consider is from 20MB to 40MB. If you are going to be working with a database then you should estimate the size of the data file by multiplying the size of each record in characters by the total number of records. If you divide by 1024 this gives you the number of KB the data file will need and the disk drive that you need should be at least twice this size to allow for a backup copy to be stored.

If you are planning to run Windows, then the recommended size of drive increases considerably. Windows applications are greedy and can take anything from 5 to 15MB of disk space per application. Also, the many ancillary files such as fonts and bitmapped images take a great deal of space. You can run Windows using a 40MB drive quite successfully as long as you only want to run a word processor and spreadsheet. If you are interested in DTP or graphics packages then 65MB to 100MB is to be recommended.

Generally speaking, installing a drive of 32MB or less on a machine is pretty straightforward; over this limit, with versions of PC-DOS or MS-DOS before 4.0, it involves 'splitting' the drive into two or more sections, known as partitions. If you are planning to install a drive over 32MB then it is worth considering using MS-DOS 5 or DR-DOS 6 which make large hard disks as simple to set up and use as small hard disks.

The technical details of hard disks are discussed more fully in Chapter 7 but it is worth making some simple points here. When it comes to the speed of a hard disk, it has to be admitted that a fast hard disk can make as much difference as a fast processor. There are two parameters that govern how fast a hard disk works - access time and data transfer rate. Access time is usually quoted in ms (milli-seconds) with 65ms being very slow, 25ms being average and down to 16ms or better being very fast. The faster the access time the more expensive the drive. Data transfer rate is more dependent on the type of drive and drive controller card used. Of the standard types of drive, MFM-ST506, RLL-ST506, SCSI, ESDI and IDE, (see Chapter 7) there is a great deal of overlap in performance but generally MFM is the slowest, with RLL slightly faster. The remaining three, SCSI, ESDI and IDE, turn in very similar performance figures - even though in theory SCSI has the potential to be very much faster than it is in practice. Currently it isn't the case that a higher transfer rate necessarily involves a higher price. Many low cost IDE drives offer higher transfer rates than sophisticated SCSI and ESDI drives!

One factor that is not generally realised is that you cannot use any disk drive with any type of machine. XTs are particularly restricted in that they can only use ST506 and SCSI drives. AT machines can be set up for drives over a wide range of capacities but even here you can encounter difficulties. In other words, once you have decided on the motherboard that you are going to use, you may not have a completely free choice of disk drives.

Which graphics?

The selection of which type of graphics you need involves choosing the type of graphics card and monitor. As in the case of hard disks many of the details of graphics cards and monitors are described in more detail later (in Chapter 8). However, it is worth summarising the potential choices:

» MDA - Monochrome Display Adapter - 80x25 line text only

» HGA - Hercules Graphics Adapter - 720x348 monochrome

» CGA - Colour Graphics Adapter - 640x200 2/4 colours

» EGA - Enhanced Graphics Adapter - 640x 350 64 colours

» VGA - Versatile Graphics Array - 640x480 256 colours

» SVGA - SuperVGA - 1024x768 256 colours

Notice that SVGA includes all of the VGA modes and VGA includes all of the EGA modes. Both VGA and EGA can work in CGA and MDA modes. There are also some other graphics adapters - such as TIGA, 8514/A and XGA - that work at even higher resolution or offer other performance improvements but these are expensive and specialised.

VGA graphics are the current standard and you should aim to buy at least a VGA card that can be upgraded at a later date to Super-VGA (SVGA). The only reason for buying older CGA or EGA cards is their low cost. If you don't want graphics, then a text only MDA card is remarkably cheap - if you can find one. If you only want monochrome graphics Hercules compatible graphics cards are almost as cheap.

If you are planning to buy a graphics card now and upgrade to something better at a later date, then it is important to realise that a monitor suitable for MDA text or Hercules graphics will not work with CGA, EGA or VGA and cannot be modified to do so. Equally, colour CGA or EGA monitors cannot be made to work with VGA. In short, a text or MDA monochrome monitor will only work with an MDA or Hercules card; a CGA colour monitor will only work with a CGA card; an EGA monochrome or colour monitor will only work with an EGA card and none of them can be upgraded to work with any other graphics standard, especially VGA. You also need to be aware of the fact that there are some older low resolution VGA monitors that will not work at the highest VGA resolutions.

The most sensible upgrade route is to buy a VGA graphics card. If you cannot afford a colour monitor buy a VGA monochrome monitor which can later be replaced by a VGA colour monitor if you discover that the applications you run on your machine require, or would benefit from, colour.

As Hercules, CGA and EGA have all been superseded by the VGA standard, it is possible to find many low-priced CGA and EGA cards and monitors. Unless you have a very undemanding application it is advisable to steer well clear of CGA graphics, no matter what the price. This is because the resolution of a CGA monitor is so poor that you run the risk of straining your eyesight if you work with one for any length of time. EGA, on the other hand, might prove a reasonable choice at the right price and for the right application.

Of course, if you are planning on using a CAD package or intensive graphics then you would benefit from a resolution even higher than SVGA. Unfortunately, the cost of monitors and display cards with performances better than SVGA are disproportionately higher. At the time of writing the cost of a monitor increases in reasonable steps with its specification until you move beyond SVGA when the price leaps to over £1000 for the monitor. There are also very few well accepted standards beyond SVGA and this makes buying any high performance graphics system something of a risk.

If you are planning to use Windows, then it is worth mentioning that the resolution not only affects the quality of the image presented, but the amount that you can see at one time. A lower resolution display usually involves scrolling to see parts of the image currently off the screen. To see the difference in resolutions offered by CGA, EGA, VGA and SVGA you can look at the screen dumps overleaf which give a reasonable impression of the differences.

It's worthwhile bearing in mind that monochrome monitors potentially offer better resolution (sharpness) than colour monitors since they do not have a matrix of coloured dots on screen; the screen has a uniform, all-over coating of a single-colour phosphor. As a result, many users actually find monochrome monitors less fatiguing to work with for text applications.

If you decide that you need colour, especially high resolution colour, then there are a few extra factors that you need to take into account before selecting the exact system that you are going to buy. The most important of these is the refresh rate, i.e. the number of complete images displayed per second. The standard refresh rate for VGA displays is 50Hz, i.e. 50 images per second, which produces a more or less steady image. Some users find 50Hz uncomfortable in bright light and so you

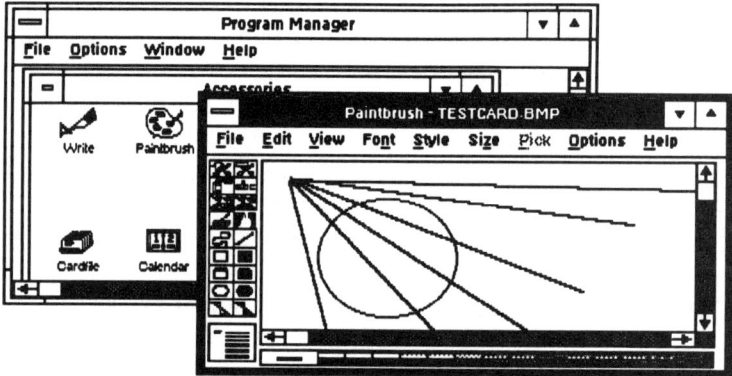

CGA 640x200

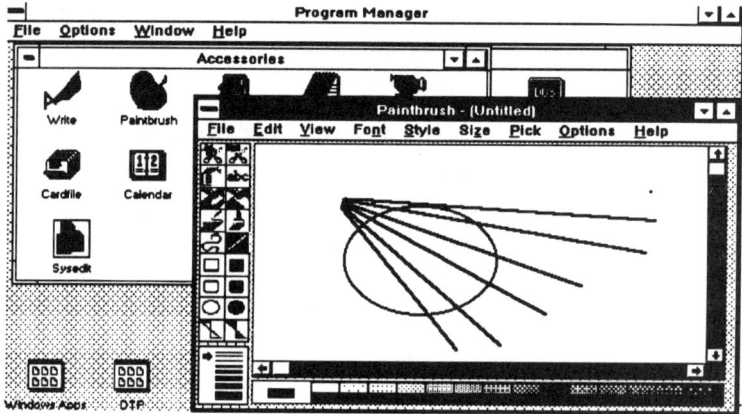

EGA 640x350

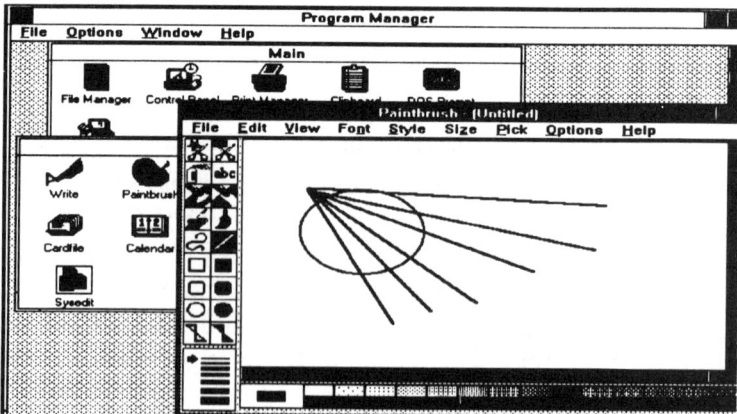

VGA 640x480

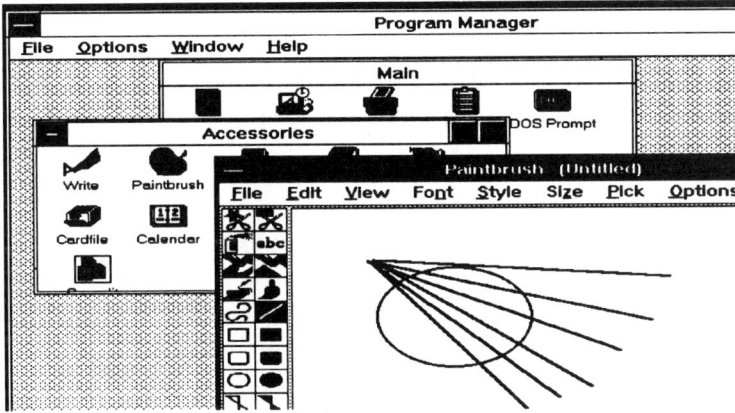

SVGA 800x600

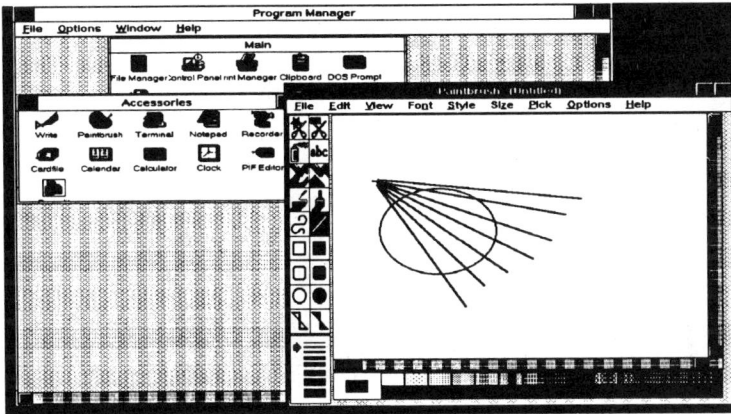

SVGA 1024x640

can find VGA graphics cards and monitors that will work at 70Hz or more. These higher frame rates do seem to produce a crisper image, but many people can only just perceive the difference. What is much easier to see is the flicker produced by a 50Hz interlaced monitor and display card. At the highest SVGA resolutions, lower cost monitors cannot keep up with the data rate needed to draw 50 images per second and so an interlaced scanning method is used which cuts the refresh rate in half. At less than 50 images per second the flicker is very easy to see, especially in areas of grey tone. Notice that this is only a problem in

768x1024 SVGA mode. The solution to the problem is to buy a display card and monitor that will work at 768x1024 without the need for interlace. This situation is anomalous in that better usually means having something extra, but in this case of better means non-interlaced!

The second most important factor in the cost of a monitor is its versatility. Back in the early days, when EGA and VGA were both current standards, the best monitors you could buy were 'multi-sync' or 'multi-frequency' monitors that would work with any graphics adapter including proposed future standards. You can still buy multi-sync monitors but, unless you have a very special need, it is much cheaper to buy a dedicated SVGA monitor that will also work with all standard VGA modes. This is a limited form of multi-sync, in that the monitor will only work with a VGA display, but this is really all that most users need! Also, notice that an SVGA monitor can either be interlaced-only or can be capable of working with a non-interlaced display for a slightly higher cost.

The final determining factor in choice of a colour monitor is its dot pitch. This is simply the space between the phosphor dots on the screen, and the closer together they are, i.e. the smaller the dot pitch, the clearer the image. However, this isn't always the case in practice because it is quite possible for bad design to produce a poor image even when working with a high quality display. The only true test is to actually look at a sample monitor in use. Even this isn't foolproof in that identical models will vary one from another in their display quality, and you can improve the look of a monitor by careful alignment.

Floppy drives

Every PC needs at least one floppy drive, if only to allow software to be installed. (The only exceptions to this rule are diskless workstations which are connected to a network and so can make use of drives installed on other machines.) There are two sizes of disk drive in use: the older 5.25" and the newer 3.5". To confuse matters even more, each of these sizes comes in two different types with different storage capacities.

The 5.25" drive is standard on the XT class of machine and in this case only stores 360KB per diskette. This is a pitifully small amount of storage for a modern machine and it is being rapidly phased out. A high capacity version was introduced for use with the IBM AT and this stores 1.2MB. The lower capacity drives are also referred to as 40 track and the higher capacity as 80 track drives. Most, but not all, high capacity drives can read and write low capacity 40 track diskettes. (Some early high capacity drives did not have this ability or could only read low capacity diskettes.)

The 3.5" drive uses a much more robust and reliable diskette and this is certainly the format of choice. If you can afford only a single drive, then a 3.5" drive is recommended. Two formats are in common use: 720KB and a high density 1.44MB. As in the case of the 5.25" disk drives, a high density drive will read and write both types of diskette.

Both 5.25" and 3.5" high capacity drives need to use special high density diskettes to work reliably. Many users think that 5.25" high capacity drives are unreliable because they attempt to use low capacity diskettes formatted to 1.2MB. This is something that you can do because the hardware makes no attempt to stop you, but it is notoriously unreliable. If you try to do this, you may get large numbers of sector errors or bad sectors reducing the effective capacity of the disk.

In the case of 3.5" diskettes there is a distinguishing mark between the two types of diskette and most hardware does use this to stop you from formatting a low density diskette to high capacity. A high density 3.5" disk is usually marked 'HD' and there are two square holes punched in one edge as opposed to one square hole in a standard capacity diskette. It is not a good idea to punch the extra hole in the casing of a standard density 3.5" disk so that it can be formatted to twice its certified capacity. It may work, but the magnetic medium is neither designed nor guaranteed to retain data at the higher density and sooner or later, data loss or corruption may occur.

An interesting problem can occur because some machines, notably IBM PS/2s and many Amstrad systems, do not make use of the extra hole to distinguish a high capacity diskette from a low capacity one. This allows users to format a low density diskette to 1.44MB. This causes no problems, provided the diskette remains reliable in use, until it is used to exchange data with another user whose machine does use the extra hole to detect the difference between diskette types. In this case, the machine will refuse to read the diskette that is formatted to 1.44MB because it recognises it as a standard 720KB diskette. If a replacement 720KB diskette copy cannot be obtained, the only solution is to drill or punch the extra hole in the diskette, so allowing the machine to recognise it as a high density diskette.

Many commercial systems are now provided only with a 3.5" drive as standard, and 5.25" drives are less fashionable these days! As always, this provides the opportunity for lower prices for 5.25" - (especially 360KB) drives. However, be warned that there are many non-standard PC drives that are very low cost and, while they may work, they will not be capable of reading a standard PC diskette. For example, there are 720KB 5.25" disk drives which partially work in a standard PC. There are also many drives intended for machines such as the BBC micro that are described as 80 track drives, but these are not the same as the high density drives used by the PC. It is important that you verify both the number of tracks and the capacity of the drive. That is, a 5.25" drive should be a 40 track/ 360KB or an 80 track/1.2MB drive.

If you can afford two floppy disk drives, get one of each size - a 360KB and 720KB for an XT and a 1.2MB and a 1.44MB for an AT. You can only use higher density drives on XTs if you have a special - and more expensive - floppy disk controller.

There are a couple of important points to remember about 3.5" drives. Most older versions are slightly thicker than the more modern 'slimline' types - they are half height as opposed to one third height. Some computer cases will take both sizes of drive, but check carefully before buying. A number of manufacturers supply their drives with 5.25" frames into which the smaller drive fits, and at least one supplies a 3.5" drive which has a front panel the same size as a 5.25" drive. Many 5.25" frames are detachable, and the 3.5" drive can be used on its own.

Finally, you will also come across 3" disk drives. These are used on machines such as the Amstrad PCW range. A 3" disk drive can often be used in place of, and treated by software as if it was, a standard 5.25" drive. You can even buy utilities that will read diskettes created by other machines, but it is very important to realise that the 3" drive is virtually unused in the PC world and it is being rapidly phased out. In short, a 3" drive is only of interest if you want to exchange data with another 3" drive user.

Buying direct

If you are building your own system or thinking about an upgrade, you should now have a good idea of the sort of facilities you want and what you need to put it together, so a checklist is helpful. Unless money is no object you ought to investigate the market. Time spent looking through the advertisements in the popular computing press will soon enable you to locate those firms which sell individual components at reasonable prices - although some of them don't offer as good a deal in terms of after-sales service or speed of delivery.

Unfortunately, there are a few rogue firms about, and if you can, always pay by credit card - then you will have the backing of the card issuing company if problems are experienced. One or two firms tend to debit your credit card account several days, weeks or even months before your goods are dispatched. Sometimes, a polite letter or 'phone call will produce a response, but if this does not work a letter to the advertising manager of the magazine in which you saw the advertisement, copied to the firm, will often achieve results. Do keep copies of your order, any invoices or delivery notes and always keep copies of your correspondence, or notes of telephone conversations. It's very easy to forget exactly what you have said or ordered over the phone, as I have found out to my cost!

It's always a good idea to ask questions about the items you are buying - the response of the salesperson over the counter or on the 'phone is a useful guide to what sort of reaction you will get if you ring up later with a query or complaint. The most frequent source of problems for any constructor is the handbook or users' guide supplied with motherboards or adapter cards. Some problems result from unfamiliarity with the English language on the part of the person who wrote the manual - remember that most computer hardware is imported from the Far East. Other difficulties may occur because of design changes which have occurred since the manual was published. A good supplier should be able to help you.

Having said all this, you have to keep in mind that when you purchase a module for the lowest price, the dealer cannot afford to spend much time solving problems for you. It is important that you invest the time in learning about the general principles of the PC and plan exactly what you want and what you are going to do. Occasionally you may need to show some ingenuity or at least some common sense. If you are worried about getting stuck, then ask the dealer if they will fit the module for you if necessary and how much they will charge. In the last resort it is worth discovering how willing the dealer is to accept a return or to swap the module for a different one.

Despite all the potential difficulties, buying modules directly by mail order **does** work most of the time.

Thinking about cost

One of the most difficult things in the world is trying to work out what is the best value for money. For example, if I offer you a 124MB drive for £259 or a 143MB drive for £389, which is better value? You can also get carried away on a 'ladder' of prices. For example, if you decide that a 20MB drive will do and discover a best price of £148 then it is very tempting to conclude that 30MB is only a small step away at another £20. The problem is that once you have taken this small step another leads you to 40MB and so on up until you are committed to spending many times what you originally budgeted! Of course, good sense usually prevails and you can work out a compromise, but it would help to have a way of examining prices.

One good aid in deciding value for money is to draw a graph of 'Price versus Performance'. For example, if you draw a graph of price against storage capacity for the speed or type of disk drive you are interested in, you can see if there is any advantage in buying a larger drive. You could also work out a MegaBytes per Pound index and see more directly

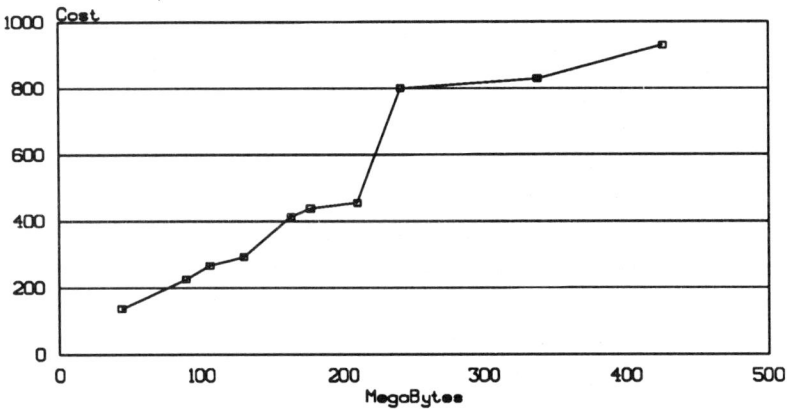

Figure 3.1
Cost v Size for IDE drives

what was the best value for money. At the time of writing, a graph of cost against capacity for fast, i.e. 20ms or better, IDE drives produces the graph in Fig 3.1. You can see that there is a large jump in cost when you move above 200MB. This can also be seen in the graph of MegaBytes/Pound in Fig 3.2. In this case you can see that the number of MegaBytes that you get for a pound falls after 200MB but returns to the optimum once you are over 300MB.

Do not assume that these figures will be true for all time - they most certainly will not! You should draw your own graphs to discover the current state before buying. In the case of disk drives, another useful measure is to compare the cost of buying a disk drive of twice the capacity of the drive you are considering, with the price of two drives of that capacity. The reason for this being a useful comparison is that when you run out of disk space you are most likely to add a second drive of the same type as the first; this ensures complete compatibility, and so it makes sense to compare the cost of two drives with the price of buying a single unit now. For example, if you were to choose a 150MB unit from the graphs shown here, the cost would be £293, and so buying two to give 300MB would cost £586 compared to £830 for

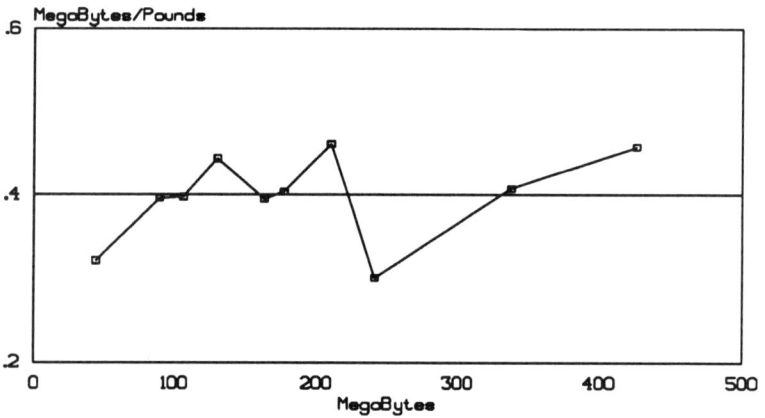

Figure 3.2
MegaBytes/Pound v Capacity

a single 300MB drive. However, if you buy a 100MB drive at £240, then the cost of a pair at £480 has to be compared to £420. Decisions such as these can be difficult, but information of this sort can help put costs into perspective. Always remember, however, that in the case of disk drives, MegaBytes per Pound is likely to increase with time and so the cost of an upgrade of any given size is likely to be less if postponed for as long as possible.

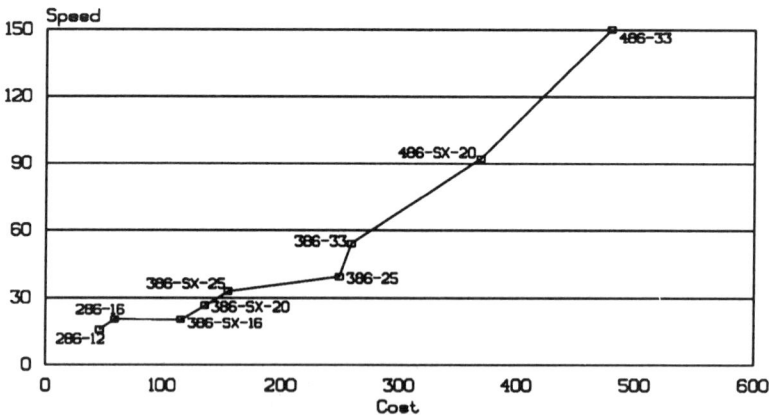

Figure 3.3
Speed v Cost for motherboards

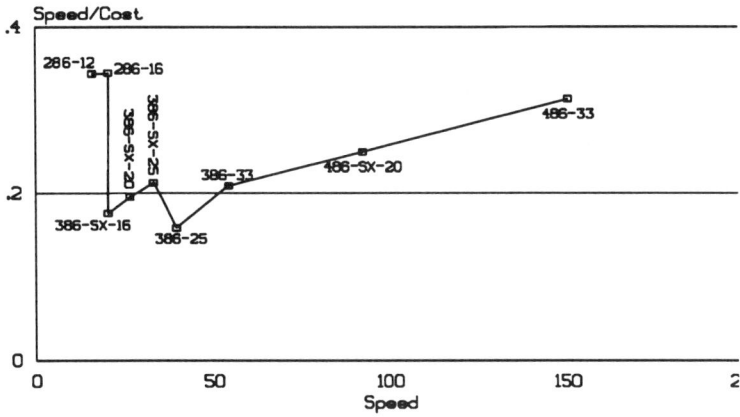

Figure 3.4
Speed/Cost v Speed

You can apply the same technique to motherboards if you substitute a measure of processing power in place of disk capacity. The only problem is finding a suitable measure of processing power. For motherboards in isolation a reasonable measure is the Landmark speed, which gives the clock rate at which a standard 8MHz AT would have to be run to turn in the same performance. You can see a plot of Cost against Landmark speed in Figure 3.3 and a plot of Speed/Cost against Speed in Figure 3.4. In this case the results are less conclusive and only really show what a remarkable bargain 286 boards are and that there is little point in buying a 386 25MHz machine when a 33MHz model costs so little extra.

Making up your mind

To help you choose the components of your system you may find the following tables helpful.

Choice of motherboard

To choose the sort of motherboard you need, look down the list of applications and find the application in which you are interested with the largest power rating. This should be used to select a type of motherboard from the subsequent list which matches or exceeds this power requirement:

Application	Power rating
Word processing	1-4
Games	2-6
Scientific (number crunching)	7-9
Computer-aided design	7-9
Presentation graphics	6-7
Ilustration graphics	7-9
Desktop publishing	6-9
Office management	5
Database	1-6
Spreadsheet	1-6
Windows	6-9
Programming	3-6

Motherboard power ratings

Type	Power rating
XT 4.77MHz	1
XT-Turbo 10-12MHz	2
286 8-10MHz	3
286 12-16MHz	4
386SX 16MHz	5
386SX 20-25MHz	6
386DX25-33MHz	7
486SX 20MHz	8
486DX-33MHz	9

Of course this list is very subjective, but it does give a good indication of the sort of machine you need for each type of application.

Video choice

To determine which type of video you need, find the highest rated application in the list below and then match it against the performance of the video cards listed.

Application	Video rating
Word processing	1
Games	5
Scientific (number crunching)	1
Computer-aided design	7 or better
Presentation graphics	4
Illustration graphics	7
Desktop publishing	7 or better
Office management	2
Database	1
Spreadsheet	1
Windows	5-7
Programming	1

Video standard	Rating Mono	Rating Colour
MDA	1	0
HGA	2	0
CGA	0	1
EGA	3	4
VGA	5	6
SVGA	0	7

Notice that some applications such as spreadsheet, database or scientific may have extra requirements if they also involve graphics, but these should be included under the presentation graphics category. Notice also that these basic applications would be better with high quality monochrome rather than low quality colour. Unless the budget is tight, and only the basics are desired, avoid standard monochrome or CGA/EGA.

Hard disk capacity and speed

You can gauge the size and speed of disk needed for the main applications using the table below. However, notice that capacity also depends on the number of applications you are planning to run. A rule of thumb is to allocate 10MB per application, plus 20MB for Windows.

Application	Capacity	Speed
Word processing	1	1
Games	2	1
Scientific (number crunching)	2-4	2-3
Computer-aided design	3-4	2
Presentation graphics	3	2
Illustration graphics	3	3
Desktop publishing	4	3
Office management	3	2
Database	3-6	3
Spreadsheet	3	1
Windows	4	3
Programming	2-3	2

Capacity		Speed	
20MB	1	65ms slow	1
32MB	2	20ms medium	2
65MB	3	10ms fast	3
100MB	4		
200MB	5		
300MB	6		

Extras

The extras that your machine needs also depends on the applications you are going to be using. In many cases, it is better to consider the extras after you have had your machine for a while and discovered exactly how you are using it. In some cases, though, it is better to plan ahead. For example, if you are going to need a mouse then it is better to include a serial port on your list of extras from the word go, because a serial port can often be included on an adapter card serving another purpose - disk controller, multifunction card or the motherboard itself. It's good practice to have two serial ports, which most serial cards will support. Make sure that the supplier actually provides the appropriate bits to give the card full functionality. The reason for two serial ports is that a mouse will use one, leaving the second free to drive a modem or to be used with file transfer programs. If you forget the serial port then an alternative is to use a mouse that comes with its own interface card - a so-called bus mouse - but these are more expensive. Most machines also need at least one printer port and if one isn't supplied on the video card you are using, then you will have to buy a separate adapter.

Application	Extras
Word processing	High quality printer
Games	Games port, mouse, sound board.
Scientific (number crunching)	Maths co-processor
Computer-aided design	Digitiser, plotter, maths co-processor.
Presentation graphics	Colour printer, mouse.
Illustration graphics	Mouse, laser printer
Desktop publishing	Mouse, laser printer
Office management	Mouse
Database	Printer
Spreadsheet	Printer
Windows	Mouse
Programming	Mouse, printer

In general, it is easier and cheaper in the long run to buy a standard multi-function card consisting of at least two serial ports, a parallel port and a games adapter port.

Key points

» Your first step is to decide on the general class of motherboard you need. This governs the overall configuration of the machine and what it is sensible to pair it with.

» Deciding on the size of hard disk drive is difficult but important.

» When choosing video hardware you should think about upgradability in the future.

» To get a better understanding of the relative values of the choices of hardware you should attempt to draw cost versus power graphs. This is relatively straightforward for disk drives and motherboards, but less so for video hardware.

Chapter 4
In detail:
Motherboards

The most important component in any machine is the motherboard. In this chapter we look in detail at the types of motherboard that are available and their characteristics.

Since the motherboard is the major component in any machine, you need to know something about it. However, there is no need to examine it down to the level of the individual chips. A general appreciation of differences in design that affect performance, price and their expandability is dealt with in this chapter.

Choosing a motherboard

Assuming that you have chosen the general type of motherboard, i.e. 286, 386SX, 386DX, 486SX or 486DX, what other considerations are there? Essentially these come down to three points:

» Size - will the motherboard fit into the case that you intend to use?

» Number of slots - how many 8- and 16-bit expansion slots does the motherboard have and is it enough?

» Type of memory - this affects both the speed of the motherboard within its class and how much memory you can easily install.

The size of the motherboard really matters only in the sense that it is important that it fits in the case! However, you might want to put together an ultra small desktop unit, and in this case you need a half-size motherboard. There is also a side argument that smaller motherboards are more reliable because they generally have fewer chips, but this is a very small consideration as motherboards are generally very reliable anyway! The question of size is examined in more detail later in this chapter.

The number of expansion slots a motherboard needs to provide is very difficult to quantify because of the wide range of possible configurations. For example, if you have a system with a separate floppy and hard disk controller, a serial card, a video card, a parallel card and a mouse card, then you have used up six slots. On the other hand, if you use a motherboard with built in IDE hard disk and floppy controller and you use a video card and a combined serial, parallel plus mouse card, you only need two slots! In most cases it is safe to assume that you will need one slot for a disk controller - either floppy only or hard disk plus floppy controller. The video card needs another slot, and a combined I/O card another, making a total of three. Most full-sized motherboards have eight slots. In the case of an AT motherboard these are usually two 8-bit and six 16-bit slots. Smaller motherboards typically have six slots, all 16-bit in the case of AT motherboards. In either case, this is enough, unless you are planning to use lots and lots of additional adapter cards. One consideration that is often overlooked is that, although the slots on the motherboard are all identical, they may not all be treated equally by the case in which you install the motherboard! The amount of space allocated to a slot in a case varies from full-length to half-length. In most cases this only matters if you are planning to use a number of older or more specialised adapter cards. Most modern mass-produced adapter cards have been reduced in size so that they are only half the length of the original adapter cards.

The third and final consideration is much more complicated: memory. As already mentioned, the memory configuration of a motherboard affects both its speed and the maximum amount of memory that you can fit in without having to resort to expansion cards. Memory is such an important subject that it is dealt with in detail in the next chapter, but it is still worth outlining the basic ideas here.

In the case of slower motherboards - 286 and 386SX machines up to 16MHz - there is no need for manufacturers to make special provision for memory to keep up with the processor. In these cases, memory design has little or no effect on performance as long as fast enough memory chips are used. After 16MHz the problem of making memory chips fast enough to keep up with the processor is too difficult. The simplest solution is to introduce wait states - short pauses that give the memory time to catch up with the processor. Clearly, wait states slow down a machine and so are undesirable. There are two basic alternatives: interleave and caching. Interleave is the organisation of the memory into banks which are used alternately. As one bank is being used the second bank has time to catch up with the processor. Interleave is a simple method, but it has the disadvantage that you have to install memory in pairs of interleaved banks to make it work. There are situations in which not enough memory is installed to allow it to work. It also isn't as effective as caching.

Caching is the use of a small amount of very fast memory as a sort of buffer between slow memory and fast processor. Exactly how caching works is explained in the next chapter, but all that matters for the moment is to know that its use produces the fastest machines. Cache memory is typically 64KB, 128KB or, in extreme cases 256KB. The 486 also has an 8KB cache built into it. This is one of the reasons that it is intrinsically faster than the 386. You can still find 486 motherboards that don't use additional cache memory, but most now do provide a secondary cache to supplement the basic 8KB. Notice that cache memory doesn't add to the total amount of memory that a machine has. If you installed 1MB of RAM and have 256KB of cache, you do not have 1MB plus 256KB of memory. The 256KB of cache memory has to be counted entirely separately from the memory used to run a program.

There are various modifications to interleaving that make it more efficient, such as page interleaved and column mode access, but it is still slower than caching. This means that given a particular type of board running at a given clock speed, the order of processing power is:

> 1 or 2 wait states
> page interleaved
> cached

and the larger the cache, the faster the board.

As important as the speed aspect of memory configuration is the total amount of memory that you can fit to the motherboard. Older motherboards tended to use DIL chips, and the maximum amount of memory on such motherboards is usually very limited. For machines 16MHz or slower this isn't too much of a problem in that you can use memory expansion cards plugged in to the standard expansion slots. The only disadvantage of this method of memory expansion is cost. In the case of machines that work faster than 16MHz, then the standard expansion bus simply isn't fast enough, and so memory fitted using expansion cards results in wait states having to be added. Some motherboards have special double-sized 32-bit memory expansion slots to try to get over this problem. This is fine, but the expansion cards are expensive and very difficult to get hold of and often specific to a single motherboard.

If you can, you should try to find a motherboard that can accommodate 8 to 16 MB or better of memory without using an expansion card. This usually implies using one that accepts SIMM or SIP modules directly on the motherboard. A complicating factor is that the largest amount of memory that you can fit to a motherboard is usually quoted assuming that all sockets will be filled with devices of the largest capacity. If this isn't the case, then you can only reach the upper limit by removing the lower capacity devices and replacing them with higher capacity devices. This is really only a potential problem when it comes to memory upgrade time, and it is discussed in more detail in the next chapter, but it is worth keeping in mind when you settle on the amount of memory to be installed initially.

The details of memory installation and configuration are discussed in greater detail in the next chapter.

There are a number of other minor considerations in choosing a motherboard. For example, most motherboards have a socket for a co-processor and it is important to know the type and speed that is used. Another consideration is the type of BIOS fitted. The BIOS is the control program that starts your machine up and tests it. Most of the time you can ignore it, but it is also responsible for configuring your machine and in this role it can limit the type of hard disk that you can use. In most cases a modern BIOS produced by AMI, Phoenix or Award is to be recommended and currently there are advantages in choosing the AMI BIOS.

Expanded and extended memory

The difference between expanded and extended memory is a difficult technical topic which is discussed more fully in the next chapter. However, there is a need to say something about how it affects motherboard selection. Put simply, modern AT 286 and 386 designs use **extended** memory, and as time goes on, this is likely to become the only sort of memory that is required. Indeed in 386 based systems it is already the only sort of memory that you need worry about, because there exists software that will convert extended memory to expanded memory without the need for any hardware modifications. However, if you are buying an XT or a 286 motherboard then there is still a need to worry about expanded memory. In both situations it is simpler if the motherboard has the ability to convert a nominated amount of memory into expanded memory via hardware. If the motherboard doesn't have the hardware needed to implement expanded memory, then the only solution is to buy a memory expansion card that does support expanded memory.

EISA and MCA

So far the only types of expansion bus that have been mentioned are the 8- and 16-bit types found in the XT and AT motherboard. The 16-bit version of the expansion bus is usually referred to as the ISA or Industry Standard Architecture bus. There have been a number of attempts to

The ROM BIOS

All PC systems have a ROM BIOS which contains several routines that are designed to operate the system. There are small differences between the standard IBM ROM BIOS chips and those of other manufacturers such as Phoenix or AMI, but they all carry out pretty well the same basic functions and are said to be compatible. The BIOS for an XT machine is not compatible with that for an AT. The main functions of the ROM BIOS may be summarised as follows:

Power-On Self Test - The POST routines test the motherboard, memory, keyboard and adapter cards and will report on any problems or failures which they find.

Basic Input/Output System - This controls almost all the activities of the system which are concerned with any form of input or output, and it allows user programs to have easy access to system features by communicating with a BIOS program module, rather than directly with the particular device, such as a floppy disk or video card.

Bootstrap Loader - This strange name disguises a most important feature - searching for an operating system on disk. Once an operating system is found, it is loaded into memory and takes control of the computer.

In most cases the type of ROM BIOS that you are using has little effect. However, it can restrict the type of hard disk that you can use in a 286/386 AT. Older BIOSs can also cause problems on 286 ATs when you try to run advanced operating systems such as Windows or applications such as Lotus 1-2-3 Release 3. The reason is that the BIOS is involved in switching from real to protected mode and early BIOSs were written before the details of how to do this were standardised. Oddly, the keyboard controller chip is also involved in switching operating modes and in most cases this, too, has to be replaced along with the BIOS to make the machine work correctly. One of the problems with trying to update the BIOS is that there are no companies within the UK specialising in BIOS upgrades. The address of one in the USA is listed in the contacts at the end of this book.

improve or replace the ISA bus. IBM introduced the MCA (Micro Channel Architecture) bus in their range of PS/2 machines and several other manufacturers responded by introducing the EISA or Extended Industry Standard Architecture bus. At the time of writing, motherboards using the EISA bus are available but they are expensive. There are currently no MCA motherboards available other than in complete machines from IBM and a very few other manufacturers. The EISA bus has the advantage that you can plug original ISA bus cards into it, and so from this point of view an EISA motherboard has no disadvantages other than price. By comparison the MCA bus is completely non-standard and best avoided. You don't really need to consider an EISA bus motherboard unless you are building a machine that needs to transfer large amounts of data very rapidly across the expansion bus. In practice, it is best to work the other way around and identify any EISA adapter cards that you would like to use before deciding that you need an EISA motherboard.

In the future the price of EISA motherboards may fall and there may be no penalty against using them. Until that time it is worth knowing that there are very few applications that benefit from their use and none at all if you don't also use specific EISA adapter cards.

Upgrading

Changing the motherboard in an existing machine is a very reasonable way of upgrading its performance. Indeed, given the price of memory expansion cards and new motherboards, it is often a reasonable way of simply increasing the amount of memory a system has! The considerations in choosing a motherboard for upgrade are very similar to buying one for any other purpose but there are some additional factors.

If your existing machine is a standard, desktop, metal-cased XT or AT type design, then you will probably be able to replace the motherboard with little difficulty. In fact the older the design, the easier it is likely to be. The early clone designs stayed as close to the original IBM as possible, and so installing new motherboards should be very easy indeed. Later clones tended to try to find advantages that would make them more attractive, and so went in for half-height and compact case designs. Even in these cases, you would usually find a full-sized motherboard, however, and so replacement might be a bit more difficult but still possible. In short, the closer to the original XT or AT dimensions and internal design your machine is, the easier the upgrade task.

Of course, a big worry is whether or not the new motherboard will have the correct mounting holes. This problem is discussed later in the section on fitting and removing a motherboard. The only problem is likely to arise in replacing an XT board with an AT board and, even in this case, a little planning should still make it possible to fit the new board. At the worst you will only have to buy a new case to fit the new board - an expenditure of around £50 - so don't let this potential problem put you off too much.

Another factor to take into account is the re-usability of any existing DIL chips or SIMMs that you may have left over from the old motherboard. This might not just be a matter of "does the board have sockets for them", because you also have to check that the original chips are fast enough.

After you have installed the new motherboard, we come to the question of which bits of the old system you can keep. If you are upgrading from an AT system to a new AT motherboard, the answer should be all of it. An AT hard disk and controller, serial/parallel, video, keyboard, the lot, should just work as before.

If you are upgrading from an XT, then things aren't quite as easy. The video, serial and parallel ports should work OK. But you will almost certainly need a new hard disk controller and keyboard, unless your original keyboard is switchable or auto-sensing.

Notice that there are some XT class machines, such as the Amstrad 1512/1640 which have non-standard motherboards with built-in video, serial and parallel ports. Machines that use such non-standard motherboards are best left alone; there is very little to gain in trying to fit a standard motherboard, because there are very few modules that can be re-used along with it. In these cases, it is much simpler to buy a new case and start from scratch.

Standard sizes

Although there are no universal standards for motherboards, in practice they all follow more or less closely the original designs introduced by the IBM XT and AT. Of course, manufacturers have attempted to improve the original and you will find some motherboards which are physically smaller and others which are larger than the originals. In almost all of these cases, the board can still be fitted using the same

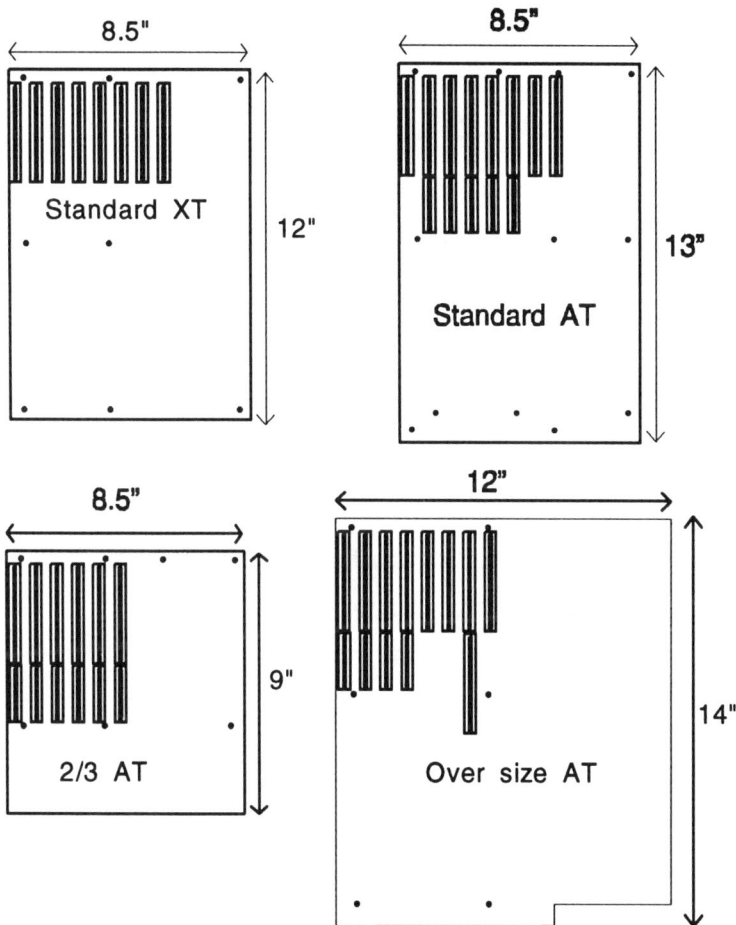

Figure 4.1
Motherboard sizes and mounting hole patterns

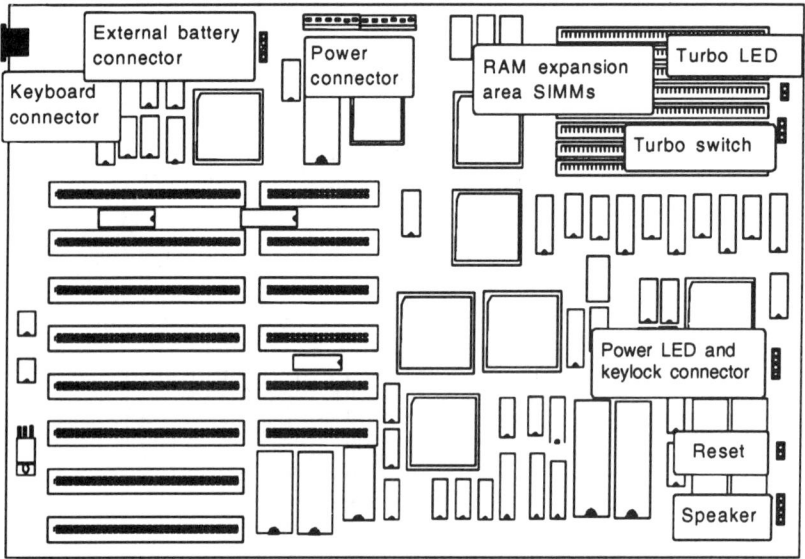

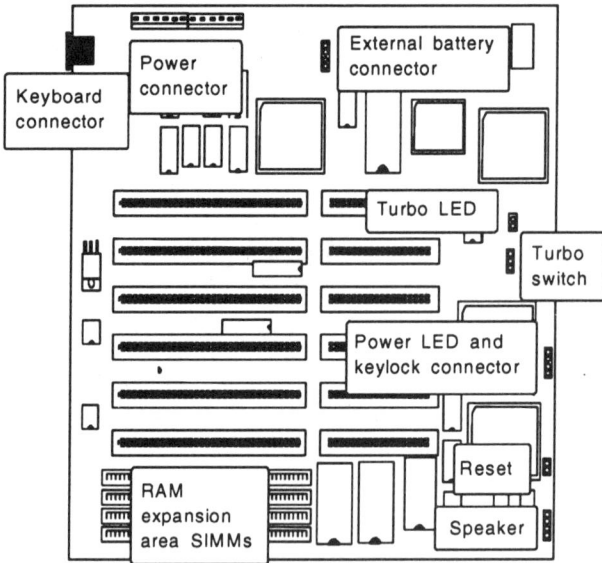

Figure 4.2
Motherboard layouts

mounting holes as the original. However, the size of the motherboard is important if you are considering an upgrade.

The original XT board was approximately 12" long by 8.5" wide. (As it was designed in the USA its measurements are in inches rather than centimetres.) Current XT boards tend to be between half and two-thirds the length of the original.

The original AT style of board was the same length as a standard XT motherboard but usually about an inch wider, see Figure 4.1. As in the case of the XT motherboard, newer AT motherboards are often only two-thirds as long as the original. There are also some huge AT motherboards designed in the days when it needed a lot of chips to provide a reasonable amount of memory. Even these huge boards can be accommodated inside many standard size AT cases but you need to make sure!

All motherboards are built to a similar style - power connector on the top right-hand side, a series of slots for adapter cards and a keyboard connector (usually) along the top edge. The memory is usually found on the left-hand side of the motherboard, below the adapter slots. The remaining connections can be almost anywhere on the motherboard but at least their function is the same.

The standardisation of the power connectors, slot and keyboard positions means that boards can be used in many different types of cases and upgrading a system can be readily achieved by removing an existing motherboard and replacing it with another, see the section *Upgrading* at the end of this chapter for more information.

In most circumstances it is better to opt for an AT motherboard, but there are still some XT motherboards that offer particular advantages, such as price or a large number of extra features. The following table summarises the technical differences between typical XT and AT design.

	PC-XT type	PC-AT type
Processors supported	8088/V20, 8086/V30 80188, 80186	80286, 80386SX, 80386DX, 80486SX, 80486DX
Expansion slots	8-bit ISA	8- and 16-bit ISA 32-bit ISA for 386/486
External data bus	8-bit (8088)	16-bit (286/386SX) 32-bit (386/486)
Internal data bus	8-bit (8088) 16-bit (8086)	16-bit (286) 32-bit (386/386SX/486)
Bus speed	4.77MHz	8MHz
Real time clock	Optional on early models	Yes
Configuration	Switches	Jumpers and CMOS memory
Battery backup for clock	On later models	Yes, and for CMOS memory
Maximum RAM	1MB	16MB on board
ROM BIOS	8KB	32KB 286 64KB 386/386SX
Hard disk BIOS and Drive Tables	HD controller	Motherboard ROM

The most important differences are that XT motherboards use different disk controllers and different keyboards from AT motherboards. In simple terms, though, the XT design is far less flexible and powerful than the AT.

Standard connections

All motherboards have the same set of connectors, and it is important to know what they are and what they do. In the descriptions that follow the colours indicated are the ones most commonly used for the connecting wires to each connector. Note: N/C means Not Connected and Key means that the pin is removed for identification.

Hardware Reset - XT and AT

Marked:	Reset
Colours:	Black/Black
Function:	This is used to connect to the hardware reset push button usually mounted on the front of the case.
Connections:	Two pins shorted together reset the machine.
Not used:	Leaving unconnected means that there is no way to reset the machine other than by switching it off.

It doesn't matter which way round the reset connector is installed.

External Battery - AT and some XTs

Marked:	Battery or Ext. Batt or similar
Colours:	Red/Black
Function:	Supplements on-board NiCad battery.
Connection:	Four pins in a line:
	Pin 1 + DC
	Pin 2 N/C or Key
	Pin 3 Ground
	Pin 4 Ground
Not used:	Leaving unconnected makes the motherboard use the built-in NiCad battery, if one is fitted.

Some motherboards use 6V external batteries and some use 3.6V ones. It is important use the correct voltage. If you are in any doubt about the connections or the voltage leave the external battery unconnected. It **does** matter which way round you connect the external battery connector!

Speaker - XT and AT

Marked:	Speaker
Colour:	Red/Black
Function:	Connects speaker to motherboard.
Connection:	Four pins in a line:

                    Pin 1: Data

                    Pin 2: N/C or Key

                    Pin 3:N/C

                    Pin 4:+5V

Not used:	No sound from your machine!

It doesn't matter which way round you connect the loudspeaker connector.

Power LED and Keylock - AT and some XTs

Marked:	Power
Colour:	Green/White (Power LED) Green/Black (Keylock)
Function:	Indicates when power is applied to motherboard and locks the keyboard input off or on. The Power LED connector connects to an LED on the front panel of the case; the keylock connector to a keyswitch.
Connection:	Five pin connector:

                    Pin 1:+ve power LED

                    Pin 2: N/C or Key

                    Pin 3: Ground

                    Pin 4: Keyboard inhibit

                    Pin 5: Ground

Not used:	Not connecting to the power LED has no effect other than that there is no visual indication of when the machine is on. Not connecting to the keylock connector simply means that you cannot lock the keyboard.

Sometimes the Power LED is placed as a separate connector making the keylock connector a four-pin connector. The cable to the power LED and the keylock switch are often separate. It **does** matter which way round you connect the power LED and keylock connector.

Turbo LED - AT and some XT Turbos

Marked:	Turbo LED
Colour:	Yellow/White
Function:	Indicates the speed of the motherboard high or low.
	Pin 1 LED Anode i.e. +ve
	Pin 2 LED Cathode i.e. -ve
Not used:	Not connecting the Turbo LED has no effect apart from there being no indication of the current speed.

It **does** matter which way round you connect the Turbo LED connector. Many larger cases use this connector to drive an LED display of the speed in figures rather than just an on/off light.

Turbo Switch - AT and some XT Turbos

Marked:	Turbo Switch
Colour:	Yellow/Black or Grey/Grey
Function:	Sets the speed of the motherboard high or low.
Connection:	A two-pin connector. Shorting the pins together sets the motherboard to run at a slow speed.
Not used:	Not connecting the turbo switch connector has no effect other than that the motherboard runs at its highest speed. There is usually a software way of setting the motherboard to run at a slower speed.

It doesn't matter which way round you connect the turbo switch connector. Some motherboards use a three-pin connector for the turbo switch. In this case, shorting pins 1 and 2 sets one speed and shorting pins 2 and 3 sets another. This is less common and non-standard.

The Keyboard Connector - XT and AT

Marked:	Keyboard
Function:	Connects the keyboard to the motherboard.
Connection:	Five-pin DIN style connector mounted at the rear of the motherboard:
	Pin 1:Keyboard clock
	Pin 2: Keyboard data
	Pin 3: N/C
	Pin 4: Ground
	Pin 5: +5V
Not used:	It doesn't make any sense to try to use a machine without a keyboard!

Note that XT and AT keyboards are different.

The Power Connectors - XT and AT

Marked:	Power Connector
Function:	Supplies power to the motherboard from the power supply.
Connection:	Two 6-pin connectors:

(nearest the keyboard connector)

Pin 1: Power good	orange
Pin 2: +5V	red
Pin 3: +12V	yellow
Pin 4: -12V	blue
Pin 5: Ground	black
Pin 6: Ground	black
Pin 7: Ground	black
Pin 8: Ground	black
Pin 9: -5V	white
Pin 10: +5V	red
Pin 11: +5V	red
Pin 12: +5V	red

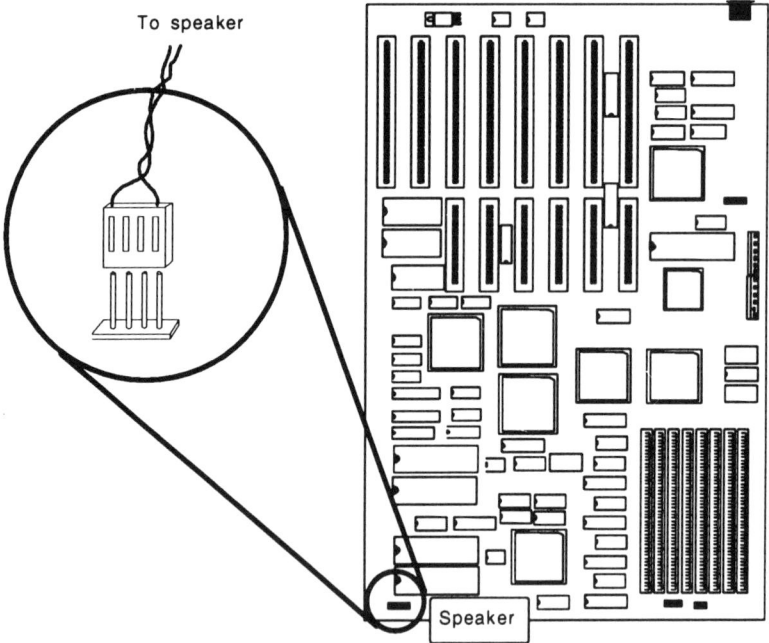

Figure 4.3
Using the motherboard connectors

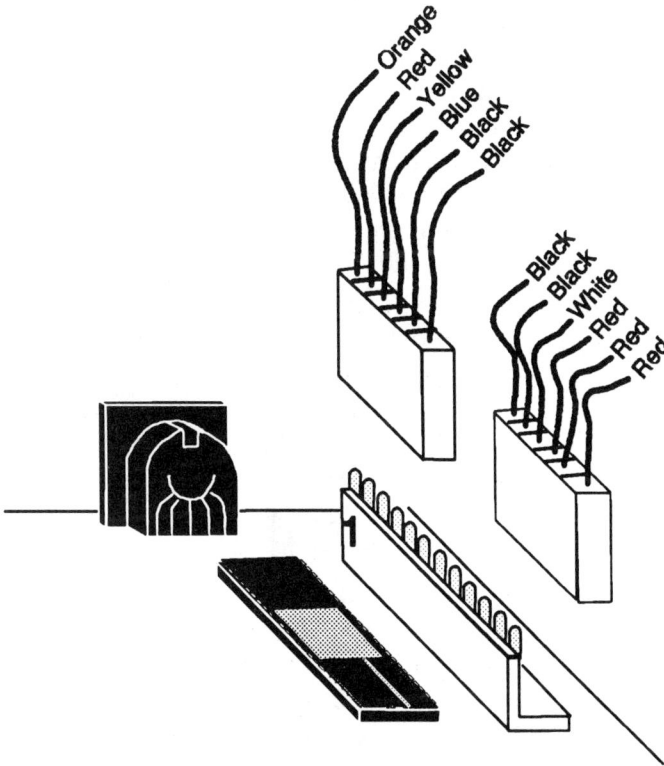

Figure 4.4
Power connectors

The colours indicated next to each pin are the standard colours used in the majority of power supply connectors. If you are in any doubt about which connector is which, then **do not connect the power supply**. This is the only connection to the motherboard that has the potential to damage it if wrongly connected. A good visual check is to make sure that the two connectors are plugged onto the board so that the **black** wires on each connector are adjacent to each other. Notice that some motherboards place the power connectors one behind another and in this case the 'black together' rule cannot be used!

Jumpers and DIP switches

Nearly all hardware has to be configured in some way or another to take account of the system that it has to work in. The standard way of doing this is to set jumpers or DIP switches according to the instructions in the manual. A jumper is nothing more than a small plug that can be fitted to short together a pair of pins. Leaving the jumper off selects one option and putting it on selects the alternative. Sometimes jumpers occur in sets that work together to select an option.

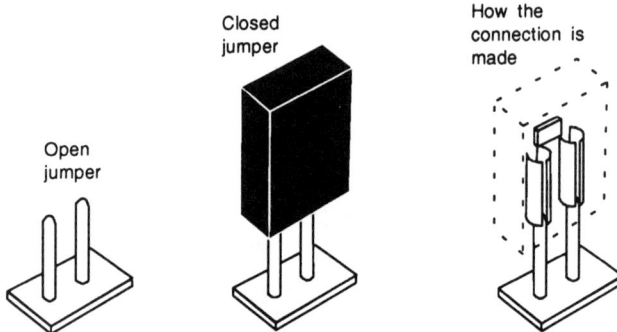

In situations where settings are likely to change often, jumpers are too much trouble and banks of DIP switches are generally used. There are two types of DIP switch - slide and push.

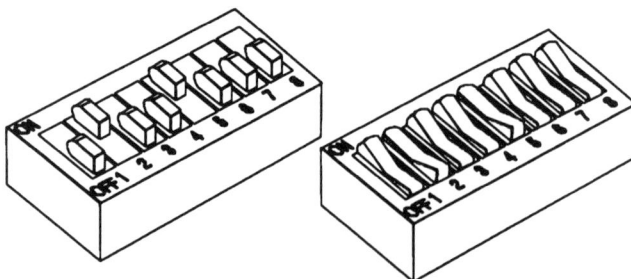

A motherboard generally has jumpers or DIP switches to set a wide range of options including whether a co-processor is fitted, the amount and type of memory, colour or monochrome video etc.. As motherboards become more sophisticated the number of jumpers and DIP switches is being reduced because of the ability of the motherboard to 'auto-sense' the correct configuration.

Fitting and removing motherboards

Fitting and removing a motherboard isn't a difficult job once you know how it is held in place. Motherboards are mounted on stand-off supports. The top end of a stand-off, see Figure 4.5, fits through a mounting hole in the motherboard. The springy sides of the stand-off hold it in place like barbs on a hook. Typically, the bottom of the stand-off slides into a slot in the base of the case. To mount the motherboard, stand-offs are fitted into holes that correspond to slots in the base and then the motherboard is inserted and slid sideways until the stand-offs are held firm in the narrow part of the slot, see Figure 4.6. This arrangement supports the motherboard, but there is nothing to stop it from sliding back out. To fix it in place there are stand-off nuts, see Figure 4.7. These screw into threaded holes in the base of the case and the motherboard is fixed to them by another bolt. The bolt is usually insulated from the motherboard using a fibre washer. One of the bolts, however, should be fitted without a fibre washer to make an earthing contact to the case. You can tell which mounting hole should be the earthing contact because it will be surrounded by a ring of bright, unlacquered copper. There are usually at least two stand-off nuts to secure a motherboard, but there can be more and there can be as few as one!

Occasionally you will come across plastic spacers which fit into holes in the case or edge gripping stand-offs that clip onto the edge of the motherboard and slot into the base in the usual way, see Figure 4.8. Edge gripping stand-offs are particularly useful when fitting a motherboard that doesn't have enough mounting holes!

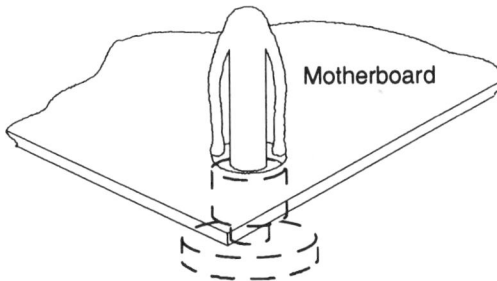

Figure 4.5
Stand-off pillar

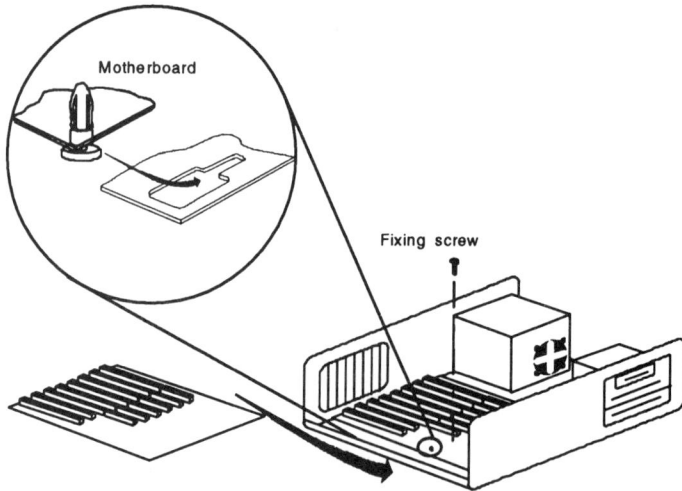

Figure 4.6
Sliding a motherboard into place

Removing a motherboard is rather easier than fitting one because you don't have to work out which holes in the motherboard are for stand-off pillars and which are for stand-off nuts. All you have to do is unscrew the fixing bolts, slide the motherboard to one side and then lift it up out of the case.

Some cases make it difficult to remove a motherboard without taking off a side panel or some other piece of metal work. You should always examine a case to see how the motherboard can best be removed before starting the job. When you remove the connectors from the motherboard, see if they are labelled - if not then label them after examining the labels on the motherboard by the relevant connectors. If the motherboard isn't labelled, and you don't have access to a manual, then you can always work out what the connectors are by tracing them

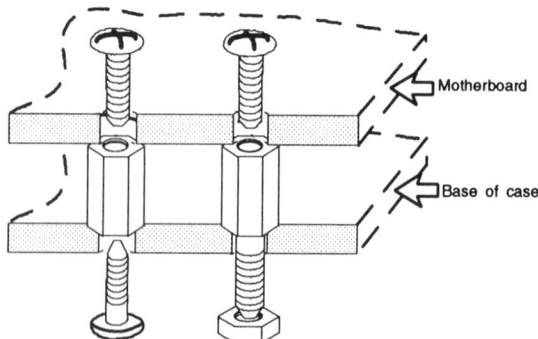

Figure 4.7
Two types of hexagonal securing stand-offs

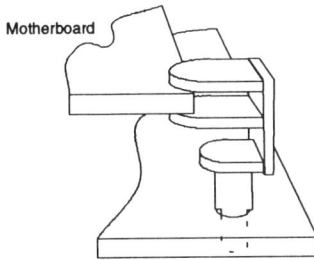

Figure 4.8
Edge gripping stand-off

back to the front panel. For example, the loudspeaker connector will trace back to the loudspeaker, the keyboard lock to the keyboard lock keyswitch and so on. This is, of course, the method to use if you have taken off the connectors without remembering to label them in the first place. A more difficult problem is when the motherboard being removed isn't labelled and you don't have a manual that shows what each connector is. In this case it is important to make a sketch of the connectors and mark their function and orientation by tracing the cables **before** disconnecting them.

A fixing kit, including stand-off pillars and connecting cables, is usually supplied with a new case rather than with the motherboard. If you are replacing a motherboard, then take care not to lose the stand-off pillars because you will need them to fit the new motherboard.

PC cases have developed a vast range of different drilling patterns for the mounting pillars. There are two basic patterns however - that used on the original XT and that used on the original AT. Some replacement boards claim to conform to the XT 'form factor' (size) but this doesn't necessarily make them any more suitable for use in an XT case. If you are replacing a standard AT board with a replacement AT-sized board you should find it easy. The only difficulties arise with replacing an XT board with an AT board. Even so, in either case you could find yourself a mounting pillar in the case or hole short in the board. This may sound a serious problem but it is usually easy enough to solve. The solution is to use additional clip-on edge supports or stand-off pillars that aren't secured to the case. As long as you have enough screws to hold the board in place, the only concern is that the board has enough support. Interestingly, the area where the board needs most support, i.e. around the expansion slots, is one area where the holes are usually drilled to match any case.

Motherboard design

The design of motherboards has changed over the years to reduce the number of chips and overall size of the board. Early XT motherboards used large numbers of logic chips and left very little space for memory expansion. As time went on more of the general logic on the motherboard was incorporated into larger and larger chips. Now, when you look at a modern design, you are more likely to see three or four very large 100-pin chips than a large number of smaller chips.

The use of large chips to integrate the functions of many smaller chips has resulted in two changes: it has been possible to make motherboards smaller and still provide more space for memory expansion; it has also been used as a way to implement more features on the motherboard. For example, many advanced, 'planar' motherboards have serial and parallel ports built in. Some specialised 'support chip sets' have even been used to extend the power of the processor. For example, some Chips and Technologies chip sets provide memory management features for the 286 that make it capable of being used in the same way as a 386 - provided you can find suitable software.

Simpler XT motherboards are usually only double-sided PCBs. This means that they have only two layers of electrical connections between the pins of the chips - one on the top and one on the bottom. More complicated AT motherboards make use of between four and seven layers of connections embedded within the PCB.

Another change is the use of surface mounted components. In this case each chip is soldered, using a machine, to the front face of the board. This has replaced the traditional method of inserting component leads through the PCB and soldering on the reverse side. The advantage of this approach is that it makes motherboards smaller and cheaper to manufacture. The disadvantage is that it makes them virtually impossible to repair unless you have a sophisticated surface mount soldering workstation. By using sockets for the most expensive components, this approach has more or less made motherboards a disposable commodity. If a fault occurs in one of the socketed chips then it can be replaced, once it has been located. If the fault occurs in a surface mounted component then it is usually easier to replace the motherboard.

Motherboard checklist

To help you gather information on the different types of motherboard that are available from a supplier you should fill in the following table. This is especially useful if you are gathering information by phone - in which case, remember to fill in at least the telephone number of the supplier!

Supplier	Tel
Manufacturer	
Product name/Id	
CPU type	8088/ 8086/ 286/ 386SX/ 386DX/ 486SX/ 486DX/ other
Clock speed	( )MHz
Memory architecture	wait states/interleave/cache cache size ( )KB max. cache size ( )KB
Memory type	DIL/SIP/SIMM sizes ( ) speed ( ) ns
Maximum memory	( )MB
Number of expansion slots	( ) 8 bit ( ) 16 bit
Custom memory expansion	Yes/No Cost £( )
Expanded memory support	Yes/No
Size	XT full/half AT full/half
Other features	
Price	
Delivery time	In stock/1 week/1 month/longer

Key points

» Factors that are important in choosing a motherboard of a given type are: size, number of expansion slots, and memory configuration.

» Memory configuration affects the speed of the design and the maximum amount of memory that can be fitted without the use of an extra memory expansion board.

» The fastest motherboards use a cache - a small amount of fast memory that acts as a buffer between the fast processor and the slow main memory.

» Upgrading a system by replacing its motherboard is a viable approach, except where a combination motherboard was originally fitted.

» Motherboards come in two distinct types and sizes: XT and AT. You can also find half-sized motherboards that will fit in place of either an XT or AT motherboard.

» There are a number of standard connections that have to be made to nearly all motherboards - including keyboard, key lock, power LED etc..

» Motherboards are held in place by a small number of bolts and plastic clips. When these are removed the motherboard will usually slide out.

» Mounting kits are usually supplied with cases. When a board is being replaced it is important to keep and re-use the fixings.

Chapter 5
In detail:
Memory

Memory is not only an important consideration when choosing your system, it is a recurring factor in the decision to upgrade. In this chapter we examine the theory and practice of memory.

While many aspects of computing grow ever simpler, the subject of memory seems to become more complex and more critical. It doesn't matter if you have an XT, AT, 386 or the very newest 486, you could always do with more memory to do justice to the latest applications. You may need more memory simply to run a program or to make it run faster. You may need more memory to accommodate the demands of a multi-tasking system such as DESQview or Windows. Whatever the reason, a careful initial choice of motherboard can make the memory upgrade problem simpler and cheaper. If, on the the other hand, you already have a motherboard that is restrictive in the amount or type of memory that it allows you to add, then you need to know enough to make a sensible choice of upgrade route.

On-board memory

One of the biggest changes in the design of PCs in recent years has been the incorporation of larger and larger amounts of memory on the motherboard. If you look at the original PC you will discover that it had very little memory on the motherboard and the expectation was that you would add more, using an expansion board plugged into a free expansion slot. Because it was impossible at the time to fit a large amount of memory on the motherboard, it was obvious to the designers that users would have to resort to an expansion board for additional memory.

This need to use an expansion board for memory focused attention on the speed of the expansion bus. Memory is the most demanding of system components in terms of its data transfer rate. Other system components are limited in their speed of operation by mechanical and other factors, but memory has to read and write data at the highest rate at which the CPU can work. In practice, the speed of memory has been well behind that of the CPU for some years, but it is still the only component in a system that gets close to the transfer rate at which the processor can work , and this makes it the most demanding.

As a result, the original XT bus (8-bit) was upgraded to what we now call the ISA (16-bit) bus and progress then led to the EISA (32-bit) and the MCA (16/32-bit) bus. You will read many statements about how much faster the MCA and EISA buses are than the original ISA bus and these are all true, but as far as memory **expansion** is concerned they are more or less irrelevant. The reason is that, while all of the high speed bus development was going on, the system designers effectively abandoned the expansion bus as a way of connecting memory to the processor in favour of a direct custom connection. That is, they used an internal bus and mounted large amounts of memory on the motherboard - a complete change in philosophy but an obvious one.

At first this resulted in motherboards with dozens of chip sockets waiting for memory chips to be plugged in. These motherboards are still usable and may even have a cost advantage because they use fairly old fashioned chips. Their main disadvantage is the amount of current consumed and the heat they produce, so if you are using such a motherboard be sure to use a large case with a good fan! To allow even more memory to be fitted many manufacturers added their own proprietary sockets to allow special adapter boards to be fitted. While this might look like the introduction of new expansion buses to compete along with EISA and MCA for the future, notice that these buses are 'memory only' and not general purpose. They are fast and simple rather than fast and sophisticated.

The main reason for the introduction of special memory expansion boards was quite simply the impossibility of accommodating all of the chips needed to provide the sort of upper limits on memory that seemed reasonable at the time. The 286 can address a maximum of 16MB and this has become a target maximum for all systems, even though the 386/486 can actually work with more. You might think that 16MB is a lot of memory and you would never need more, but then 64KB looked a lot in the days before the original IBM PC and 640KB seemed excessive at that time! Any limit should be viewed as a potential future problem.

Even though specialised memory expansion boards allow memory to be added up to the 16MB limit, they present a serious problem due to their lack of standardisation. This means that a custom memory upgrade is available only from the manufacturer of the motherboard. Because motherboard designs change fairly rapidly, you may discover that, only a few months after buying your motherboard, you cannot buy the memory upgrade card that it uses! If you wish to use a motherboard that has a custom memory expansion card, then it is advisable to check with the suppliers that they actually stock the specific board you require before you make a purchase (many do not) and then buy it at the same time as the motherboard. You can of course leave it unpopulated with memory chips until you actually need it.

SIMMs and SIPs

The solution to the lack of standardisation of the memory expansion buses and boards came about in an unusual way for the computer industry. Instead of the computer designers setting a standard, the chip manufacturers produced a new range of components that removed the need for memory expansion cards altogether. Take nine 1Megabit chips, assemble them into a small module, and you have the equivalent of a 'super-chip' storing 1MB. By using surface mounting chips the memory module could be made a lot smaller than the equivalent in standard DIL chips and sockets.

The only disadvantage of such modules is the chance that one of the memory chips may fail and so result in the need to scrap the whole module. In practice, the reliability of memory chips is such that you needn't worry. There may even be some improvements in reliability as a result of having fewer mechanical/non-soldered connections. Just regard the entire module as a single chip and forget any idea of internal repairs!

Two different types of memory module have become common: SIMMs (Single Inline Memory Module) and SIPs (Single Inline Package). SIMMs are small PCBs with standard edge connectors that fit into a special SIMM socket. SIPs have a single row of pins that fit into a corresponding row of small sockets. In practice SIMMs are easier to fit because there is no danger of bending a pin, but apart from this there is little to choose between them.

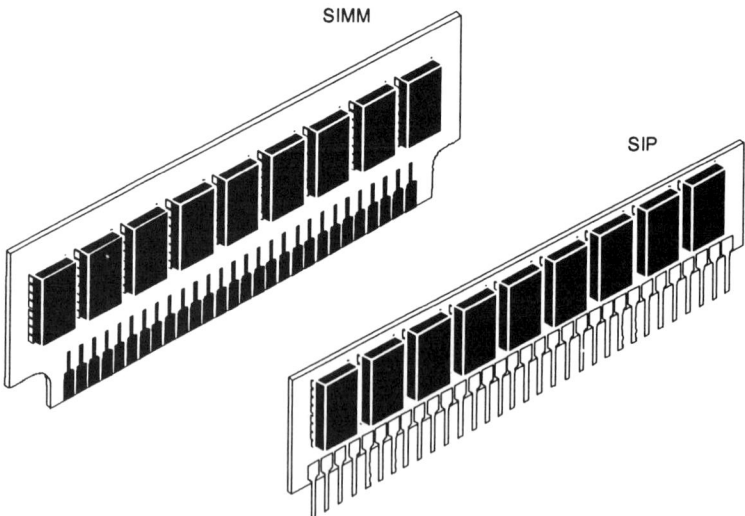

Figure 5.1
A SIMM and a SIP

What is important about SIMMs and SIPs is that they have established a sort of standard for memory expansion. Now, instead of having memory expansion boards, the memory can be accommodated on the motherboard by way of rows of SIMM or SIP connectors. With the current generation of chips it is relatively easy to provide the typical 16MB on the motherboard and very soon 64MB on a motherboard should be entirely possible!

Upgrading slower machines

So far the discussion has concentrated on memory for fast machines, but if you are considering a machine that runs at 16MHz or less then the situation is slightly easier. In this case it is possible to fit memory using the ISA expansion bus with no loss of speed. This means that you can quite easily perform a memory upgrade by buying a memory expansion card and the necessary chips. However, you shouldn't consider this as the only option. It is quite possible that the price of a memory upgrade card, plus suitable chips, will be equal to the price of a new motherboard plus chips to the same memory capacity. Even if the motherboard upgrade is slightly more expensive, you might still prefer it because of the extra features it offers.

A mixed approach

It sounds as though there are only two types of motherboard - all-DIL and all-SIP/SIMM. In practice, many take the hybrid approach of having banks of traditional DIL chip sockets and a few SIP or SIMM sockets as well. For example, smaller XT boards - and some ATs as well - use 64KB x 4 and 256KB x 4 chips to make up the first 640KB of base memory . This has the advantage of a low cost starter system with the possibility of increasing memory by adding SIMM modules later.

A summary

You should now be in a position to understand the different types of memory technology that you will encounter. A rough classification is:

» **Early PC - memory expansion cards**
Low motherboard memory capacity using DIL chips. No proprietary memory expansion bus so extra memory has to be fitted using the XT, or the ISA bus. In many ways the PS/2 range can be thought of as similar to early PCs in that they often rely on the MCA bus for expansion.

» **Middle PC - mixture of on-board and proprietary bus**
A higher motherboard capacity using SIP/SIMM/DIL. Usually a proprietary expansion bus fitted for emergencies.

» **Late PC - mainly motherboard expansion**
A very large motherboard capacity using SIMMs. If a proprietary bus is available then it is only intended as a rarely used facility.

Types of memory module

Memory modules, be they chips, SIPPS or SIMMS, differ in three basic ways - the total amount of memory that they provide, the organisation of that memory, and the speed of access. If you want to buy memory for your machine, then all you need to do is consult the manual that came with it for the details of the required type and speed. However, it helps to know, if only to remove some of the mystery, just a little more about the way memory is organised.

Information is transferred between memory and the processor over a data bus. The smallest data bus is eight bits wide and so any memory has to be able to supply at least eight bits at a time. Some memory chips are organised so that they can only supply one bit at a time - in this case you would need eight such chips - see Figure 5.2.

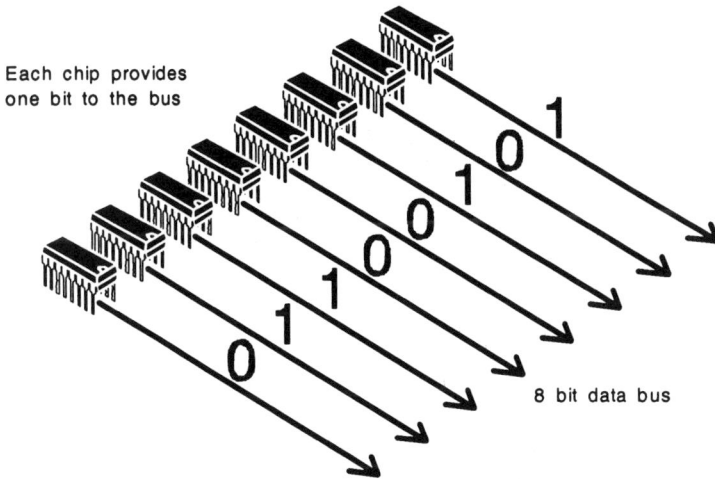

Each chip provides
one bit to the bus

8 bit data bus

Figure 5.2
Eight one bit chips are needed for an 8-bit bus

If you use chips that are organised so that that each can supply four bits each, then you need only two such chips - see Figure 5.3.

This neat picture of needing eight bits is slightly spoiled by the use of an additional bit - the parity bit - to detect errors. The parity bit is set

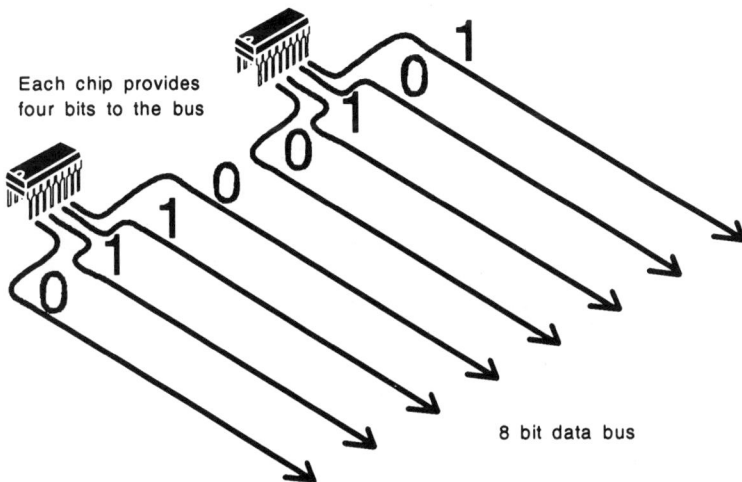

Each chip provides
four bits to the bus

8 bit data bus

Figure 5.3
Two 4-bit chips are needed for an 8-bit bus

by hardware to indicate whether there are an odd or even number of bits set to one. Obviously, if one bit changes, the setting of the parity bit will be incorrect and the accidental change will be detected. Not all machines use a parity bit, and its practical value is arguable - see the box *The importance of parity*. If you include the parity bit, then you need to use a memory organisation that provides nine bits in total.

The organisation of a memory chip is usually indicated by writing the total amount of memory and the number of bits that it supplies. So for example, a 256Kx4 chip provides 256K by 4 bits (where K stands for 1024) and if you put two of them together you get a full 256KB, i.e. 256Kx8 bits.

Many systems use different types of memory chip to reach a particular capacity. For example, an XT with 640KB of memory will have two banks, each containing nine 256Kx1 chips, and two banks containing nine 64Kx1 chips (64+64+256+256=640). This can seem quite complicated but as long as you do the arithmetic it should all make sense.

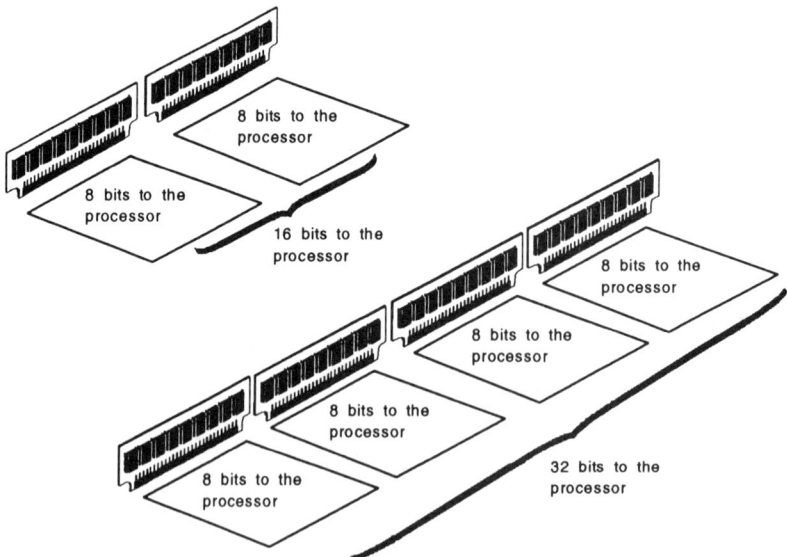

Figure 5.4
Adding memory to a 16- and 32-bit bus (ignoring parity)

If the data bus is 16 bits wide this means that you have to add chips to give 16 bits plus two parity bits if used. For example, many 286/386SX machine use 256Kx9 SIMMs and these have to be added in pairs to make 18 bits. Full 386/486 machines need memory to be added in 32-bit chunks, so in this case you would need to add four 256Kx9 SIMMs - see Figure 5.4. The smallest chunk of memory that you can add is often referred to as a 'bank', although the terminology is far from standard. Banks are explained in more detail in the next section.

To summarise:

» You have to add chips or memory modules that provide the same number of bits as the data bus.

That is:

» in 8-bit XT systems you have to add 9 1-bit chips

» in 16-bit 286 and 386SX systems you have to add 18 1-bit chips

» in 32-bit 386/486 systems you have to add 36 1-bit chips

(Remember that the extra bits over and above the width of the bus have to be added for parity checking.)

Upgrade paths - banks

The arrangement of banks in a machine explains why not all memory capacities can be reached without removing existing memory devices. For example, if your machine has two memory banks that take either two 256Kx9 or 1Mx9 SIMMs, then with one bank full of 256Kx9 SIMMs the total memory capacity is only 512KB (i.e. 256KB+256KB). By adding another pair of 256Kx9 SIMMs you can reach 1MB. Using a pair of 1Mx9 SIMMs you would reach 1.5MB (512KB+1MB), but to go higher you would have to remove the existing 256Kx9 SIMMs and replace them by four 1Mx9 SIMMs giving 4MB. In the case of a 386/486 the SIMM modules would have to be installed (and similarly

The importance of parity

Many users know that 1 Byte is eight bits. So why do we always have to buy memory in blocks of nine bits? The answer is parity error checking. When IBM introduced the PC they were used to big computers which all used error checked memory. An extra bit is added and set to one if the number of data bits set to one is odd. If a single data bit is changed, then you will know because the parity bit tells you that there should be an odd or even number of data bits, and the reality will be different. The IBM PC was the first mass market machine to have parity error checking and it was almost certainly a mistake. Parity checking increases the amount of memory sold by around 10% - in a 16MB computer there is an extra 2MB dedicated to parity checking. So is there any real benefit?

The sort of faults that cause a parity error fall into two classes - permanent chip errors and transient errors. Permanent chip errors can be detected by the Power-On Self Test or POST, so there is little advantage in parity checking except in a machine that is left on for very long periods and so doesn't get its share of POST. Even in a machine of this sort, running a memory testing program every now and again, or even as a background job, would find such problems without the use of parity checking. So parity checking is only really needed to detect transient errors - that is, a change in a bit in memory that occurs without the chip in question failing a memory test at a later date. What sort of things cause such transient errors? The only reasonable candidates are power spikes and cosmic rays. The cosmic ray idea is that a high energy alpha particle shoots through the case of your machine and changes a single bit in its memory. In all the years that I have been using a PC, I have never seen a single transient event. Power spikes have always been large enough to reset the machine and high energy cosmic rays must be scarce! Any parity errors that I have seen have always been due to a faulty chip that a memory test program would have found without the need for the parity bit.

Some recent clones dispense altogether with parity and they work just as well as types which still use parity checking.

removed) in blocks of four making the choices even more restrictive and expensive.

Sometimes it is possible to be confused by the number of SIMM or SIP sockets on a motherboard. The number of memory banks is not equal to the number of sockets. For example, suppose you have four x 9 bit SIMM connectors on a 286 or 386SX motherboard, what memory configurations are possible? You might think that the smallest amount of memory that you can install is whatever you can plug into a single SIMM socket. But if you want a 1MB machine you can't simply plug in a 1Mx9 SIMM because that doesn't fill a bank. As the 286 or 386SX uses a 16-bit data bus, you have to fit pairs of 9-bit SIMMs. In other words, each pair of SIMM sockets is a bank. In this case, to reach 1MB, you have no choice but to use four 256Kx9 SIMMs because these

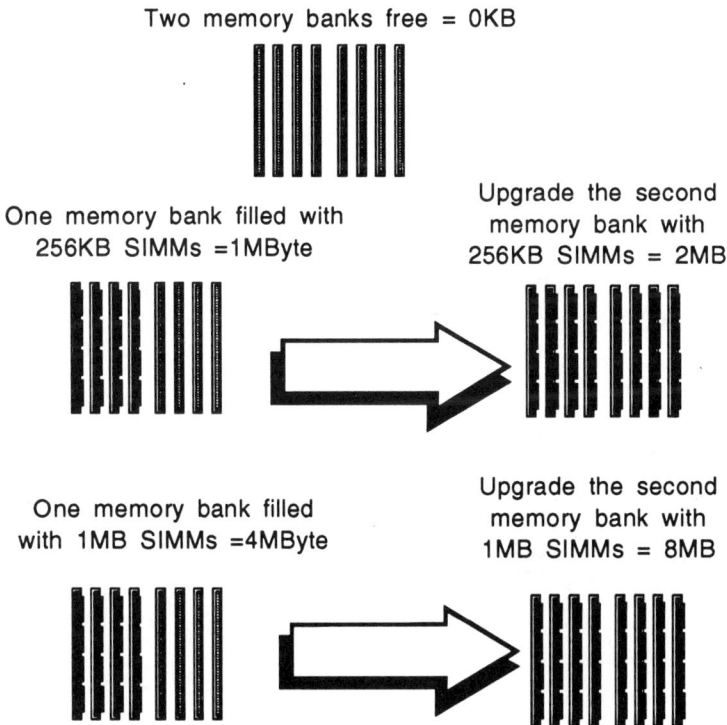

Two memory banks free = 0KB

One memory bank filled with
256KB SIMMs =1MByte

Upgrade the second
memory bank with
256KB SIMMs = 2MB

One memory bank filled
with 1MB SIMMs =4MByte

Upgrade the second
memory bank with
1MB SIMMs = 8MB

Figure 5.5
The maximum amount of RAM achievable depends on what you
install in the first bank

completely fill two banks. Now you might be able to see what the problem is. To meet the requirements of future memory expansion you need to use 1Mx9 SIMMs, but to make up complete banks you have to fit 256Kx9 SIMMs. If you now change your initial memory specification to 2MB of RAM, then the whole picture changes. Now you can fill a single bank with two 1Mx9 SIMMs and upgrading to 4MB is just a matter of plugging in two extra 1Mx9 SIMMs. You can save having to throw away a megabyte when you upgrade by fitting an extra megabyte in the first place! This not only applies when you are buying a new machine, but when you are performing a partial upgrade. The rule is that for maximum upgrade potential always opt for a memory size that can be achieved using as few complete memory banks as possible.

Notice that all of these arguments apply equally well to memory expansion cards, as well as memory fitted to the motherboard.

The final complication is that some machines make use of banks in pairs to speed up processing - see *Interleave* in Chapter 7. The idea is that if the machine has two memory banks then it can access each one in turn giving the memory longer to retrieve data. This makes it possible to use slower and cheaper memory devices. If you fill banks in pairs then the machine's performance will be improved by up to 25%. In short, you don't have to fill pairs of memory banks but it does speed the machine up to do so.

Speed

As well as the exact type of memory chip or module that you need, each type comes in a range of speeds. The speed of a chip affects its price and, while it is a waste to use chips that are faster than necessary, using chips that are too slow will cause problems. As a rule of thumb, the following access speeds should be regarded as the **minimum** for the indicated system clock speeds:

System Clock (MHz)	Motherboard memory (ns)	Chip marking	Expansion memory (ns)
8	150	-15	150
10	120	-12	150
12	100	-10	120
16	100	-10	120
20	80	-80	100
25	80	-80	100
33	70	-70	100

Memory access times are measured in nanoseconds (ns). 1 nanosecond is one thousand millionth of a second,

i.e 1ns=0.000000001 second

There are considerable overlaps in these figures. For example, you can find lots of 16MHz 386SX machines that will work quite happily on 100ns memory but some need 80ns. If in doubt, install the next highest speed. What happens if you get it wrong? Well, you don't get any puffs of blue smoke or fireworks and you don't damage the chips. In many cases they will even appear to work - until the machine warms up a bit. Memory chips that are too slow may actually work fast enough when cool, only to start to generate memory errors when they reach working temperature. If you have installed chips that are too slow, one solution is to introduce wait states which cause the memory to run slower, but the processor has to wait for the memory to catch up with it. You can often set the number of wait states using the setup routine in the system BIOS. Notice, also, that the speed of memory needed on an expansion board never needs to be faster than 100ns because the expansion bus cannot work any faster!

Access times are indicated on chips as a two-digit number. This means that for slower chips the access time in nanoseconds is 10 times the speed marking, while for faster chips the speed is given by the marking. As a matter of interest, the SRAM chips used for cache purposes on fast 386 and 486 machines have an access time of 25 - 35 ns, and this is the speed at which the main memory chips would have to work to keep up with the processor. DRAM chips with this speed would be prohibitively expensive. (See the box that follows for more details of SRAM and DRAM)

Types of chip

Memory chips and modules are made by many manufacturers and they all have their own type numbering systems and speed designations, although there is usually some degree of similarity once you know what you are looking for. Manufacturers and type numbers are given in Table 5.1.

The smallest capacity of memory currently used is known as a 64Kx1. Nine (very occasionally eight) of these are needed to give 64KB of PC memory. The next size up is the 256Kx 1. Again, nine are needed to make up 256KB of PC memory. The largest size commonly found at present is the 1Mx 1. Similarly, nine are needed to give 1MB of PC memory. These chips are usually packaged with 16 or 18 pins, 8 or 9 on each side and are known as DILs.

Other DIL memory chips exist - such as the 64Kx4 (two of these and a single 64Kx1 are needed for 64KB of memory) and the 256Kx4 (two of these and a single 256Kx 1 are needed for 256KB of memory). Both types are met with, particularly on small size boards where space is at a premium. You will often find 64Kx4 chips on VGA cards, where eight will be used to give 256Kx8 of memory. The difference between their use on video cards and motherboards is that video card memory is not parity-checked for errors - it isn't necessary for modern boards and most manufacturers reduce the chip count still further by omitting any memory chips used for parity checking.

Table 5.1

	64Kx1	64Kx 4	256Kx 1	256Kx 4	1Mx 1
Generic	4164	41464	41256	414256	411000/511000
Fujitsu	MB8264A	MB81464	MB81256		MB81C1000
Hitachi	HM4864	HM50464	HM51256	HM514256	HM511000
Hyundai	HY5164	HY53C464	HY51C256		
Intel	2164				
Micron Technology	MT4264		MT1256	MT4C4256	MT4C1024
Mitsubishi	M5K4164		M5M4256		M5M4C1000
Mostek	4564				
Motorola	MCM6665				
National Semicond'r	NMC4164				
NEC	uPD4164	uPD41464	uPD41256	uPD414256	uPD421000
OKI	M3764	M41464	M41256	M514256	
Panasonic	MN4164		MN41256		
Samsung	KM4164	KM41464	KM41256	KM414256	KM41C1000
Siemens	HY4164	HY41464	HY41256		
Texas Instruments	TMS4164	TMS4464	TMS4256	TMS44256	TMS4C1024
Toshiba	TMM4164	TMM41464	TMM41256		TC511000

Dynamic + Static RAM =Main memory and cache

Many users are confused or misled by the terms dynamic and static RAM or DRAM and SRAM. The trouble is that 'dynamic' sounds better and has all the connotations of 'doing something' whereas static sounds slow. In fact, your preferences should be reversed because SRAM is generally faster, more difficult to make and hence more expensive. All of the megabytes of memory in your machine will be DRAM as it is the only type that is cheap enough to make it possible for you to buy it by the megabyte. However DRAM isn't fast enough to keep up with processors that run faster than 10MHz and so this leads to the introduction of wait states - short pauses necessary to allow the memory to catch up with the processor. There are various ways of avoiding or minimising wait states while still using DRAM. The most common method these days is to use caching. A cache is a smallish amount of SRAM fast enough to keep up with the processor. The processor reads and writes directly into the cache, which in turn deals with the slower DRAM memory. With luck, most of the data that the processor wants to work with can be held in the cache so allowing it to work without wait states most of the time.

Obviously, the larger the cache the better, but this follows a law of diminishing returns. Once you get beyond 64KB of cache then there isn't much improvement. The exception to this rule is if you are multi-tasking and then larger caches are a good idea. Some machines allow you to upgrade the cache by fitting extra RAM chips. Notice that increasing the size of the cache doesn't increase the amount of memory available to run a program - it simply makes the machine faster, if you are lucky.

Considerations for cache upgrades are much the same as for main memory upgrades, but with the following differences - cache memory is always fast (around 25ns) SRAM and it is always in the form of DIL chips. Also notice that a RAM cache isn't the same as a disk cache - but they do work on the same principles. A RAM cache speeds up the operation of RAM memory and a disk cache speeds up the operation of a disk.

This is not a complete listing of all possible manufacturers' chips. Some of the above may only be found in older equipment, or sold as second user items; there are also other manufacturers whose products will bear similar numbers to the above but which will sometimes bear different letter codes. In all cases, it should be possible to work out what type of memory chip is involved. The generic number is frequently used in advertisements and magazine articles.

SIPs and SIMMs appear to have many different numbers, - even more confusing than those for DILs. It is best to purchase these from a reputable supplier and then to mark them yourself with a permanent ink marker so that you do not insert the wrong type (if you have more than one size). Be particularly careful to obtain the correct type - some machines use 8-bit modules (no parity) while others use 9-bit with parity. Always check with your supplier that you are getting the correct type of chip, since SIPs will not fit SIMM sockets and vice-versa.

SIMM looks set to be the single standard for memory modules in the future, with SIP modules being used occasionally; 64Kx1 DIL chips are already referred to as 'obsolete'.

Memory use

Although not strictly concerned with the installation or upgrading of memory, it is necessary to know something about the use to which a machine puts the memory you install. Memory in PCs may divided into three types, depending on how it can be used: conventional, extended and expanded.

» Conventional memory

This exists between 0 and 1024KB (or 1MB) and of this, 640KB is usable by DOS and the remaining 384KB is reserved for video RAM and the ROM and RAM of other attached devices such as disk controllers. At the top of the conventional memory, the ROM BIOS is given a 128KB slot and immediately below this is an area that can be used by video cards and other add-ons. Technically, DOS could utilise any unused locations between 640KB and 1024KB - in practice up to a maximum of 96KB extra - but this can usually be achieved only by the use of software which alters the position of the video RAM within the memory map. Such software is included in MS-DOS 5, DR-DOS, QEMM386 and 386MAX but this only works on 386 systems. Some 286 systems based on the Chips and Technologies chipset can perform the same trick with the help of suitable software.

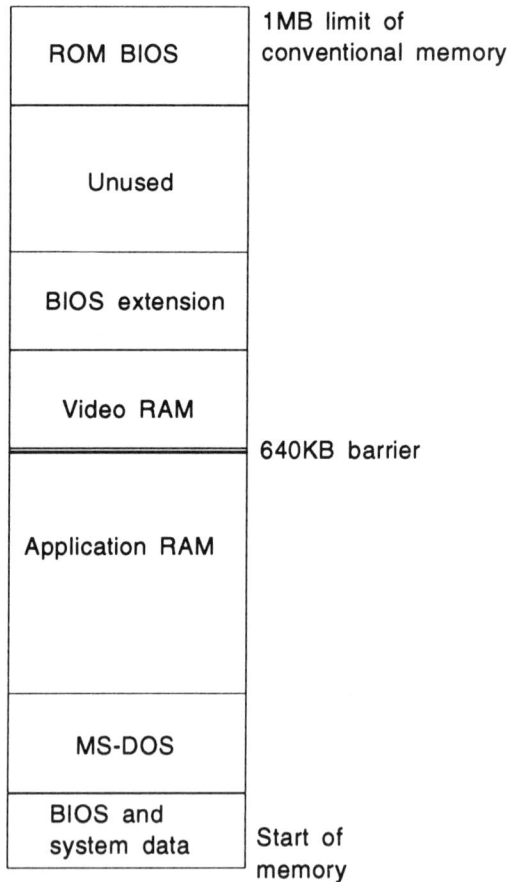

ROM BIOS	1MB limit of conventional memory
Unused	
BIOS extension	
Video RAM	640KB barrier
Application RAM	
MS-DOS	
BIOS and system data	Start of memory

Figure 5.6
Conventional memory

» **Extended memory**

This is just ordinary memory that happens to live above the 1MB limit. It isn't any different from conventional memory, i.e. the first 640KB, but it can only be used by a 286 or 386 processor while running in a different mode - protected mode. The earlier 8086 and 8080 can't make use of memory above 1MB at all because they can't run in protected mode, only in real mode, and have no facilities for managing more than

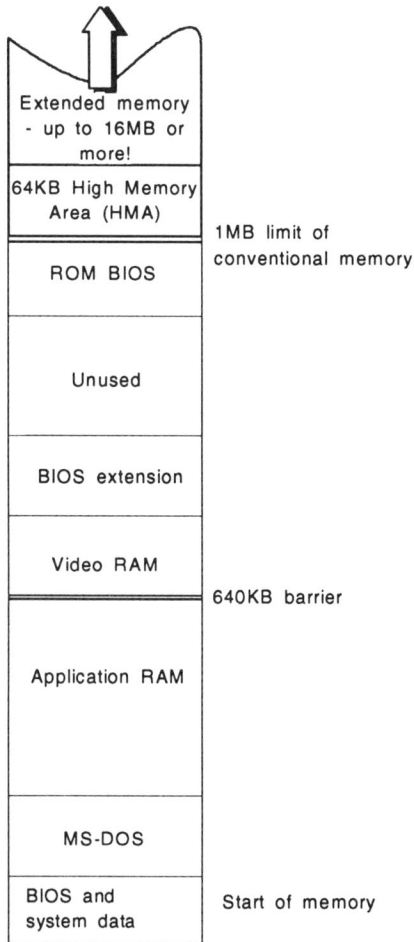

Figure 5.7
Extended memory

1MB. Also, most MS-DOS software can't get at extended memory because they only work in real mode, although this is becoming less true as applications become more sophisticated. New operating systems such as Windows and OS/2 can make use of extended memory. Also, on 386 based systems extended memory can be converted to expanded memory by the use of memory managers, such as QEMM 386, 386MAX, and the utilities that come with MS-DOS 5 and DR-DOS.

» Expanded memory

This is a form of bank switched memory. It breaks the 640KB barrier by allowing blocks or banks of memory to be switched in and out of the same area. It's a bit like swapping diskettes in a disk drive - the drive may only have a capacity of 360KB, say, but by 'bank switching' diskettes in and out of the drive, its storage capacity can be effectively much larger. As long as you keep this model in mind, then understanding expanded memory should cause you no problems. The simplest form of expanded memory uses a small 64KB swap area called the page frame. (In fact, the smallest expanded memory block that can be swapped is 16KB and this is generally referred to as a sub-page or sub-page frame.) This is the sort of expanded memory that you need to increase the amount of data that you can work with. You can make use of it to run more than one program at a time, but only by an inefficient process of swapping an active program from conventional memory to expanded, while an inactive program goes the other way. Notice that the program has to be copied in 64KB chunks from conventional memory into the page frame and vice versa. This is slow, but much better than swapping to and from disk! Expanded memory can be added to any type of processor, even the oldest XT design. For this reason many programs can make use of expanded memory, but cannot use the simpler, and now more common, extended memory. Notice that on all machines, apart from the 386/486, additional hardware has to be provided to implement the bank switching.

In the future, expanded memory will certainly become obsolete because extended memory is so much simpler and faster in use. However, for the moment it has to be admitted that expanded memory is still very important as it represents the only way to break the 640KB barrier with

1MB limit of
conventional
memory

| ROM BIOS |
| Unused |
| Page frame |
| BIOS extension |
| Video RAM |

640KB
barrier

| Application RAM |
| MS-DOS |
| BIOS and system data |

Start of
memory

Any expanded
memory page
can be switched
into the page
frame

Expanded
memory pool
divided into
frames

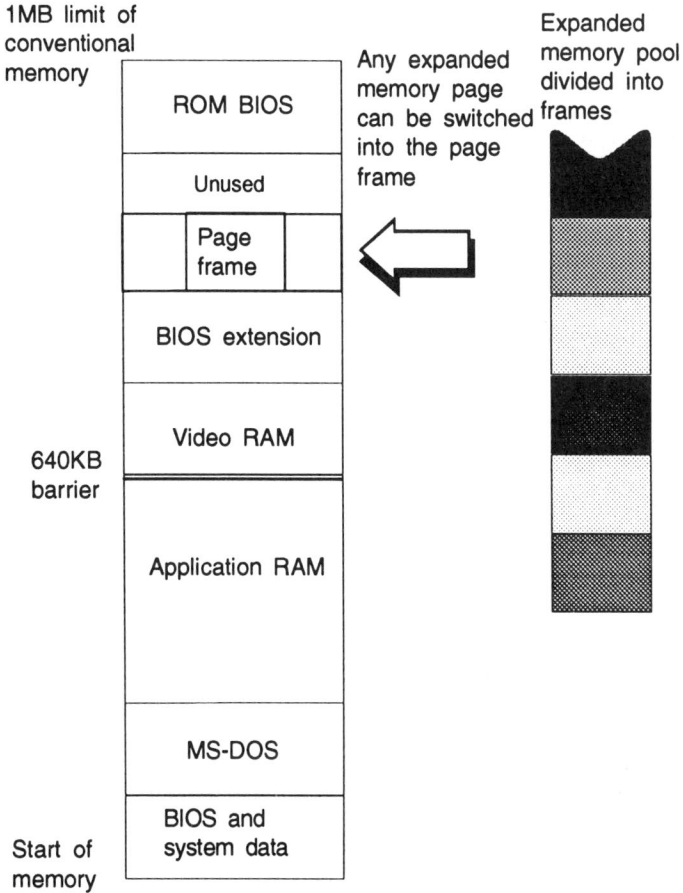

Figure 5.8
Expanded memory

many applications programs such as spreadsheets. If you are using an XT design then it is the only way of extending memory beyond 640KB. General recommendations are:

» **XT 8088/86 machines** - expanded memory is the only way to break the 640KB barrier but in most cases it would be more cost effective to upgrade the motherboard to a 286 or 386SX than add an expanded memory adapter card.

» **286 machines** - hardware based expanded memory is still necessary although it is possible to find programs that convert extended memory into expanded. If possible, choose a 286 motherboard that supports expanded memory without the need for extra hardware.

» **386/486 machines** - expanded memory isn't an important consideration because of the ease with which extended memory can be converted to expanded using nothing more than software.

The general recommendation concerning XT machines need not be taken as a binding one, because there are many users who find that expanded memory added to their XT has prolonged its life well beyond their expectations. Also see the box *The larger frame*.

Buying memory expansion cards

The important question to ask yourself is whether or not you need extended memory, expanded memory or both. Some early memory cards would only provide one or the other but these days most memory cards are configurable. Even so, the question of expanded memory is still an important one if you need a full LIM/EMS 4.0 large frame capability - i.e. if you have an XT class machine and want to run a multi-tasker such as DESQview. If you need large frame EMS, then installation of a card isn't quite as simple as you might be led to believe. In particular, if you want to take advantage of a large frame, then you have to free up a large chunk of memory in the first 640KB region. This

The larger frame

If you really want to increase the number of programs that you are running on an XT class machine then you need large frame or full EEMS 4.0 standard expanded memory.

The difference between this and standard expanded memory is that a large chunk of the conventional memory area can be swapped, not just a tiny 64KB block - hence the name large frame expanded memory. Using this larger frame, multi-tasking programs such as DESQview can swap almost the entire conventional memory area in a single operation. Many expanded memory cards are either not capable of this sort of large frame operation or they are not correctly set up to work in this way. Multi-taskers such as DESQview can still swap programs using small frame expanded memory, but as each program has to be passed through the page frame in 64KB chunks, this is considerably slower. This accounts for the reported performance differences in multi-tasking a simple XT machine.

The DESQview manual recommends setting up any expanded memory as large frame expanded memory, with as large a frame as possible. You can tell the difference between setting up large and small frame expanded memory because in the case of large frame you generally have to disable most, if not all, of the memory on the motherboard so that it can be replaced by memory switched in from the expanded memory pool. Another problem to look out for are older expanded memory cards that create large frame expanded memory using software rather than hardware. These are much slower than true EEMS 4.0 expanded memory cards.

Multi-tasking using expanded memory is a technique that is becoming less popular as multi-tasking on 286 and 386 becomes easier and cheaper. Even so, if you want to make more use of an existing XT machine, and you can find an EEMS 4.0 standard card cheaply enough, it does work well enough to run three or four programs at the same time using DESQview.

generally means disabling or relocating the memory on the motherboard, and how difficult this is depends very much on the type of machine that you have.

Also, remember that ISA bus memory cards will introduce wait states when used with 286 machines that run faster than 10MHz - no matter how fast the memory chips you fit! The speed limitation is due to the bus and not to the memory card itself. The wide range of memory expansion cards that were available until recently seem to be being phased out in favour of a much smaller selection of cards that implement both expanded and extended memory using SIMMs. Indeed, if you need a memory card to use up some DIL chips that you have left over from a motherboard upgrade, say, then you might have difficulty locating one.

One type of memory upgrade card that hasn't been mentioned so far is the conventional memory upgrade. In the early days of PCs, the motherboard could hold less than the full 640KB of memory and to reach 640KB you needed an add-on card. Some current expanded/extended memory cards have the ability to 'back-fill' conventional memory to bring it up to the full 640KB but again, this is a type of card that is rapidly disappearing.

Buying memory upgrades

So, once you know which chips you need, the only problem is to shop around for a good price. You should try to find a reasonable price, but watch out for really cheap offers. These are often manufacturers' overstocks, i.e. chips bought for a product that wasn't built in the numbers anticipated. There is nothing wrong with manufacturers' overstock unless it has been recovered from built units. Removing memory from cards for re-sale isn't a good idea unless the devices are re-tested and offered with a guarantee.

Another point to note is that if your machine has a well known brand name you don't need to feel trapped into buying their proprietary upgrade card - there are alternatives and they work.

Installing memory

The actual installation of memory is very easy. If you are using DIL chips then the task is a little more difficult than SIMM or SIP modules, but still not difficult. The biggest danger in inserting a DIL chip is that you bend one of the pins under the package rather than insert it into the socket. In most cases of a memory upgrade failure involving DIL chips the cause is a bent or twisted pin.

To insert DIL chips into a socket with a reasonable chance of success you should first 'form' the pins to make them at right angles to the body of the chip - see Figure 5.9. You can do this by pushing the chip gently against the edge of a table, using a small pair of pliers or using a special chip insertion tool. Once you have the legs formed you can place the chip into the socket and push firmly down. The chip should go in in one movement and you can check for bent pins by looking carefully along the side. To remove a chip it is better to use a chip removal tool, but as these are expensive a reasonably safe alternative is to use a thin flat-bladed screw driver and lever up each end of the chip a little at a time. Notice that memory chips have to be inserted the correct way round (see Figure 5.10) and this is usually indicated by a notch at one end or a small depression in one corner. This mark should be matched

---

Warning!

Nearly all RAM chips are very prone to damage by static. They are usually supplied in an anti-static packaging in which they should remain until you are going to use them. Before you handle RAM chips or modules make sure that you earth yourself by touching a radiator or something metal that is connected to earth - a water pipe will usually do. This will get rid of any high voltage static charges that you might have built up. To be completely safe it is better to work on an earthed metal surface while installing the chips. A large sheet of aluminium foil that is touching a radiator or water pipe will do but the simplest solution is to work on a metal draining board if one is available!

Before straightening   After straightening

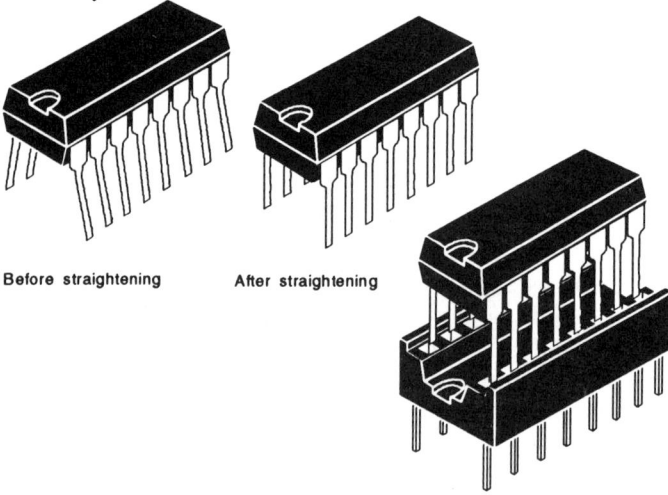

Figure 5.9
Inserting a DIL chip

up with the notch or cut off corner on the chip socket or a dot marked on the PCB.

Another slight complication that you need to be aware of is the use of dual sockets. To enable two different types of chip to be used, some motherboards and memory cards have a two-sized chip socket that when laid out in a rectangular array can be very visually confusing. The two common types are an 18/16-pin and a 20/18-pin socket - see Figure 5.11. All you have to do is choose the type of chip that you are

The 'pin one' end of a chip is marked by a semi-circle or a dot

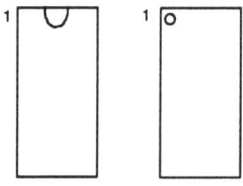

The 'pin one' end of a socket is marked by a semi-circle, notch, or dot on the motherboard

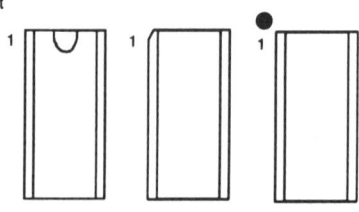

Figure 5.10
Lining up a DIL chip with its socket

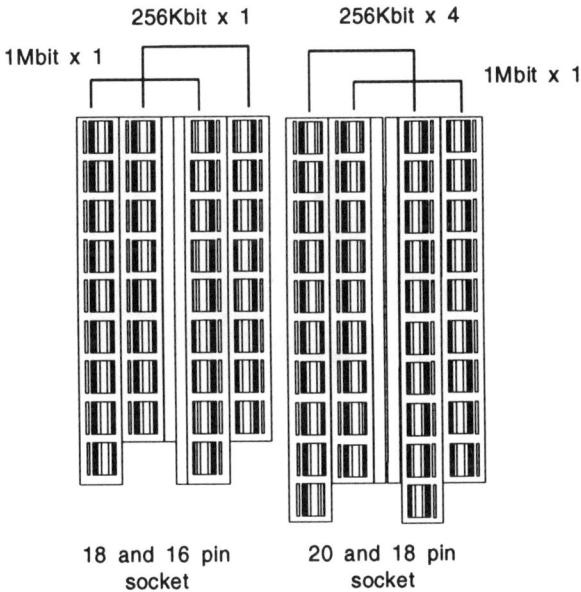

256Kbit x 1   256Kbit x 4

1Mbit x 1

1Mbit x 1

18 and 16 pin
socket

20 and 18 pin
socket

Figure 5.11
Two types of dual socket

going to fit and use the correct portion of the socket. Usually the first
chip is the most difficult to fit correctly because after this you at least
have something to guide your eye.

Installing SIP or SIMM modules is much easier and quicker than DIL
chips. The SIP is mechanically the simpler in that the printed circuit
board holding the chips has a row of pins sticking out of the bottom
edge. A SIP socket is just a row of holes ready to accept the pins. To
insert a SIP all you have to do is line up all of the pins in the socket and
push with a firm, steady force until the pins sink into the sockets. The
only danger here is that a pin will miss the socket. The only
complication is that SIPs come in 30- and 32-pin types and it is
important to make sure that you use the correct type.

A SIMM looks more like a standard expansion board in miniature. It
has edge connector 'pads' along the bottom edge. Early SIMM
connectors were, likewise, just expansion sockets in miniature, and the

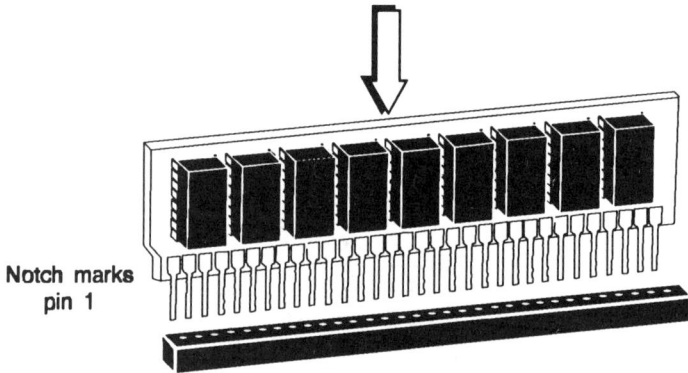

Figure 5.12
Inserting a SIP

SIMM was installed by pushing, and removed by pulling. This isn't a good method for such a small card and modern SIMM connectors use a different approach: to insert a SIMM into a modern connector you place the module into the slot at an angle and rotate it into the upright position where two clips hold it in place. Removing a SIMM is just the same operation in reverse - just like it says in all the best build-it-yourself manuals! It is important that you identify the type of

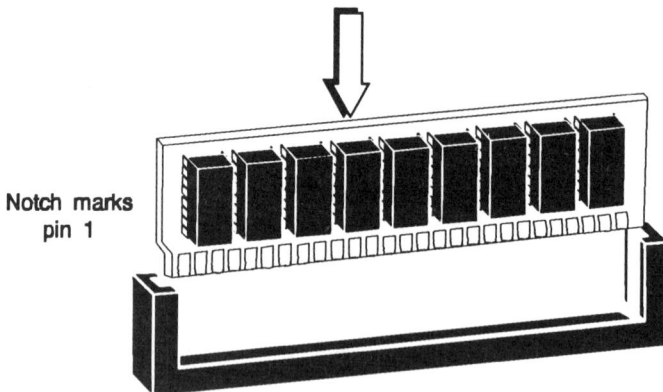

Figure 5.13
Inserting an old style SIMM into a push fit socket

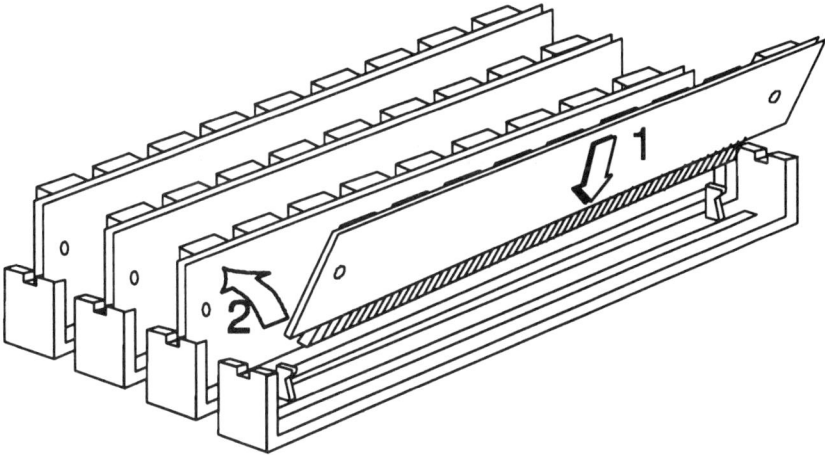

Figure 5.14
Inserting a SIMM that rotates into place

SIMM connector in use, because trying to rotate a push/pull connector, or push/pull a rotate connector will only result in unhappiness.

Some machines require you to set DIP switches or jumpers on the motherboard to let it know how much memory you have installed and even which size of chip. The only way that you can find out how to do this is to look at the original manual as there is no standard, or even commonly accepted, method. Most modern motherboards don't need any setting, though, because they discover the amount of memory installed by looking for it when they first start up. In this case, if the machine reports less memory than you think you have installed, the chances are you haven't installed it properly.

Installing SRAM chips to upgrade a cache is exactly the same, but in this case you will certainly have to alter jumpers or switches on the motherboard to let it know how much cache memory is available. Again, the details of how this is done are far from standard and the only way of finding out how to do this is to consult the motherboard's manual.

Key points

» Modern motherboards allow large amounts of memory to be fitted without the use of an expansion card. This makes many of the arguments about improved expansion buses, such as EISA or MCA, largely irrelevant for the average user.

» It can be cheaper to upgrade the motherboard than add a memory expansion card to a slower machine.

» Memory modules and chips come in different sizes and widths. For example, 1Mx9, 64Kx9 and so on.

» The smallest amount of memory that you can add to a machine is one whole bank. For a 8088 a bank is 9 bits wide, for a 286 and 386SX it is 18 bits wide and for the 386/486 it is 36 bits wide. The width of a bank is simply the width of the databus plus one parity bit for each byte, i.e. for each 8 bits.

» DIL memory is being slowly but surely superseded by SIMM and SIP modules.

» You have to make sure that you buy fast enough RAM chips for the processor with which they are to be used.

» There are three types of memory: conventional, extended, and expanded. The distinction is relatively unimportant for 386 machines, but vital for 286 and XT machines.

Chapter 6
<u>The grey box</u>

A computer's case is its most visible attribute. In this chapter we consider how different types of case make a machine more or less suitable for particular purposes.

You may not think that a computer's case is very important, but it is. Not only is it the part that you see most often, it also governs how many drives you can fit, how many and what type of expansion cards you can add, and how easy it is to get inside and make modifications. All this contributes to how reliable the system is. If you are planning a completely new system then you have to spend a little time selecting a suitable box.

Upgrading

If you are planning a motherboard upgrade, then you should also consider a new box. It can add as little as £50 to the cost of the upgrade and might improve the usability of the machine. All this may be true, but why would you ever want to buy a new case for your machine? The answer is that when you upgrade the motherboard it is very tempting to buy a new box to put it in. Essentially what you are doing is to part build your own machine by moving the hard disk, video and expansion cards to a new motherboard in a new box. What you have left over may look like at least 50% of a computer but it is really only a shell - a motherboard in a box. You might be able to recoup some of its value second-hand, or you might be able to put some low cost/low performance expansion cards with it - an old monochrome card plus monitor and a single floppy, for example - to make it useful for less demanding applications.

Types of case

The question addressed in this chapter is "what do you want from a computer case?". The answer depends on the type of machine you need and the type of user you are. The most important question is how often you will need access to the interior of the machine? As you are planning to upgrade or build your own machine you are likely to be the type of user who needs to get inside to fit new boards and even change the configuration. In this case, accessibility is a most important consideration. A desktop case might be easy to get into, but you have to remove the monitor that is sitting on top of it first and that generally means clearing the desk. If this doesn't sound like a problem then a desktop case, possibly with a flip top to make it even easier to get into, is a good idea. Otherwise I would recommend a tower case of some sort, if you can justify the extra expense.

The traditional reason for using a tower case is so that you can have lots of disk drives and plenty of room for expansion. In practice, the number of drives that you can install in a tower isn't that much greater than in a desktop case - typically 5 or 6. Also, with devices shrinking there isn't as much need to worry about how many full height or even 5.25" half height devices you can fit. If you restrict yourself to the 3.5" form factor, then a desktop case is almost as good. A tower case is usually roomier and so fitting a lot of devices is easier but it is the fact that you can stand it on the floor that is its real great advantage. This means that you can keep your desk clear and get at the insides of the computer without having to find somewhere for the monitor to sit. If you don't feel like the expense or have a need for a full tower case then a desktop mini-tower is the next best thing. This isn't as roomy and it takes up desk space but you can still get inside without having to move the monitor.

Getting inside

If you build your own machine then you will certainly know exactly how to get inside the case. However, removing the outer cover of a machine for the first time can be a problem. There are a great many different fixing methods. The traditional arrangement for a desktop case is to use a small number of fixing screws at the back of the case but you may find fixing screws along the side of the case as well.

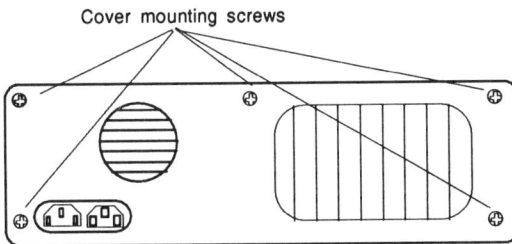

Cover mounting screws

Once these screws are undone, removing the cover is a matter of pulling forward and then lifting up.

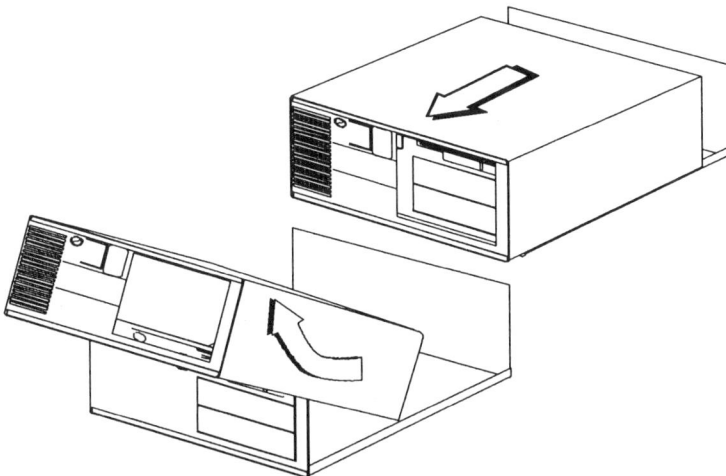

Sometimes it is necessary to spring the sides at the back of the case apart to ensure that they clear retaining clips at the front. Some modern cases work in reverse in that you have to lift up the back edge to allow the front panel to clear the switches etc. that poke through.

Getting inside a tower or mini-tower case is usually very easy once you have decided which type of external cover is being used. If you look carefully at the outer case you should be able to see if it is a single piece of steel folded to make an upturned U or if each side is separate. In the case of the upturned U all you have to do is remove the fixing screws at the back and then lift it off with a pivoting action.

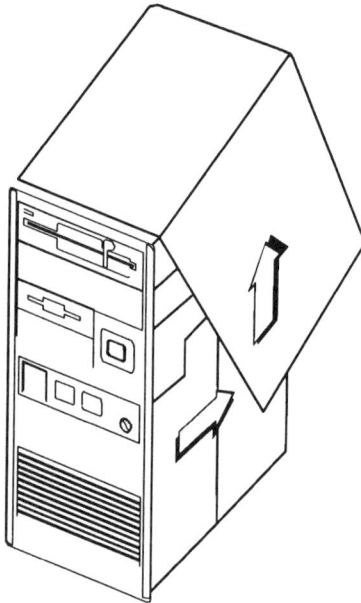

As for a desktop case you may have to spring the back edge of the case around a retaining bracket at the rear.

For a tower case with separate side panels these usually have fixing screws and spring retaining clips. Once the fixing screws are removed a sharp pull at the bottom edge should free the side panel completely.

One complication is that some cases appear to have no retaining screws whatsoever. This is usually because there is a false rear panel, usually made of thick plastic, which is held on using spring clips. The solution is to remove this first by levering it off with a screwdriver to reveal the fixing screws.

If you frequently remove the cover of your machine then it is worth investing in a power screwdriver. Even a budget model takes the trouble out of removing and replacing cover screws.

Other features

There is a range of other technical points that are worth looking out for - the size of the power supply, the number of drive mounting bays and their type etc.. How important each of these is depends on what configuration you are likely to be running. For example, if you are only planning to use a single hard disk and two floppies then a 200W power supply should be enough, but there is some wisdom in the idea that you can never have too big a power supply.

A similar wisdom applies to disk drive bays - better too many than too few. But beware of a case with so many bays that it prevents easy access to the motherboard. How easy it is to remove and install the motherboard is another important consideration.

Fixing kits and instructions

Most cases are supplied with a fixing kit of one sort or another. However, what is included varies quite a lot. Stand-offs and screws for mounting a motherboard are the minimum you should expect. How to install a motherboard was described in Chapter 4. You should identify all of the motherboard mounting components that have been supplied and work out how you are going to use all of them before attempting to fit them to the motherboard and case.

Not all cases provide enough mounting pieces for the number of disk drive bays that they have.

Most cases do not come with any instructions of any kind. You can argue that, being mechanical, the way they are supposed to work should be obvious to anyone. In the main this is true, but occasionally a less than obvious feature, such as a side panel that has to be removed to allow the motherboard to slide in, would benefit from documentation.

In the absence of an assembly diagram you should spend a little time examining the case to discover what can be removed and what is fixed. Don't simply try to force the motherboard and drives in without thinking it through!

There are two general types of drive mounting: side slides and cradle. Side slides were first introduced in the original IBM AT. A pair of side slides have to be bolted to each side of a drive, which can then be slid into place, see Figure 6.1. The only problem with side slides is that, often, not enough are provided with the case. It is possible to buy extra side slides but this can be expensive (around £5 a pair) and quickly add to the total cost of the case. Cradle mounting is simpler in that the drive is simply bolted directly to the case, see Figure 6.2. It has the disadvantage that you cannot remove the drive without access to the both sides of the cradle. Notice that drive bays come in a range of sizes - full height 5.25", half height 5.25", half height 3.5" and slimline (1/3rd) height 3.5". Unless you are planning to install very high capacity or very old fashioned drives, full height bays are more or less redundant. The current standard is half height for 5.25" drives and slimline for 3.5" drives. Some cases also come with 3.5" to 5.25" conversion trays. The topic of installing drives is discussed further detail in Chapters 7 and 8.

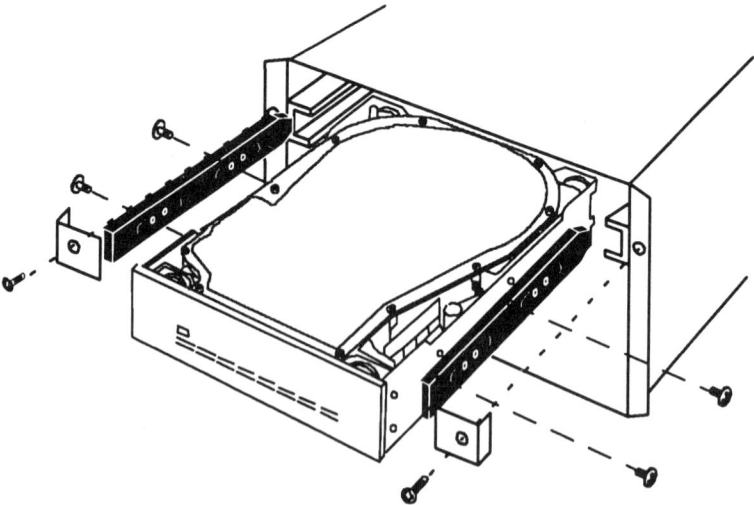

Figure 6.1
Side slide mounting

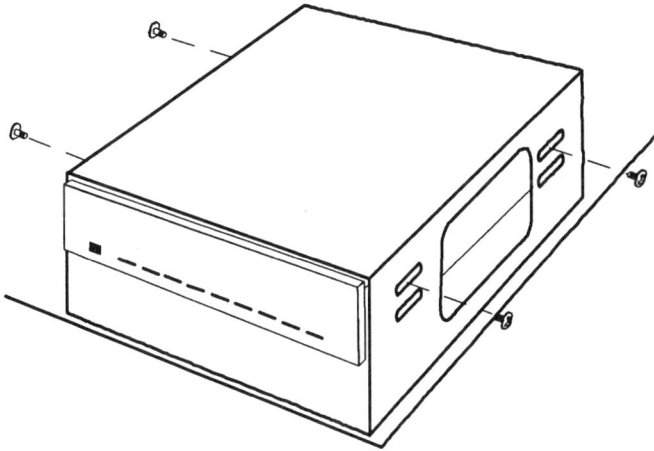

Figure 6.2
Cradle mounts

As well as mounting drives, there is also a need for a case to accommodate a number of D-type sockets. These are the sort of sockets that are used for serial and parallel ports. Often the first few such connectors are actually mounted on the adapter boards to which they belong.

However, some cards use cable-connected sockets which have to be mounted on the case. Most cases have a number of suitably sized holes or knockouts ready to accept the two standard sizes of D-type sockets - 15 pin and 25 pin. If you are planning to use more than one or two extra D-type sockets, for example if you plan to use the machine to run

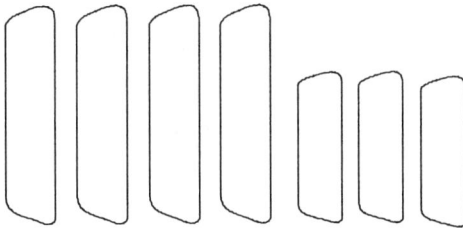

Figure 6.3
D-type cutouts

a multi-user system or a bulletin board, then the number of D-type cutouts a case has might be an important factor in its selection.

Connections

The connecting cables between the switches and lights on the front panel are also usually supplied with the case. If possible you should choose a case that comes with labelled connectors. Otherwise a few minutes spent labelling the connectors by tracing them back to their front panel connections will repay the effort in time saved in the future.

Sometimes a power splitting cable or convertor will be included to provide a power connection for additional 5.25" or 3.5" drives. If you discover that you need more drive power connectors then additional power splitters can be bought separately. Power splitters are also sometimes used to provide power for a numeric speed indicator. Notice that all of the main power connectors for disk drives and to power the motherboard are part of the power supply. You should find out how many of each type of connector the power supply has.

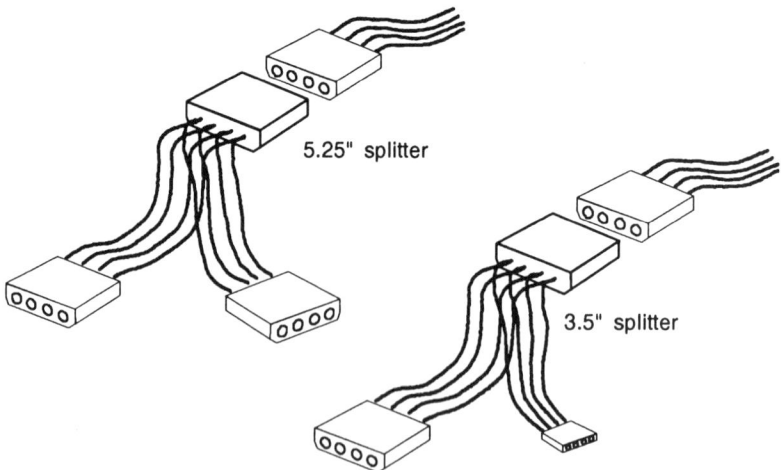

Figure 6.4
Power supply splitters

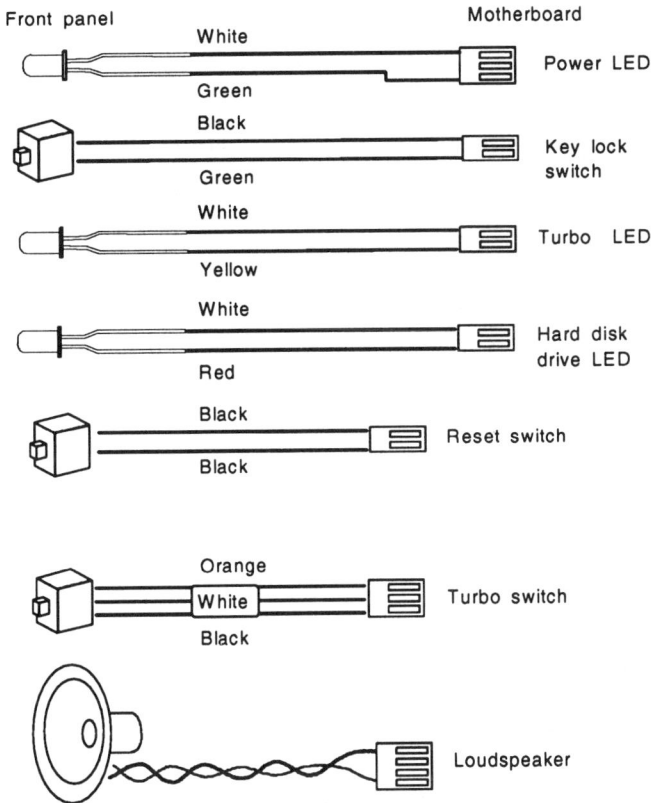

Figure 6.5
Connecting cables

Also included in the fixing kit is a loudspeaker and this can be mounted in the case in any of a number of possible ways, ranging from double sided tape to a specially made plastic mount.

A less standard item is the external battery connector. This is most often included with full sized tower cases. It is usually mounted using double sided tape somewhere near the external battery connector. Notice that it is important to check that the voltage supplied by the external connector is the same as that used by the motherboard.

Although there is no standard colour coding for the connections to a motherboard the following are reasonably common.

Red/White	Hard Disk Activity Light
Green/White	Power On LED
Yellow/White	Turbo LED
Green/Black	Keylock switch
Red/Black, Grey/Grey	
or Orange/White/Black	Turbo switch
Black/Black or Blue/White	Reset switch

Adapter card mounts

One of the areas in which all cases have standardised is that for expansion cards. A big difference, however, is how much space they give to accommodate the length of an expansion card. Many smaller cases restrict the length of card that can be inserted in at least part of

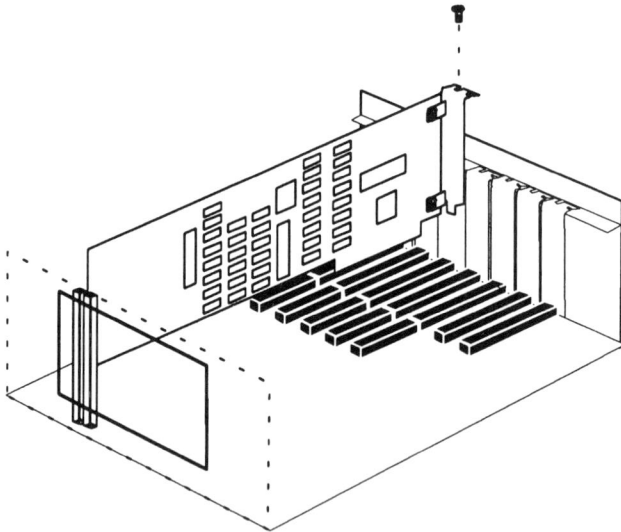

Figure 6.6
Expansion card fittings

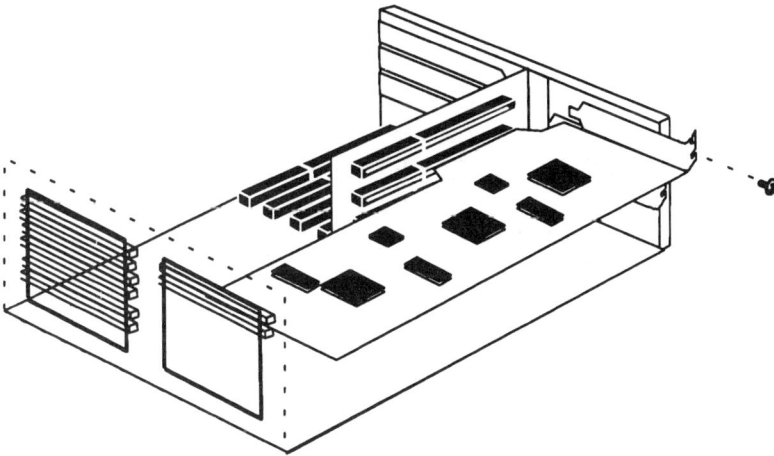

Figure 6.7
Slimline case

the area to half of the standard length. For the full length cards a plastic guide is usually included which clips onto the metalwork to hold the end of the board. For half length and shorter cards there is generally no need to secure the free end. The metal bracket on the adapter card is simply screwed to the case after the card has been plugged in. Blanking plates should be fitted where adapter cards are not in place. The reason for this is that not using the blanking plates results in the air flow from the fan being altered so that it all passes out though the holes in the expansion area.

Whilst on the subject of cooling fans it is worth noting that, in most situations, the only cooling fan needed is the one that is fitted in the power supply. Some larger cases do provide mounting holes for additional fans, but these are only needed if you are running large numbers of disk drives in the one case.

Some slimline cases come with a right angle convertor to turn one of the expansion slots through 90 degrees so allowing expansion cards to be fitted sideways.

Speed indicators

One of the optional extras often found in slightly larger cases is a numeric speed indicator. Whilst these are completely unnecessary, some people like them and are prepared to spend extra time and money on them. The only problem is that the instructions that come with speed indicators are usually very obscure - so much so that setting the speed indicator to work can be the most difficult problem in building the entire machine! Unfortunately, all speed indicators are slightly different so it isn't possible to give an accurate account of how to set one up in all cases. However, it is possible to describe the general principles and show how they apply in one particular case. Once you understand the general principles and see one case, others are easier to deal with.

The first thing to understand is that a numeric speed indicator doesn't show how fast the machine is running by measuring its clock speed - it isn't anything as clever. The speed indicator is simply a slightly improved version of the Turbo LED found on most front panels. When the machine is switched into turbo mode the Turbo LED is on, and when it isn't in turbo mode the Turbo LED is off. The same on/off approach applies to the speed indicator with the difference that when the Turbo LED is on, the numeric indicator shows digits that give the highest speed at which the machine runs. When the Turbo LED is off, the indicator shows numerals corresponding to the lowest speed.

Once you understand the on/off nature of the speed indicator, setting one up seems a lot simpler. It involves two steps:

» connecting the wiring necessary to supply power and an indication of the turbo state

» setting jumpers or switches so the the numerals that display in both turbo on/off are correct

Connecting the wiring is slightly different in each case, but there has to be a connection to the power supply and one to either the Turbo LED on the front panel or to the Turbo LED connector on the motherboard. There is also the slight problem of whether high speed turbo mode is indicated by a high or a low signal on the Turbo LED. In each case there is usually a slightly different wiring diagram. The most usual condition is that Turbo LED low indicates a high speed turbo mode.

Ones digit setting

Tens digit setting

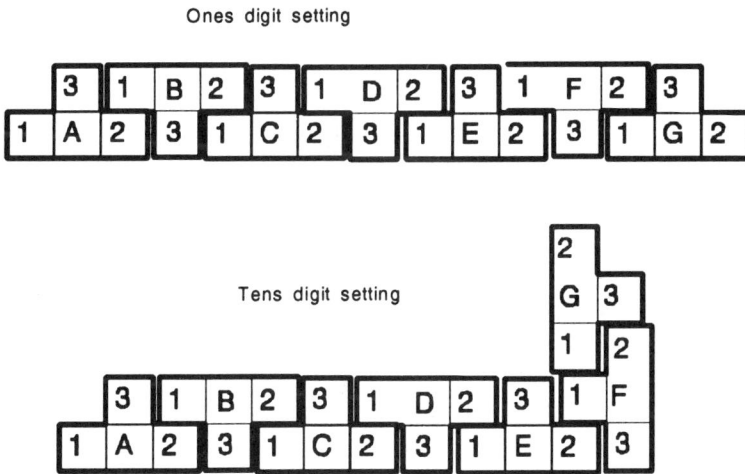

Figure 6.8
Speed indicator connector blocks

In the example speed indicator (SB-056 display fitted to a Procase 617 series) there is a single connector block that has to be wired differently according to whether Turbo low or Turbo high indicates a high speed mode. The display is supplied pre-wired for Turbo low.

The next step is to set jumpers to produce the required two sets of figures. For example, if the turbo speed is 20MHz and the standard speed is 16MHz then the tens digit has to be set to show a 2 or a 1 and the units digit has to be set to show either a 0 or a 6 according to the state. How the jumpers are set obviously depends on the exact design of the display. In the case of the example display, the jumpers are arranged so that each jumper has three possible positions according to whether it is placed on pin 1, 2 or 3. Jumper settings are indicated as A2, B3 etc., meaning jumper A is placed on pin 1, jumper B is placed on pin 3 and so on, see Figure 6.8. A table is provided which gives the jumper settings according to the digits that are to be displayed in the two modes. In the case of the tens digit changing from 2 in turbo to 1 in standard, the jumper settings are 2A, 2B, 1C, 2D, 2E and 2G (notice that there is no F setting). If you set the jumpers in this way, then the tens digit will change from 1 to 2 when the Turbo LED signal goes from high to low. The jumpers for the units digit have to be set in the same way. Also notice that the numbering of the jumper positions is different if Turbo LED high indicates a higher speed.

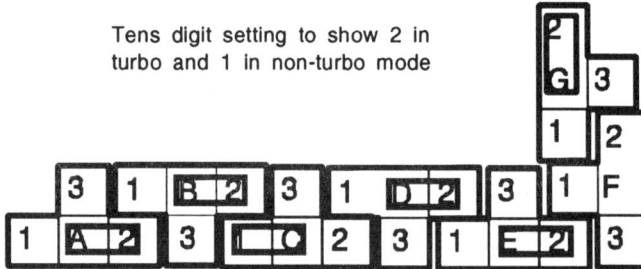

Tens digit setting to show 2 in
turbo and 1 in non-turbo mode

Figure 6.9
Setting the digit speed

If you are having difficulty setting the speed indicator do not worry too much. You cannot damage the motherboard by setting it incorrectly. The only result will be that the indicator will either fail to light or it will show the wrong clock speeds. Also notice that you are free to choose any display digits that you want - so setting 99MHz is perfectly permissible although quite useless, as is ignoring the speed indicator altogether!

Buying advice

Buying a case is difficult because they are fairly low value items and this makes dealers unwilling to spend much time discussing their advantages and disadvantages. Another problem is that case manufacturers intend the majority of their products to be used by clone manufacturers and so they go to some lengths to cover up not only the identity of their products but also their own identity. To make selection easier use the checklist given on the next page. However, don't expect to get complete answers.

Case checklist

When selecting a case of any particular type, desktop, tower or mini-tower you should discover the following details.

Supplier	Tel
Model identifier	
Type	Desktop/ Slim line/ Tower/ Mini-tower
Access	Slide off/Flip top/Side panel
Number and type of drive bays	( )5.25" full/half height ( )3.5" half/slim height
Drive mounting type	Side slides/brackets
Expansion slots	( ) full size ( ) half length
Fixing kit	Mounting components Yes/No External battery Yes/No Loudspeaker Yes/No Drive mounting parts Yes/No
Connectors	Full set Yes/No Labelled Yes/No
Power lead	Yes/No
Numeric speed indicator	Yes/No
Number of D-type cut outs	( )
Extra fan mounting	Yes/No
Power supply	( ) Watts ( ) 5.25" power connectors ( ) 3.5" power connectors
Instructions	Yes/No

Key points

» The type of case you need depends on the number of drives and other devices that you intend to fit and on the amount of access to the interior that you anticipate needing.

» The fixing kit and connections that are supplied with a case vary greatly in composition.

» Digital (numeric) speed indicators can be difficult to connect and configure correctly but they are not essential and can be left unconnected.

Chapter 7
In detail
Hard Disks

Choosing and installing a hard disk drive and its controller raises many questions and these are addressed in detail in this chapter.

The type and quality of hard disk that you use affects a machine's overall performance more than any other component excepting the motherboard. In particular, the seemingly simple choice of hard disk or no hard disk results in an immense difference in the usability of the entire system.

Disk drive capacities are always increasing, but since the introduction of Windows 3 the size of a typical drive has doubled from around 40MB to the 90-100MB mark. As a result, many users are considering buying a new high capacity drive as a replacement unit. The choices for a drive upgrade are very similar to first time installation.

Drive types

There are currently four common types of hard disk drive available: ST-506, ESDI, SCSI and IDE. The actual disk drives themselves work in more or less the same way. What differs is the way that they are connected to the PC - the disk drive to PC interface.

The oldest interface is the ST-506/412 which was introduced with the original IBM PC around 1980. Its name comes from the model numbers of the first two common hard disk drives used with the PC which were supplied by Seagate.

The ESDI and SCSI interfaces have been around for some time but really only became important with the move to more powerful PCs based on the AT design. ESDI - Enhanced Small Device Interface - was introduced in 1983 by the Maxtor Corporation as a high-speed, high reliability interface with a data transfer rate (see later) double that of the ST-506/412 standard - roughly 1 Megabyte per second (MB/s). SCSI, Small Computer Systems Interface, pronounced 'scuzzy', has been around for quite some time in one form or another and it is used for a wide range of other interface applications apart from hard disks.

The ESDI and SCSI interfaces differ markedly from the ST-506/412 interface because they are much more complex and sophisticated. The full ESDI specification allows for advanced features such as more than 1024 cylinders and higher numbers of sectors per track per drive than normally allowed (see later). However, in practice ESDI has been more or less superseded by SCSI for large capacity drives.

The IDE (Integrated Drive Electronics) interface is the newest and, at the moment, the most confusing. The fact that it is about to change its name to ATA (AT Attachment) when it is converted to an ANSI standard doesn't help! IDE interfaces are becoming more common as far as AT machines are concerned. Since most of the control logic is based within the hard drive, an excellent rate of data transfer is assured and the card which plugs into the bus is small and cheap. In addition to the hard and floppy disk controller, some IDE interfaces have serial, parallel and games ports - which saves on expansion slots! For new machines, the IDE approach is worth considering very seriously, and it is probably the drive type of choice.

Tracks, sectors and heads

Physically, all disk drives work in the same way, by recording magnetic pulses onto the surface of a disk. Data is recorded in concentric tracks and disks differ in the total number of tracks that they have. By using more than one disk and more than one read/write head the number of tracks can be increased still further - see Figure 7.1. The set of tracks, one per surface, that the heads can read in one location is called a cylinder. The ST-506/412 standard is limited to drives with no more than 1024 cylinders and this restricts the maximum size of drive that can be built without changing to ESDI, SCSI or IDE. Each track is also divided up into a number of fixed size chunks of data called sectors. Standard drives have 17 sectors per track, but higher capacity drives can have in more sectors per track than this.

When you are configuring a drive for use you need to know the number of heads, cylinders and sectors per track it has - see later.

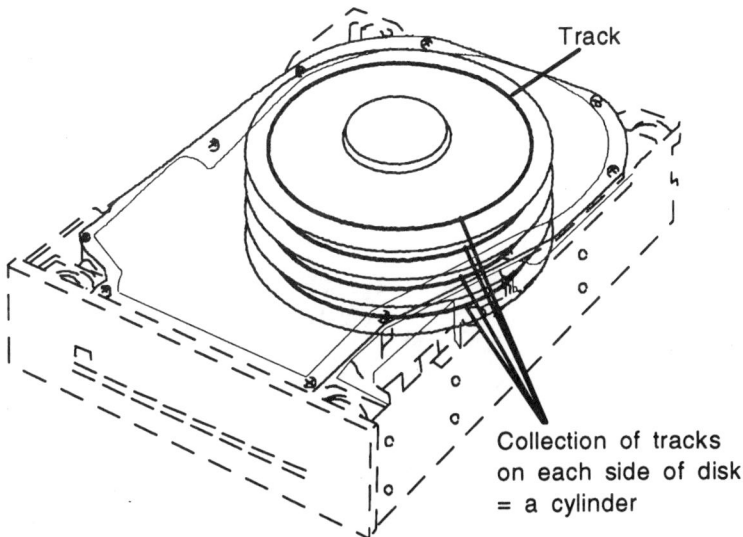

Track

Collection of tracks
on each side of disk
= a cylinder

Figure 7.1
Tracks and cylinders

Data transfer rate

The most interesting question to be answered is why a drive's interface type is important? After all, it might be of interest to an electronics engineer that a particular drive is SCSI rather than ESDI but what does it matter to the user? The answer to this question relates mainly to the issue of data transfer rate, although there are some secondary considerations.

Data transfer rate is simply the speed at which data can be transferred to or from the drive, usually measured in kilobytes per second (KB/s) or megabytes per second (MB/s). The transfer rate gives you some idea of how long it would take to read or write a file. For example, if a disk has a transfer rate of 250KB/s then a 10KB document could be read in four hundredths of a second, and a 1MB drawing file would take 4 seconds. In practice, the times to read or write these files would be longer because of other overheads that will be discussed later, but the general principle is the faster the transfer rate the better.

Each of the disk drive interfaces has a different typical transfer rate. The ST-506 is generally recognised to be the slowest, but there is little to choose between the remaining three. In theory, the SCSI interface should be the fastest but in practice it is often no better than the ESDI or IDE interface. The difficulty is that, although each of the interfaces has a theoretical maximum transfer rate, they rarely perform as well in practice. Some typical transfer rates are shown in the table below:

Interface	TransferRate (in MB/s)
ST-506	0.1-0.9
ESDI	1.2-1.8
SCSI	1.0-5.0
IDE	1.0-5.0

As you can see, in practice there is a considerable overlap in each of the ranges. However, you can normally conclude that the slowest of all drives is an ST-506, with ESDI and most SCSI taking the middle ground, and IDE and some SCSI drives (SCSI-2 in particular) being the fastest of all.

Disk controllers

So far we have talked about disk drives as though they were the only component to be considered. In fact a complete disk drive system is composed of the drive, a controller card and cables to connect the two. In the case of the IDE interface the controller card is built into the disk drive itself, and so doesn't appear to be a separate part of the system. Some machines have a direct IDE connector built onto the main board and in this case installation is just a matter of plugging in the drive cable. In a machine that doesn't have a built in IDE connector, then you do need what looks like an interface card, but this doesn't carry much in the way of electronics and is mainly there to convert the IDE connector to the standard AT expansion slot. However, most hard disk controller cards also contain the interface electronics necessary to operate a floppy disk and this makes even the IDE card slightly more complicated. You can buy interface cards for each of the standards - ST-506, SCSI, ESDI and IDE - with or without floppy disk support.

The performance of a disk drive system depends on the drive and the controller and this is a fact that is often overlooked. For example, you can buy a fast ST-506 drive in the expectation of good performance, but you will be disappointed if you use an inappropriate controller. Controllers ,as well as disk drives, differ in the speed at which they will transfer data. For example, if you connect a standard ST-506 drive to a PC/XT 8-bit controller, then the data transfer rate will be around 150KB/s. If you connect the same drive to a standard PC/AT 16-bit controller, then the data transfer rate will jump to 300KB/s. If you go to the trouble of finding a high performance disk controller, then you can reach 500KB/s. Note that this range of data transfer rates is achieved using the same disk drive. You could say that the type of disk drive determines the highest data transfer rate achievable using the best possible disk controller.

The data transfer rate depends on the speed at which data can be sent between the PC and the controller and the controller and the disk drive.

Clearly, the overall data transfer rate is set by the slower of the two. The different types of disk interface have an effect on the maximum rate of data transfer between the disk and the controller, but the rate of transfer between the controller and the PC is mainly determined by the nature of the ISA bus and the speed of the processor in use.

MFM and RLL

ST-506 disks come in two types - MFM and RLL - and these have maximum disk-to-controller transfer rates of 600KB/s and 900KB/s respectively. As IDE and other more sophisticated drives become more common the issue of MFM versus RLL is becoming less important, but it is still relevant if you are upgrading or using older drives. The difference between the two types of drive comes from the way in which data is coded. In the case of RLL, 50% more data can be squashed into the same space. In a standard MFM drive, each track is divided into 17 sectors, but an RLL drive typically has 26 sectors per track. The higher number of sectors per track of the RLL encoding imposes constraints on the type of drive that can be used, and a drive designated for use as MFM cannot be used reliably as RLL.

Data encoding and decoding is done on the controller card which plugs into the computer data bus and you can, to some extent, alter the characteristics of the drive by changing the controller. The nominal increase in data storage of RLL over MFM is 50%, but this increased performance imposes a lot more on the controller and the system is potentially more error-prone than MFM encoding. Data transfer is also faster with the RLL encoding. In general, I would recommend that you avoid RLL drives, unless they are part of a hard card, since the long data and control cables can pick up electrical interference from other parts of the system and make life difficult for a sub-system which is operating on very tight specifications. Even with a hard card unit, be prepared for problems as the disk ages.

Interleave

Disk controllers, even those working with the same type of disk drive, differ in their ability to move data to and from the hard disk. Older types of controller, in particular, aren't fast enough to read consecutive sectors in one revolution of the disk. What happens is that the controller reads a sector from the disk and then sends it across the PC interface and into memory, but this takes so long that the next sector passes under the read/write head before the disk controller is ready to deal with it. This means that the disk has to complete another whole revolution before the sector can be read. As a typical track is made up of 17 sectors this means that it takes 17 revolutions of the disk to read a whole track.

This problem can be reduced by making use of interleave. Instead of trying to read the sectors one after the other, a 2:1 interleave reads every other sector. As long as the disk controller can be ready to read the next but one sector the entire track can be read in two revolutions which is a big improvement on 17 revolutions. If not, then a 3:1 or more interleave has to be used. As long as the interleave is set correctly a complete track can be read in n rotations if the interleave is n:1.

The interleave factor on a disk drive can be set using software. In fact, it is set during the low level formatting - a process which is discussed in Chapter 10. The optimum interleave factor for a system depends upon the disk and the disk controller, as well as the speed at which data can be transferred within the system. This can make it quite difficult to determine the optimum interleave factor unless you have a utility that will do this for you. Notice that the penalty for setting the interleave too optimistically, that is too low, is more severe than making it too high. For example, if a disk really needs a 3:1 interleave then setting it to 1:1 or 2:1 means that it will always miss reading the next sector at each pass and therefore take 17 revolutions to read a track. Setting it to the correct interleave of 3:1 means it takes three revolutions and setting it to 4:1 (i.e on the low side) means it takes four (that is just one extra) revolutions.

Currently, AT and PS/2 controllers can transfer data as fast as the disk can present it and vice versa, giving a 1:1 interleave, but older controllers are less efficient, with interleave factors of 2:1 being fairly standard for ATs and 4:1, or even 6:1, commonly found with elderly XT controllers. The standard 4.77 MHz data bus of the XT affects the rate at which a controller can pass information, compared with the 8 MHz data bus of most AT systems. This is why you will usually find that even the best XT systems have to use interleave factors of 3:1 or 4:1.

With an interleave of 4:1, a 17 sector MFM disk can transfer data at 128 KB/s, compared with over 500 KB/s at a 1:1 interleave. RLL drives are about 50% faster and ESDI or SCSI drives are twice as fast. If you use the IBM Advanced diagnostics disk to low-level format a drive on an XT fitted with an older type of hard disk controller such as the Xebec 1210 (fitted as standard in early IBMs), then be prepared for a shock - the data transfer rate is a maximum of 85 KB/s. Current Western Digital and Seagate XT hard disk controllers have their own built-in low level formatters which use a standard interleave of 3:1 which you can override. It is not advisable to use an interleave of 1:1 on PC-XTs since data transfer is a maximum of 400 KB/s on the data bus, which is lower than the 500KB capacity needed to support a 1:1 interleave.

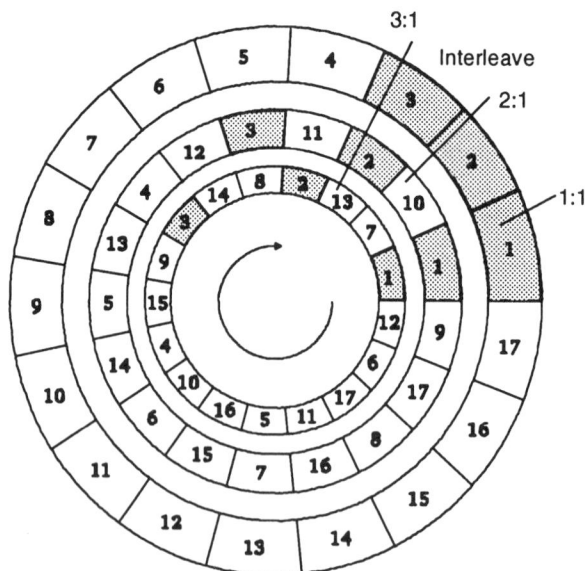

Figure 7.2
The effect of interleave

Modern controllers have confused the interleaving question by having enough memory to store a single track without needing to transfer it over the expansion bus. This means that you can use a 1:1 interleave because the controller will read each sector in turn and store it in its local buffer. Of course, the data transfer rate may still not be as fast as 1:1 interleaving would suggest, because the data is then transferred from the local buffer across the expansion bus at whatever speed the processor can manage. Still, this is the best that could possibly be achieved for that particular machine.

So, the fastest ST-506 disk system would be an RLL disk drive used with a 1:1 controller and this delivers a transfer rate of roughly 0.9MB/s. RLL disks are faster because they pack more data per track, but some users still prefer standard MFM drives because they are more reliable. An ST-506 MFM drive used with a 1:1 controller delivers a transfer rate of 0.6MB/s.

The same arguments apply to ESDI and SCSI disk systems but, because ESDI and SCSI are normally used where a high performance is desirable, they are usually 1:1 interleave anyway. This produces the fairly standard 1.25MB/s transfer rate in the case of ESDI. However, when it comes to transfer rates the range of values encountered with SCSI drives is very wide. The reason is that, unlike ST-506 and ESDI, the SCSI interface doesn't define the rate at which data is transferred from the disk to the controller. This means that it is possible to implement a SCSI system with a range of different types of disk drive hardware, and hence the final transfer rate is very variable.

SCSI

Apart from data transfer rate the ST-506, ESDI and IDE interfaces are very similar. All of them are purely for disk drives and each can support up to two hard disks. The SCSI interface, however, has an extra feature in that it can claim to be a general purpose interface. In principle, you can use the SCSI interface to connect almost anything to your machine - tape drives, floppy drives, audio synthesisers etc.. In practice, this usually turns out to be more difficult than imagined because of the lack of suitably sophisticated software drivers for the SCSI interface. The problem with SCSI is that it is a committee-based standard and no single manufacturer has dominated the market, as happened with ESDI and ST-506/412. The whole business is reminiscent of the well-known RS232 serial interface, which has the same committee-based origins and consequent problems since too much flexibility is allowed in its implementation. In time this problem may be solved, so that any SCSI device can be plugged into the same interface card, but for the moment extreme caution is needed if you plan to mix a range of SCSI devices.

A new international standard SCSI-2 is due very soon and promises to define a high speed, up to 20MB/s, interface that should work with a range of devices, including disk drives.

IDE

Although the ST-506 is slow, the real bottleneck is between the disk and the controller card. Once you are using a 1:1 controller there isn't anything you can do to increase its rate of working. The IDE interface is, in essence, a redesigned ST-506 interface that avoids this bottleneck.

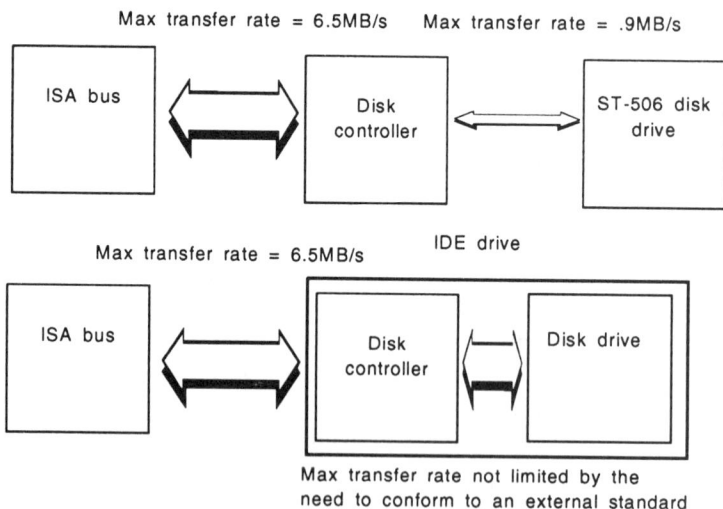

Figure 7.3
Data transfer rates on IDE and ST-506 drives

Originally, the idea of the IDE controller was to integrate the controller with the drive. Instead of having electronics on the drive coupled by cables to electronics on the controller board, an IDE drive has all of the electronics on the drive. You could say that the IDE drive uses the ISA interface directly. This not only has advantages in reducing the cost of the electronics, but it also allows an IDE drive to store data on the drive in any format it likes - as long as the electronics does the work of converting it to look like a standard ST-506 drive and controller combination. This accounts for the very high data transfer rates claimed for IDE drives. They are only limited by the maximum data rate of the ISA bus. In short, IDE drives are designed to plug directly into the (16-bit) ISA bus and this is the only interface standard that they have to adhere to. This makes IDE cheap and fast.

Newer motherboards often have a direct IDE drive connector socket. If you want to use an IDE drive with a motherboard that doesn't have an IDE socket then you need to use a very simple IDE controller card. This is often referred to as a 'paddle' card.

Access time

So far we have concentrated on data transfer rates because this is the most important measure of the speed of a disk drive and because it is usually ignored in manufacturer's specifications as it is so hard to measure. Most drive specifications dwell on the access time. This is the time needed to move the head to any given track - also known as the 'seek time'. Clearly, access time is important because it determines the lag between requesting data and starting to read it. If you are considering a particular type of drive and controller, e.g. ST-506 or ESDI, then access time is the only parameter of importance because the transfer rate is fixed. Once you have selected the type of drive you are going to use and its transfer rate, then by all means think about access time but don't choose fast access in preference to a high transfer rate.

Some drives have a voice-coil positioner, rather than a stepper motor. Stepper motor head positioning is prone to temperature and tracking errors as well as being slow, so high capacity drives now use voice-coil positioning. As a general rule, older stepper motor drives have an even number of read/write heads stated as part of the specification, while voice-coil types have an odd number - one head, not included in the total, being used to read positioning information from special tracks. Voice-coil drives can be identified by their very fast seek times - generally less than 30 milliseconds, compared with 60-100 milliseconds for stepper motor drives.

Installation and cabling

Installing a drive is a five-stage process:

» mechanically fixing the drive into its mounting bay

» connecting the cables to the drive

» connecting the cables to the controller

» configuring the drive and controller

» software initialisation of the drive

The final step concerning the software initialisation is described separately in Chapter 10 because, logically, it comes after you have physically installed the drive.

Mechanically fixing the drive into its mounting bay is a relatively straightforward operation unless you are trying to squeeze it into an awkward space. The only real complication that can occur is that you might have to remove the drive's own front panel to stop it poking out of the front of the case.

Potentially one of the most awkward stages in installing a drive is cabling. Fortunately this isn't at all difficult in practice, but it does differ slightly depending on the type of drive.

The cabling necessary for ST-506 and ESDI drives looks identical and often results in the two types of drive being confused by a casual observer. Both use a twin cable connection - one 34-way and one 20-way ribbon cable. In both cases the 34-way cable can be plugged into two drives (if two 34-way edge connectors are fitted) but a separate 20-way cable has to be used for each drive. Which drive is drive 0 and which is drive 1 is set by jumpers or switches on the drives themselves. Normally a drive can be set to be drive 0, 1, 2 or 3 (perversely labelled DS1, DS2, DS3 and DS4 on some drives). As long as you are using a standard cable, the first drive should be set to be drive 0 and the second to drive 1.

It is important that both ribbon cable connectors are connected the correct way round. Pin 1 on the drive is at the end of edge connector nearest the notch. Pin 1 on the cable connector is marked either by a small triangle and/or by a single coloured wire in the ribbon cable. See Figure 7.4 which also shows the power connector, a typical drive selector jumper block and terminating resistor pack.

There is a strange complication in that a twisted 34-way cable is sometimes used.The reason for this is that if two drives are attached, then a twisted cable automatically selects one drive as drive 0 and one as drive 1 without having to alter the settings on the drive. When a twisted cable is used the jumpers on both drives are set to drive 1 and the drive connected to the end connector will act as drive 0 and the one connected to the middle connector will act as drive 1. Notice that the same trick of automatic drive selection is used with floppy drives but

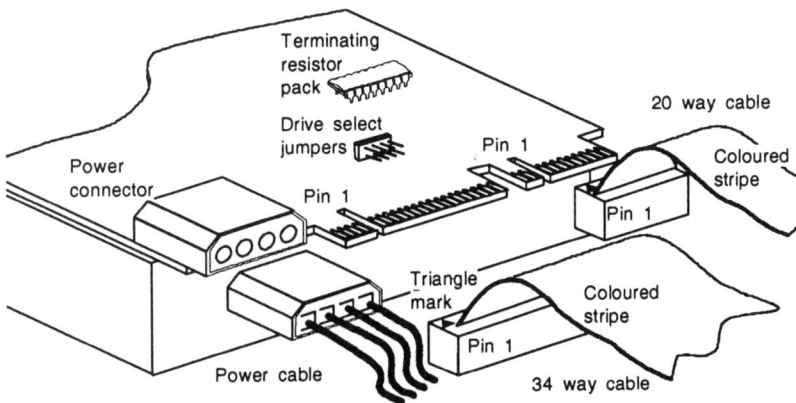

Figure 7.4
ST-506 and ESDI connectors

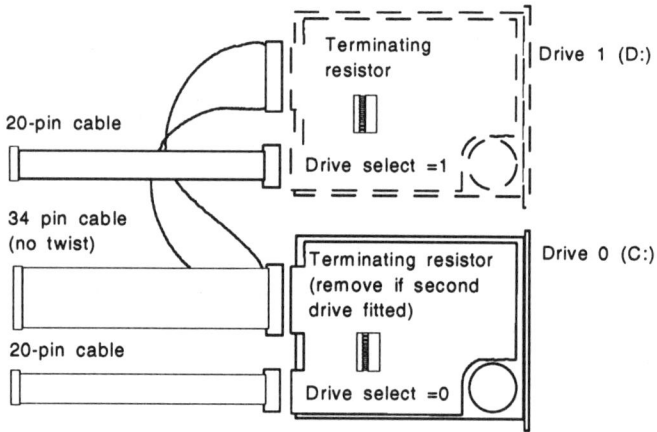

Figure 7.5
ST-506 and ESDI drive cabling

the twist in the cable is in a different place. This means that twisted hard disk and floppy disk cables are different and **cannot** be used interchangeably. Fortunately the use of twisted cabling is growing rare because even though it was designed to make installation simple in practice it results in a great deal of confusion.

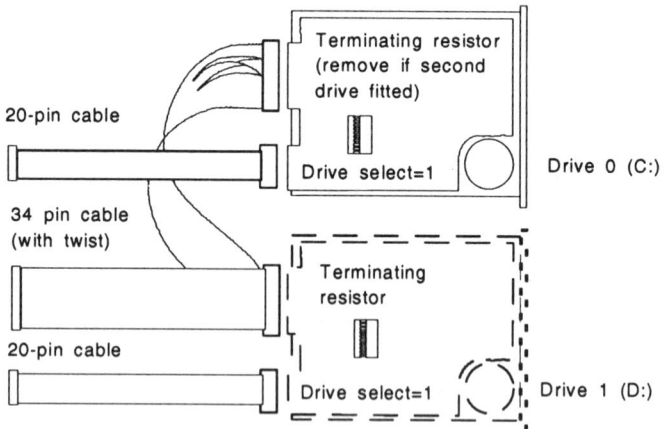

Figure 7.6
Twisted hard disk cables

The cabling for SCSI drives is usually a single, very wide, 50-way cable. Additional drives can be simply connected to this cable. The thickness of the cable makes an installed SCSI drive unmistakable.

An IDE drive uses a more modest single 40-way ribbon cable. Sometimes this can be plugged in directly to a socket on the motherboard, in other cases an IDE controller is used. Again, two drives can be connected on the same cable but exactly how the drives are configured to work together varies according to the drives.

As in the case of ST-506 and ESDI drives it is important that the cables are connected the correct way round. Cable orientation is usually marked by a coloured wire at one edge, indicating pin 1. When you plug a ribbon cable plug into a ribbon cable socket the orientation can be found either by the presence of a mating key or by the marking of pin 1 by a small triangle. In some rare cases markings are missing from the socket and you have to look on the PCB either for a triangle or for a figure 1 indicating pin 1.

Finally you have to remember to connect the power supply to each drive. Most hard disks, even if they are 3.5" drives, use the standard 5.25" power connector. Notice that this has a right and a wrong way so be careful before you try to push the connector home.

Once you know how to connect all of the cables then all that remains is to configure the drive and controller. As far as the drive is concerned all that is necessary is to set a jumper indicating if it is drive 0 or drive 1.

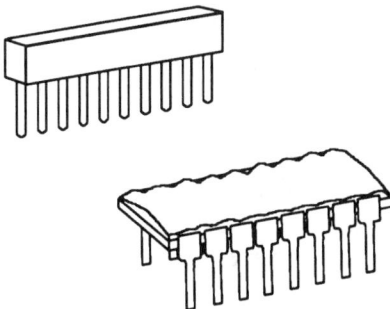

Figure 7.7
Terminating resistor packs

If two or more drives are fitted then you also have to remove a resistor terminating pack from all but the last drive on the cable. See Figures 7.5 and 7.7. Sometimes the terminating resistor can be disabled using dip switches.

If you buy a new hard disk, you should be supplied with a manual. If it wasn't supplied, then complain vigorously to the supplier. Failing this, get hold of a copy of disk PCI 235 from the PC Independent User Group, which has quite a lot of useful information on drive characteristics but not on the settings of drive jumpers - that's why the manual is so useful. Most new drives are supplied set up to work as the first hard disk in a system, so you may be able to muddle through. If the drive is second-hand, still try to get hold of the manual, otherwise you may run into difficulties. As a rule, buy your hard disk and controller card from the same place, then if you run into problems, there is only one organisation to contact for help. A new hard disk will need to be prepared for use and the methods for carrying this out are to be found in Chapter 10.

Installing a controller

Configuring a hard disk controller can be extremely complicated. If you have the manufacturer's instructions then there will be a long table of jumper settings to take into account. On XT controllers the jumpers are actually used to determine the type of the drive with which the controller is being used. In this case it is very important that the drive and controller are chosen so that they will work together. Unlike an AT controller, an XT controller governs the number of tracks, heads and cylinders on a drive that can be used.

In the case of AT controllers, the jumpers are mainly only concerned with details of configuration that rarely need alteration. Most AT controllers will work with their factory defaults. Whether you are configuring an XT or an AT, however, it is essential to get hold of the controller's instructions.

If you have a choice of controllers then for an XT hard disk controller both the Western Digital and Seagate Technology types have much to recommend them - currently MFM XT controllers are labelled as WD1004-WX1 (Western Digital) or for RLL, WD1004-27X or WD1004A-27X. The Seagate type are ST11M for MFM and ST11R for RLL. Very occasionally, you will find XT-GEN2 (or XT-GEN2R) types but these are obsolete. The difference between the two WD RLL types is that the 1004A type cannot be used as the second controller in a system.

AT controllers are also made by Western Digital and are widely 'cloned'. The most usual MFM type is the WD1003V-MM2 which can be used with a 2:1 interleave and controls up to two hard disks and two floppy drives (360KB, 720KB, 1.2MB, and 1.44MB); the WD1003V-MM1 has no floppy disk controller but is otherwise identical. The advantage of this is clear if you wish to install a specialised floppy controller which supports more than two drives. The floppy controller function cannot be disabled on the MM2.

One clone controller on the market (WA3V) also supports the same range of features as the MM2, but in addition, the drives can be low-level formatted using a built-in routine (using DEBUG with an offset:segment add) which can save problems if you haven't got the appropriate software. The WD1003V-SR1 and - SR2 are RLL versions

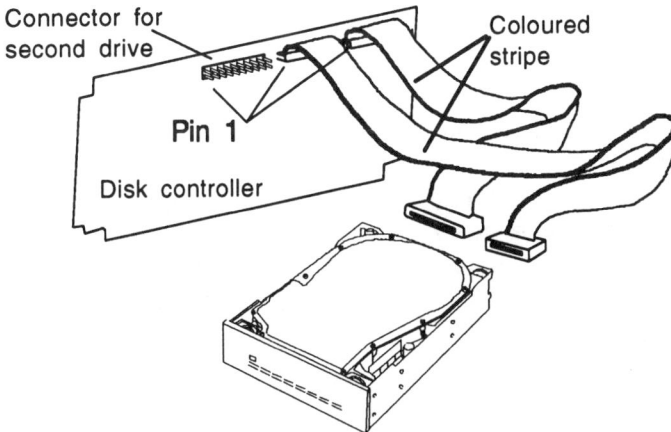

Figure 7.8
Connecting cables to the disk controller

of the same controller. For 1:1 interleave, you need the WD1006V series (MM1, MM2, SR1, SR2) or the WA6V.

ESDI AT controllers such as the WD10076V-SE1 or -SE2 (the latter has provision for two floppy drives) tend to cost about double the price of the ST-506/412 types and an intelligent SCSI controller about three times as much - and you will need a host adapter as well.

IDE controllers are so simple that they hardly have any electronics on them! Some motherboards have direct IDE connections which mean that you can simply plug the 40-way cable from the drive directly into the motherboard without using an adapter card or an expansion slot. Of course, unless the motherboard also has a built in floppy disk controller you will still need to use a separate floppy disk controller. Generally speaking an IDE controller need no configuration other than what is needed to make any floppy disks connected to it work. Typical IDE controllers are the Seagate ST07A and the ST08A both of which support two hard drives and the ST08A also supports a pair of floppies.

Upgrading

A common question is how complicated it is to add a second drive. In the case of the ST-506 and ESDI interface it is generally a matter of buying a second 20-way cable and making sure that the 34-way cable has two drive connectors. If the 34-way cable has a twist in it then you should set both drive selection jumpers (on the disk drives) to drive 0. If the cable is straight then set one to 0 and one to 1.

Adding an extra SCSI drive is, in theory, just a matter plugging it in and setting its SCSI ID (identity) to a value that isn't currently in use. In practice it is advisable to make sure that it is a type of drive supported by the SCSI controller already installed.

An IDE drive can be added by plugging it in and setting one to 'master' and one to 'slave' using jumpers on the disk drives. As in the case of SCSI it is safer to use a drive that is explicitly supported by the controller. In most cases the simplest option is to buy a second drive of the same type as the one already installed.

In most cases the difficult part of adding a second disk drive is the physical mounting - i.e. finding the right screws and making it all fit!

Hard cards

A hard card is a hard disk drive mounted on an expansion card complete with controller. As they are supplied already connected to a controller and there is no need to find a way of mounting the drive they are ideal if you are worried about fitting a standard drive. Some early hard cards were unreliable because they took more power from the expansion bus than was reasonable. They also over-heated and suffered other problems. As a quick upgrade they are a reasonable choice but in most cases a well installed standard drive is likely to be cheaper and more reliable.

Caching controllers

Some advanced controllers take the idea of using memory as a buffer one stage further. By using large quantities of memory, data and programs can be read from disk and held ready for use on the controller card. Typical disk cache sizes are anything from 4MB to 16MB making this sort of controller expensive. However, the price is falling and at the time of writing caching controllers for IDE drives are available for £200 to £300. A caching controller can speed disk access up to three to four times and at the best can result in a file being loaded almost instantaneously. They are ideal and highly recommended for applications such as CAD and DTP.

Printer port drives

Printer port drives are self-contained external drives that connect to a system via the parallel printer port. They exceptionally easy to install from the hardware point of view although they are slightly more complicated in terms of software. They are more expensive than standard drives and are slower but they do have the advantage of being portable. You can also remove a printer port drive and lock it in a filing cabinet or safe for security.

Buying advice

If you are planning to buy a new machine complete with disk drive or upgrade your disk drive in the near future then its performance will affect most of the applications software that you run. Surprisingly, although the current disk drive situation appears very complex, there is a clear cut best choice. If you can, go for an IDE drive with a fast access time. It will be cheaper and have a data transfer rate that is as fast, if not faster, than any of the other types of drive available. If your machine has an IDE connector then you don't even need an IDE controller card. If it doesn't then make sure you get an IDE controller with a floppy disk interface included to avoid having to use up an additional expansion slot with a separate floppy interface card.

The only reason for not using an IDE drive is if you are expanding an existing non-IDE system with a second drive. Even then it is worth comparing the cost with buying a new IDE system.

The success of IDE drives has resulted in ST-506 and ESDI becoming more or less obsolete. In the near future it may even be difficult to get hold of ST-506 drives from standard suppliers. On the other hand there are a large number of low capacity, 20MB or so, surplus drives on the market that are perfectly serviceable if they provide the storage capacity that you are looking for. Second user drives are best avoided because drives, being electro-mechanical components, wear out. Even if a drive can be demonstrated to be working there is no guarantee that it will continue to work reliably. Worn out drives often work reliably immediately after re-formatting only to quickly go out of alignment. Heat faults are also more common on ageing disk drives.

A hard disk checklist

When buying a hard disk you should try to obtain information on as many of the following points as possible.

Supplier:	Tel:
Manufacturer	
Model number	
Total formatted capacity	( ) MB
Type of drive	ST-506 MFM/ ST-506 RLL/ ESDI/ SCSI/ IDE/ Hard card/ Printer Port
Size of drive	3.5"/5.25" full/half height
Access/Seek time	( ) ms
Controller	Included Yes/No XT/AT Interleave 1:1 or ( )
Floppy support	Yes/No
Cables	Included Yes/No For 1 or 2 drives
Formatting software	Included Yes/No*
Other features	
Price	£( )

*Note that formatting software is discussed in Chapter 10.

Key points

»   Hard disk drives come in a range of different types: ST-506 MFM, ST-506 RLL, ESDI, SCSI, IDE, plus hard card and printer port alternatives.

»   IDE and SCSI drives are generally the fastest with IDE usually being available at the best price.

»   Hard disk controllers are different for the XT and AT designs.

»   It is important to check that a controller will support the type of drive you want to use. This is particularly so in the case of XT controllers which have to support the number of tracks, heads and cylinders for the particular drive.

»   The most important characteristic of a drive/controller combination is the data transfer rate that it can achieve.

»   Interleave is a way of optimising drive controller combinations that are not fast enough to read a single track in one revolution of the disk.

»   SCSI drives and controllers are very non-standard.

»   Cabling for ST-506 drives is easy apart from the complication caused by the use of a twisted cable to make the installation of two drives easier.

»   Hard cards and printer port drives are an alternative if you don't want to attempt standard drive installation.

Chapter 8
In detail
Floppies, Video and I/O

This chapter describes the additional features you will need to get your system going, and to enhance its capabilities.

Once you have chosen a motherboard and hard disk drive, the major characteristics of your system have been defined. With the possible exception of the video monitor, these two modules also take the largest chunks of any budget. However, there are still a great many minor decisions to be made that influence the overall usability of your machine.

The topics covered in detail in this chapter are:

» floppy disk drives and controllers

» video cards and monitors

» parallel and serial cards

» multifunction cards

Floppy disk drives and controllers

The general details of floppy disk drives have been discussed in Chapter 2. In practice there is very little to choose between different makes of drive and in most cases it is simply a matter of price and availability. There are one or two novel drives on the market at the moment such as Canon's twin 3.5" and 5.25" drive combined in a single half height unit, and the high capacity 2.88MB version of the 3.5" floppy. Only time will tell if these are long term survivors.

When it comes to floppy disk controllers, most users do not have much of a choice other than to accept whatever floppy disk controller is incorporated into the hard disk controller. After all, the performance of the hard disk controller is an important issue, whereas the floppy disk is generally an afterthought - just a way of loading software and exchanging data. The lowly status of the floppy is fairly accurate and the only real issue is storage capacity rather than transfer speed or access time.

Occasionally, however, you may have to fit a separate floppy disk controller if you are using, say, an IDE drive or perhaps even no hard disk at all. There are three current types of floppy disk controller in common use. Of these, the basic XT controller (which cannot be used in an AT) will only allow the use of 360KB and 720KB capacity drives and normally requires no adjustment. The two other types are usable on both XT and AT machines but may require adjustment of links (jumpers or DIP switches), either to set up the drive types or the address within the computer memory map. One type (for example, the Compaticard) will allow the use of up to two external drives (with two internal drives at the same time) while the other only permits two internal drives to be attached. Drive types are frequently sensed automatically by the latest type of 'intelligent' controller; these controllers will also normally allow high capacity drives to be used with XT machines.

Before altering links on these controller cards, make quite sure that you know the capacity of the drive(s) that will be fitted as drive A: (and B:). This can be quite difficult with 5.25" drives since high capacity drives

Low density 720KB diskette   High density 1.44MB diskette

MF2-DD   MF2-HD

High density hole

Write protect hole

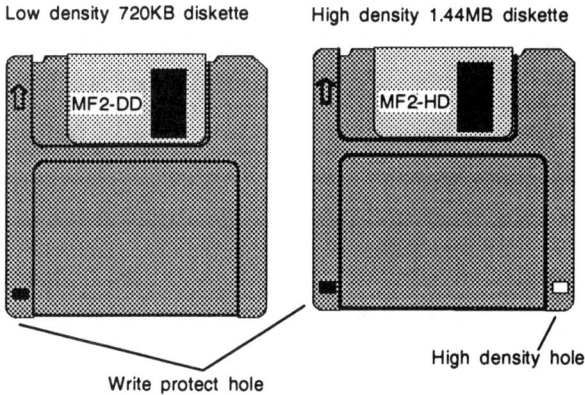

Figure 8.1
3.5" diskettes

look very similar to standard drives. If in doubt, remember that you
should have a high capacity drive in an AT system. With 3.5" drives,
the high density type can be identified quite readily as follows: Turn
the drive upside down with the front of the drive facing you and look
at the circuit board by the front of the drive. A high capacity type has
two optical sensors, one on either side. The right-hand one checks the
write-protect slide on the disk and the sensor on the left looks for the
additional hole which is only found on high density disks. If it is not
present, the disk is treated as a low-density (720KB) type. High density
5.25" drives do not have this facility and will gather the information by
examining the format of the disk. If the disk is not formatted, it will be
treated as a high density type for formatting purposes unless you tell it
otherwise.

Note that there are now AT multi-function cards that contain floppy
disk controllers.

Fitting a floppy drive

Fitting a floppy drive is very easy and there is very little to do. The
drives are physically mounted in exactly the same way as a hard disk,
the only difference being that the drive front has to poke through the
case. If the case doesn't accommodate 3.5" drives then the solution is

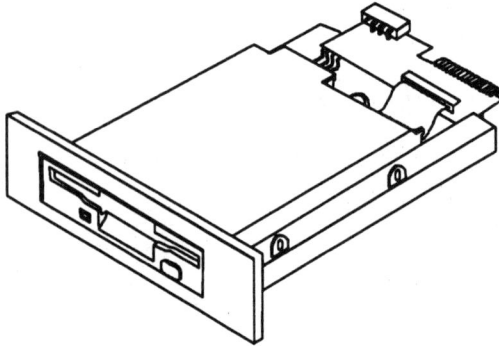

Figure 8.2
A 3.5" to 5.25" drive conversion

to buy a 3.5" to 5.25" conversion kit. This usually provides a 5.25" tray in which the smaller drive can be mounted, a power supply plug convertor and a disk cable convertor. Once installed in the conversion kit the 3.5" drive can be treated for all practical purposes as a standard 5.25" drive.

The cabling system for 5.25" drives uses a single 34-way ribbon cable. One end is plugged into the controller and then the drives are connected in turn. Which drive is drive 0 and which drive 1 is determined by jumpers or switches on the drives. If you use a standard straight cable then one drive should be set to drive 0 and one to drive 1. The

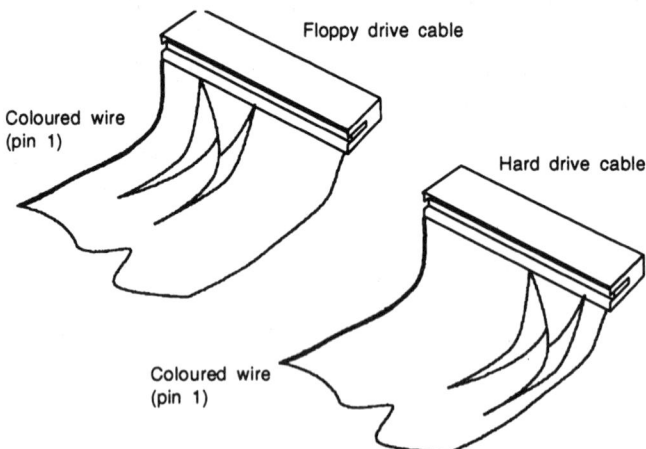

Figure 8.3
Twisted cables

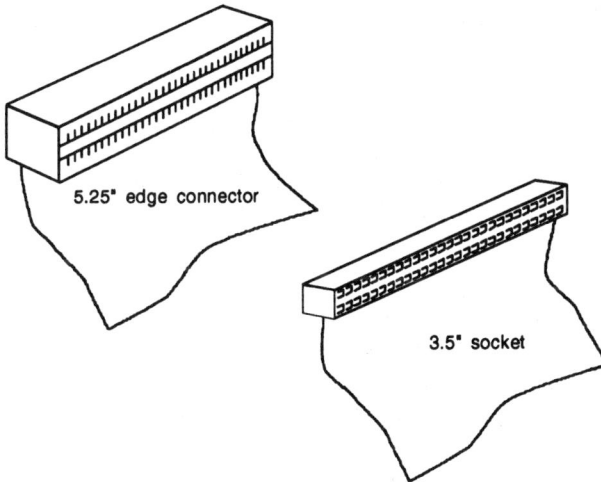

Figure 8.4
3.5" and 5.25" 34 way connectors.

terminating resistor pack on all but the very end drive on the cable should also be removed. This configuration is not often met with in PC clones.

As in the case of hard disks some drive installations use a twisted cable. In this case you should set **both** drives to be drive 1 and which is actually drive 1 and which is drive 0 is resolved by their position on the cable. Note that a floppy disk twisted cable isn't the same as a hard disk twisted cable but the 34-way straight cables are interchangeable.

Fitting a 3.5" disk is as easy but different connectors are used for both the 34-way cable and for the power connector. Whereas a 5.25" disk uses a PCB edge connector on the 34-way cable, a 3.5" disk uses a socket of the same type as used to connect to the controller card. You

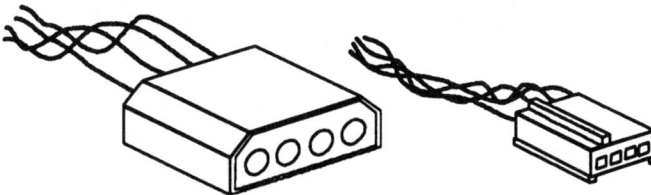

Figure 8.5
5.25" and 3.5" power connectors

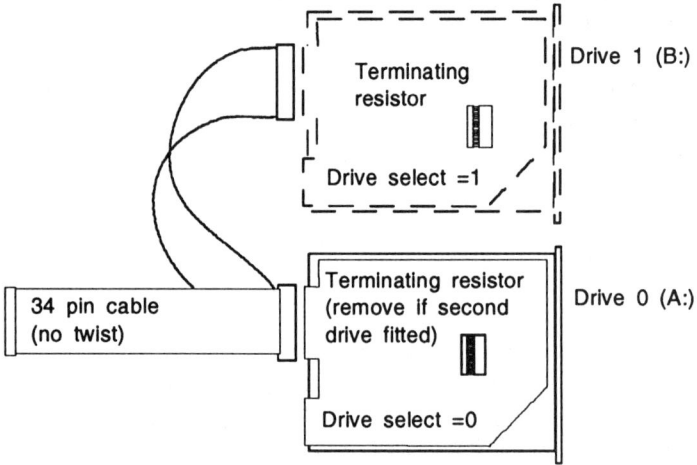

Figure 8.6
Standard floppy drive connections

can either buy a cable that has both edge connectors and sockets or use a convertor to change the socket to take an edge connector. Use whichever solution is cheaper or more readily available.

The same argument applies to the power cable connector. Instead of using the familiar 5.25" power connectors 3.5" disks use a smaller connector. Modern power supplies usually have one or two of these

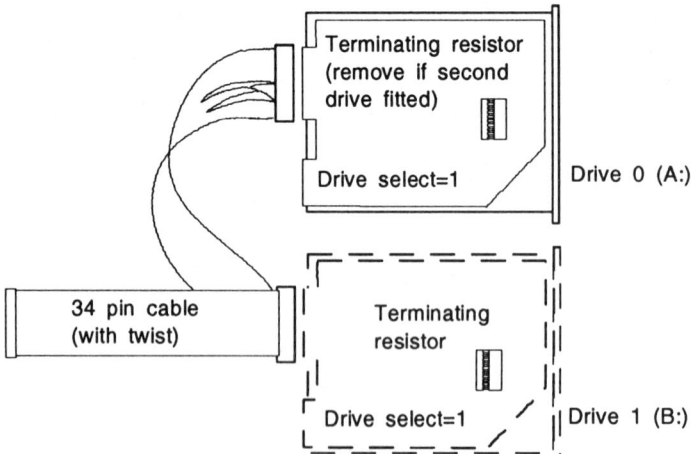

Figure 8.7
Twisted cable floppy drive connections

types of connector already fitted. If this isn't the case, then a convertor must be used.

Notice that the same rules for setting which drive is 0 and 1 apply to 3.5" drives. The only difference is that there is usually a small (sometimes **very** small) switch which can be set to drive 0 or 1.

Video cards and monitors

Monochrome monitors and adapters are the cheapest form of visual display - but in most cases offer limited ability. The cheapest monochrome adapter cards conform to the most basic IBM standard, known as MDA (Monochrome Display Adapter). They do not have the capability for high quality graphics but they display text perfectly well.

The change to colour is nearly always worthwhile. The oldest and most basic IBM-style colour/graphics standard is referred to as CGA or Colour Graphics Adapter. It will operate in two modes, 80 column by 25 row or 40 column by 25 row when displaying text, or in a 4 colour medium resolution mode or a 2 colour high resolution mode. The quality of text display with a CGA card is poorer than for an MDA card since the characters are based on an 8 by 8 matrix, rather than the 9 by 14 matrix. This means that lower case letters with 'descenders', such as 'g', 'y', or 'p' are cramped. It also makes it a poor choice for any application that requires attention to detail as well as colour - such as painting or other graphics packages. While it is now comparatively cheap and may be better than no colour at all, it is obsolescent and should be avoided if possible. Most CGA cards include a printer port.

The next standard of interest is the enhanced graphics adapter - usually referred to as EGA. Good EGA monitors can display 16 different colours on screen at a time and the picture quality with graphics can be very good. EGA cards can be set to emulate CGA and they usually do not include a printer facility. Like the CGA, the EGA is obsolescent, but can sometimes be acquired either second-hand or from one of the firms specialising in 'end of line' items.

The most satisfactory and readily available colour card which is within the reach of the average PC user is one which supports the VGA (Video Graphics Array) standard. The VGA standard is current and seems as though it will be available for the foreseeable future: VGA cards can be set up to emulate the CGA or EGA standard and usually have a 15 pin output socket - this distinguishes them from MDA, CGA and EGA cards. VGA cards can display up to 256 colours on a suitable monitor, and can also drive special monochrome monitors - but only in one colour - usually black on white!

There are also Super VGA (SVGA) cards which offer substantially higher resolution and often more colours. You will also hear of XVGA - which for all practical purposes can be ignored -unless you have bought an IBM machine in which case you can regard it as a higher cost version of SVGA!

At these higher resolutions there are also many very specialised graphics cards aimed at applications such as CAD and graphic design. For example the IBM 8514/A standard gives a similar resolution to SVGA but it can work faster as can TIGA cards. In most cases SVGA is quite sufficient.

One type of adapter which you may hear about but not be able to buy as a card for your PC-compatible is the MCGA (Multi-Colour Graphics Array). This is supplied as a built-in feature of IBM PS/2 model 25 or 30 and, like the VGA, offers up to 256 different colours.

The choice of a colour monitor is quite important and will depend upon the sort of work you intend to do with it as well as the amount you are prepared to pay. All colour monitors work in the same basic fashion, but the different standards (CGA, EGA and VGA, the last two having downwards compatibility) imply that the internal circuitry will be more complex in an EGA monitor which can emulate (imitate) a CGA, and most complex of all in a VGA since it can emulate CGA and EGA modes in addition to its own.

Size of screen is also important - a 12" (diagonal measurement) screen will have an visible area whose diagonal measurement is at least an inch smaller, and for most purposes, a 14" screen is recommended. Colour screens (whether in TV sets or computer monitors) display colours by means of a regularly-spaced matrix of tiny red, green and blue dots or bars - combinations of which can produce all the basic colours, including white. The smaller the dots, the sharper is the quality of the picture (definition); CGA and some cheap and cheerful EGA and VGA screen displays have a spacing between the centres of the coloured dots of about 0.42 mm, while better quality versions have 0.31 or even 0.28 mm. Naturally, the smaller the spacing, the greater the number of dots and the better the picture quality. The snag? They cost more.

To work with SVGA you need a higher quality of monitor. You can either buy a dedicated SVGA monitor which has been designed to work at these high resolutions or you can use a multi-sync monitor which can work at all resolutions up to some predefined ceiling. If you only want to work with SVGA then a multi-sync monitor is an unnecessary luxury.

Most video cards (monochrome, CGA and EGA) use the 8-bit bus and are capable of working in XT and AT machines. VGA cards come in both 8-bit and 16-bit versions and the latter will not usually work in an 8-bit system (although some can be set to do so by setting links). As already mentioned, the best choice on performance grounds is a VGA card and preferably one that can be upgraded at a later date to a Super VGA card. As VGA cards provide all of the video modes found in MDA, CGA and EGA there is no penalty for buying one other than cost.

All video cards contain some memory chips, referred to as video RAM, and the amount varies from 64KB in recent MDA and CGA cards with so-called Hercules Graphics compatibility, to 128KB for EGA cards. VGA cards have either 256KB, 512KB or 1MB of video memory; at least 512KB is needed for the highest video resolutions and 1MB is needed to reach 1024x768 at 256 colours. Very early IBM cards (MDA and CGA) had much less memory - the MDA with 4KB and the CGA with 16KB. The total space reserved in the computer's memory map is 128KB, so VGA adapters which use more than this have special circuitry to enable the video memory to be paged into this space as it is needed. Unless you are going to write your own programs that directly access the video hardware this is mostly of academic interest but it does explain how such large amounts of video memory can be used, even though there only ever seems to be 128KB allocated to graphics boards.

Of more practical interest is that many video cards can be upgraded by adding extra RAM chips. For example, many EGA cards come as standard with only 64KB of memory and can be upgraded to 128KB to provide extra colours and a higher resolution. Similarly, VGA cards can be upgraded from 256KB to 512KB or even 1MB to provide the highest resolution VGA and SVGA modes. Note that not all VGA cards can be upgraded in this way.

The considerations for upgrading video memory are exactly the same as for motherboard memory. You have to find the correct chips and ones that work at least as fast as the video card requires.

Configuring a video board is mainly a matter of letting it know the type of monitor with which it is going to be working. The reason that the video board needs to know the type of monitor is that it governs which video modes can be used.

There are two distinct groups of monitors in use: TTL (TTL stands for Transistor Transistor Logic) or digital, and analog. With the introduction of the VGA standard, IBM changed the way in which the display worked. Monochrome and earlier colour monitors used digital signals (where the signal is either on or off) and for colour monitors this yields a total of 8 colours. A further, separate signal (intensity) switches the colour signals to bright or dim and this increases the range of colours to 16.

TTL monitors are simpler and so cheaper to build, but they are restricted to showing a maximum of 64 colours, irrespective of the sophistication of the video card. Analog monitors, on the other hand, are slightly more expensive but they are not restricted in the number of colours that they can display. In theory, they could display up to 262,144 colours but in practice, most are limited to 256 particular colours at any one time due to the video cards in use.

TTL monitors are used for MDA, CGA and EGA adapters and analog is used for VGA. TTL monitors have a 9-pin connector whereas analog use a 15-pin connector, although some older models still use a 9-pin connector. The pin connections are shown in Table 8.1 overleaf.

Table 8.1

Pin	Monochrome	CGA colour	EGA colour	VGA mono	VGA colour
1	Ground	Ground	Ground	not used	Red video
2	Ground	Ground	Sec. Red	Green video	Green video
3	not used	Red	Red	not used	Blue video
4	not used	Green	Green	not used	not used
5	not used	Blue	Blue	Ground	Ground
6	Intensity	Intensity	Sec.Green	not used	Ground (red)
7	Video	not used	Sec. Blue	Ground (green)	Ground (green)
8	Horiz. sync.	Horiz. sync.	Horiz. sync.	not used	Ground (blue)
9	Vert. sync.	Vert. sync.	Vert. sync.	no pin	no pin
10				Sync. return	Sync. return
11				not used	not used
12				not used	not used
13				Vertical sync.	Vertical sync.
14				Horizontal sync.	Horizontal sync.
15				not used	not used

In general, you should buy a monitor to suit the graphics adapter that you are using - e.g. CGA monitor with a CGA adapter. It's worth while noting that there are many VGA cards that have both 9-pin TTL and 15-pin analog connectors. In this case it is possible to use either a TTL or an analog monitor, but the graphics modes that you can use will depend on the type of monitor that you actually connect. For example, if you connect a CGA standard monitor then the VGA card will only operate as a CGA mode card. In other words the video card only governs the range of video modes that are available but the type of monitor that you use governs which modes you can actually use.

The VGA video standard is really an AT video standard and, while it was never intended to be used with XT machines, you can find VGA cards that will work in XTs. In this case the machine might well need a BIOS upgrade to support VGA modes.

Identifying the types of video modes in which a monitor will work is complicated business, because there has never been a simple and consistent set of names used for the different types of monitor. Also, there are many monitors that were designed as intermediates between say EGA and VGA. For example, you can find TTL monitors that will work at VGA resolutions but, of course, not at the full range of colours. The situation with regard to brand new monitors is a lot simpler, and in this case you need only worry about buying either a VGA i.e. up to 640x480 resolution, or a Super VGA i.e. up to 1024x768 monitor. If you are tempted by an older monitor, then you need to determine whether it is a TTL or an analog monitor and what range of vertical and horizontal scan rates it will work at. Each graphics mode requires a different scan rate and if the monitor can work at that rate then it should be able to work in that mode. Notice that the most important of the two is the horizontal scan rate and that the vertical scan rate is sometimes optionally increased by a video card to reduce flicker. Synchronisation frequencies are as follows:

Mode	Vertical (Hz)	Horizontal (KHz)
EGA monochrome	49.4	18.2
MDA monochrome	50.0	18.4
HGA	50.9	18.8
CGA (RGB)	60.0	15.7
EGA colour	60.0	21.8
VGA 640x350	70.1	31.5
VGA 640x480	60.0	31.5
SVGA 800x600	58.0	36.0
SVGA 1024x768	40.0	32.1

Notice that the vertical scan frequencies are quoted for SVGA and assume an interlaced mode.

Installing a video card is just a matter of configuring it for use with the particular monitor, plugging the adapter card in and connecting the monitor to the card. You also have to set jumpers or switches on the motherboard to let the BIOS ROM know the type of display installed. In the case of an AT motherboard, this is usually only a matter of selecting mono or colour. Many BIOS ROMs automatically detect the type of video card in use and will inform you if you have set the jumpers on the motherboard incorrectly! Notice that, while the connector at the video card end of the cable has been standardised, the connector, if any, at the monitor's end is non-standard. This means that you must use a cable that is intended for use with your monitor or make one from the manufacturer's specifications.The latter course of action is not recommended and monitors are usually sold complete with cables and power leads.

Serial and parallel ports

Serial ports are used for bi-directional transfer of data and are used where a device such as a modem or mouse has to communicate with the system. Parallel ports are almost always used with printers and data transfer is one-way. Newer systems such as the PS/2 and many ATs have a bi-directional or limited bi-directional facility on the printer port. In general, a device that needs to input data or both input and output data to the machine will tend to use the serial port whereas output only devices such as printers tend to be connected to the parallel port. The influence of tradition and historical use is quite strong - for example, plotters tend to use serial interfaces, just like early printers and teletypes, even though they are output-only devices.

The usual type of serial communication port on a PC is designated as an asynchronous type since characters can be sent with no special timing information. Each character is divided from the preceding and following character by a stop bit and a start bit; after an initial 0 (start bit) the next 8 bits describe the character and one or two stop bits are

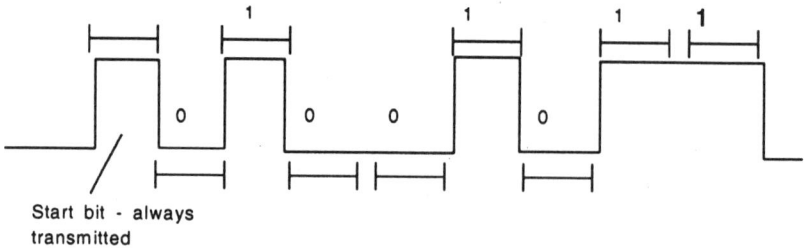

Figure 8.8
Asynchronous serial data

added - a maximum of 10 or 11 bits thus describe each character (or byte). The timing information needed to separate out each bit is obtained by examining the lengths of the start and stop bits on reception. The data is sent over a single wire and return data is received via another wire. The alternative, synchronous serial, is to send a separate clock signal using an additional wire. Although asynchronous serial does have a built-in ability to deal with speed variations, both the sending and receiving machines have to agree the overall speed or baud rate and many other parameters.

Serial port cards are almost interchangeable between ATs and XTs, although an AT serial card is not the wisest choice for an XT, nor is it possible to use an XT serial card in an AT running OS/2. The XT type may be identified by the UART (Universal Asynchronous Receiver/Transmitter, a 40-pin chip). The XT serial cards use an 8250 or similar chip, whereas ATs use the 16450. These type numbers may differ somewhat in the case of the 16450, according to the manufacturer, but the device number should include the '450' part. Serial ports on PCs conform to the infamous RS 232c standard (Reference Standard 232 revision c) and there are usually one or two in any system, referred to as COM1 and COM2, which act independently of each other.

The original standard connector for a serial port is a 25-pin D-type, but AT serial ports often use a 9-pin D-type to save space. Mice also often use 9-pin connectors but the majority of other devices use the original 25-pin connector. The solution to this problem is to get hold of a 25- to 9-pin convertor.

If you are planning to make up your own serial cables then the pinouts for 9- and 25-pin connectors are shown in the table overleaf.

9-pin connector	25-pin connector	Function
1	8	DCD Data Carrier Detect
2	3	RX Receive Data
3	2	TX Transmit Data
4	20	DTR Data Terminal Ready
5	7	GND Signal ground
6	6	DSR Data Set Ready
7	4	RTS Request To Send
8	5	CTS Clear To Send
9	22	RI Ring Indicator

When you install a serial port the only configuration that is generally necessary is to select if it is going to be COM1 or COM2. In an AT system it is possible to configure the serial port to be COM 3 or COM 4 but this isn't advisable as some software will refuse to work with COM 3 and COM 4. Also notice that if you install an internal modem then this is likely to need to be configured either as COM 1 or COM 2 because an internal modem comes with its own built in serial interface. In this case make sure that it and the serial interface assignments don't clash.

There are also a great many jumpers and switches that affect the use of the auxiliary control lines such as RTS. As some equipment doesn't make use of these lines it is occasionally necessary to disable them. However, if you are connecting a piece of equipment that was designed for PC use then it is likely that the default setting will work.

The parallel port usually connects to a printer and its eight data lines send all the bits for a single byte of data simultaneously. This is a faster method than that used for serial ports. Problems can sometimes arise if the cable from the computer to the printer - the normal attached device - is more than a couple of metres long owing to attenuation and "scrambling" of the signal. The standard connector for a parallel port is a 25-pin D-type. You can tell the difference between a serial and parallel 25-pin connector on the machine because the parallel port is a female i.e. a socket and the serial port is a male i.e a plug.

If you are planning to make up your own parallel cables then the table below which shows the pinouts should help.

Communication ports occasionally go wrong or refuse to communicate, in which case, an appropriate diagnostic program is used. I would recommend QAPLUS or the Shareware COMMHELP - the latter explains how to make the loopback plug needed to test a serial port. Both programs test the communications ports intensively, and involve the use of loopback plugs. These are easy to construct for a serial interface but nobody bothers much about the printer port loop back - its easier to use a real printer.

Pin	Function	Pin	Function
1	-Strobe	10	-Ack
2	Data 0	11	Busy
3	Data 1	12	PE
4	Data 2	13	Slct
5	Data 3	14	-Autofd
6	Data 4	15	-Error
7	Data 5	16	-Init
8	Data 6	17	-Slct In
9	Data 7	18-25	Ground

Multi-function cards

Although serial and parallel interface cards aren't very expensive - about £10 or so, if you have to buy each one separately then the cost mounts up, as does the number of expansion slots you are using. A much better alternative is to buy a single multi-function adapter card. These are available for both XT and AT systems and while they might cost a little more than a single function card they are far less expensive than buying a full range of separate adapters. If you are putting a machine together from scratch then it is advisable to find a multi-function card that does what you want even if it has extra facilities that you don't want at the moment.

A typical XT multi-function card will contain a parallel printer port, two serial ports, a games adapter port and a real time clock. You can even find them complete with floppy disk controllers.

The new generation of AT multi-function cards - for example the DFI MIO-500 - go one step further and include not only a parallel printer port, two serial ports, a games port and a floppy disk controller, but an IDE hard disk interface as well. If your machine uses an IDE hard disk drive then a single MIO-500 supplies all of the standard interfaces that your machine needs for less than £50. Add a graphics card and you have a complete machine with only two adapter cards no matter what motherboard you use.

Games and mouse ports

The discussion of multi-function cards introduces the idea of a games port. This is a standard joystick input that will accept a single analog or PC joystick. This is used by many games for accurate X,Y positioning complete with fire buttons. The games port is in fact a crude two-channel A-to-D convertor and can be used for applications other than position sensing but the details would take us beyond the scope of this book. A standard 15-pin connector is used and its pin-outs are shown in the table opposite.

Pin	Function	Pin	Function
1	+5V	9	Ground
2	+5V	10	Position 3
3	Button 4	11	Position 1
4	Button 6	12	Button 7
5	Position 0	13	Button 5
6	Position 2	14	+5V
7	Ground	15	+5V
8	Ground		

You can buy special games adapter cards that supply two complete 15-pin connectors. This allows a pair of joysticks to be connected at the same time for two person games.

It is important not to confuse the games port with a mouse port. While a joystick and a mouse are both pointing devices, they work in very different ways and they are not interchangeable. The majority of software is designed to work either with a mouse or with a joystick. The majority of current mice are designed to work via a standard serial port and in this case all you have to do is plug them into the serial port and tell the software that the mouse is on COM1 or COM2. There are special bus mice, however, that make use of a completely different type of interface via a special adapter card. There are no advantages in using a bus mouse and the serial mouse is becoming increasingly popular because of its lower cost.

Graphics and I/O checklist

The following checklist will help you gather information about graphics cards, monitors and general interfaces.

Supplier	Tel
Graphics card model	
Graphics card type	MDA/ CGA/ EGA/ VGA/ SVGA/ other
Max resolution	( ) x ( )
Max colours	( )
Extra memory needed	( )KB
Additional features	
Price	
Monitor model	
Type	Colour/Mono
Highest graphics mode	MDA/ CGA/ EGA/ VGA/ SVGA/ other
Dot pitch	( )mm
Auto mode switching	Yes/No
Cables included	9/15 pin video/mains connector
Price	
I/O card model	
Interfaces included	( ) serial ( ) parallel ( ) games ( ) IDE ( ) floppy ( ) clock

Key points

» Separate floppy disk controllers come in two types able to support either two or four disks. Many XT controllers will only work with 360KB and 720KB drives. With a special controller you can use 1.2MB and 1.44MB on an XT.

» Fitting a floppy disk is easy, but notice that there are two types of cable in use - straight and twisted - and installation is slightly different in each case. The twisted cable is the commoner.

» You may need to buy a conversion kit (to 5.25") to make the fitting of 3.5" drives possible.

» Currently the best video card/monitor combination is VGA mono or colour which is capable of upgrading to SVGA (preferably non-interlaced 256 colour) by adding more memory.

» Most machines need at least one parallel and one serial I/O ports. The best way to equip a machine with sufficient ports at reasonable cost is to use a multi-function card.

162

Chapter 9
Putting it all together

In this chapter we look at the task of putting together all of the modules described in earlier chapters to make a working computer.

If you have read the earlier chapters of this book you should have a good working knowledge of all of the important modules that make up a computer. You should even know how to install each of them (in isolation), but starting from scratch with a collection of boxes and ending up with a working computer can be a daunting task. To make this task easier you need to take a step by step approach, checking everything as you go. It is also worth knowing that it can take the best part of a day to go from a collection of cardboard boxes to a finished and fully configured machine - so don't rush.

Many of the details of installation have already been described in earlier chapters so be prepared to look back if you aren't sure.

Buying advice

By now, you will have acquired the motherboard that you need and the case, power supply and a range of boxes, containing everything from a monitor to a floppy disk drive. Don't lose the invoices, sales slips or other bits of paper since you might need to contact one of your suppliers; it's a bit embarrassing to do so if you can't remember exactly what you purchased from him or when! Check carefully that you have (with each card you have purchased) an instruction manual or leaflet and any necessary cables or connectors. If not, contact your supplier since each manual or leaflet contains essential information. Take care not to lose anything and make sure that you keep parts from each module together.

Warning!
Handling chips and boards-
the danger of static

Individual chips and some complete adapter boards are prone to damage by static discharges. It is always a good idea to take precautions against static whenever you are working with electronic components or modules. Some people are so static prone that it is even worth taking precautions when the machine is safely inside a metal box! If you find that electric shocks from static discharge are a problem then buy an anti-static mat to place under the desk or table on which the machine is sited.

When it comes to handling components or adapter boards simpler and cheaper precautions are sufficient. All you need is a sheet of aluminium foil spread out over the working area. If you want to be extra cautious then you can even attach it to a radiator or a water pipe to earth it but under **no circumstances** attach it to the mains earth. The mains earth can carry a lethal voltage under some fault conditions. Before you start working, discharge any static build-up by touching a radiator or water pipe. Wearing clothes made from natural fibres rather than nylon helps reduce static problems as does a slightly humid atmosphere.

Chips and adapter boards are safe from static as long as they remain inside their protective conductive bags or foam. These should be kept in case you ever need to return an adapter for repair.

The quality of instructions that you get with each module is highly variable. US sourced products generally have better instruction manuals but this is part of the reason for their slightly higher prices. The instructions may well be as basic as a single sheet, or even in the form of an tiny reduced photocopy. Even if the English of the manual is bad, do not despair because it is often the diagrams that give you all of the information you need.

Before you forget, note the following particulars from your hard disk if you have one: manufacturer, model and type number, and check for a defect list which is either enclosed with the drive or stuck onto it. The defect list gives a list of the cylinder and head numbers which the manufacturer has noted as being defective during testing. This is vital since a defective cylinder cannot be relied upon for storage of data. The defect list may indicate other information, such as the precise byte or sector, but these cannot be utilised. Very few hard disks are completely free from manufacturing defects and some had a couple of dozen defects adding up to 100KB or so of disk space. Usually, a new hard disk should have less than a dozen defects. Some users are outraged at the idea that a new disk should have any defects but that's the way the industry works. To put it in perspective, the number of defects usually add up to a very small percentage of the total capacity of the drive and to produce a 100% defect free drive would not be economically viable.

Most of this hard disk information will be used at the stage after installation, that is when you come to set up the drive, and the danger is that it will get lost along with the packaging. Even in the best prepared situations it is still common to have to open the case or remove the drive to read the defect list stuck to its base!

Setting up the motherboard

Before doing **anything** else, locate the box containing the motherboard and read through the users' guide, handbook or whatever. Then read it again, making particular note of the locations of any switches or links which you will need to alter in order to set the machine up in its final configuration. The details of switches and jumpers can be found in Chapter 4.

Before making any changes to the switch or jumper settings make a note of the original settings of the switches or links, just in case. Keep it with your user manual. Set the switch positions or links according to the instructions in the user guide. In particular, check the setting of the colour/monochrome switch or link, and the settings for the number of floppy disk drives and various amounts of memory, if these are present.

If you are setting up an AT board then you might also have to set links to introduce wait states. The number of wait states varies according to the speed of the memory modules that you are using. See Chapter 5 for more information. Some more recent machines allow the wait states to be set up from a built-in configuration program, so check your manual.

Check that you have the correct type and amount of memory chips and install them into the motherboard. Memory installation has been described in Chapter 5 but the following points are worth bearing in mind:

» If you are at all in doubt about what you are doing then only install the minimum amount of memory until you have established that everything is working.

» Start installing memory from bank 0 and always make sure that you install complete banks.

» If you are using DIL chips then make sure that you straighten the pins before insertion, insert them the correct way round and don't bent the pins under the chip. The most common cause of DIL memory not working on first installation is a bent pin. It can be difficult to see where each chip actually fits in the rows of empty sockets so start from an edge and work in.

» If you are using SIPs or SIMMs then make sure that they are inserted with the correct orientation.

If you are intending to use a maths co-processor (8087, 80287 or 80387), it is best to install it now. Some boards require you to alter a link or switch position if a co-processor is to be installed. For details see the box - *Installing a co-processor.*

Check the users' guide for the location of the battery (if the machine has one) - this keeps the time/date function working while the machine is switched off, and, on AT machines, may maintain the configuration information. The battery may be a NiCad Battery (rechargeable when the machine is switched on) or a disposable, plug-in type. The battery is often situated between the keyboard socket and the slots and its operation may be controlled by a selectable link. If the machine uses a disposable battery, this will be provided with the motherboard and should be connected strictly according to the manual. The red wire goes to the positive pin of the connector on the board.

This completes the initial work on the motherboard and it should be put carefully on one side preferably back into its anti-static bag or placed on its conductive rubber sheet.

The case and power supply

The next stage is to prepare the case to receive the motherboard. Check very carefully for sharp edges on the case components, If you find any sharp edges, get a file and smooth them off. Whatever you do, do not file or work on the case in any way once the motherboard and other electronics has been installed. The reason is simply that metal filings and fragments can lodge under circuit boards and chip sockets and cause malfunctions. It the case looks as if it isn't absolutely clean then vacuum clean it to remove any loose bits of metal.

Depending upon the type of case, slide off the lid (after undoing a series of screws at the rear and underneath - along the lower edges) or raise it if it is hinged. Your case will probably have the power supply already fitted, but if not, installation is straightforward and is carried out as follows:

The case should have a series of cut-outs (usually at the right and rear) which must correspond with the power switch, mains input/auxiliary output and cooling fan. Fit the power unit power switch into its cut-out and then use the short bolts supplied with the hardware to fix the power supply to the rear of the case. A couple of bolts, or tongues which latch into sockets, are normally used to fix the base of the power supply to the case.

You will also find a series of wires with connectors on one end and attached at the other to various lights, usually different coloured LEDs and switches at the front of the case. These have been described in detail in Chapters 4 and 6 and have to be plugged into the corresponding connectors on the motherboard.

The power supply connectors carry colour coded wires are reasonably well standardised in their colour coding. Red wires carry +5 volts, yellow wires +12 volts, and black wires are 0 volts. There are three other wire colours, blue, white and orange, and these may carry -12, or -5 volts, or provide a PowerGood signal to the motherboard.

Note that it is vital that you plug the two main power connectors to the motherboard in the correct way round. Failure to do so will damage the motherboard beyond repair. See Chapters 4 and 6 for more information on motherboard connectors. If the standard colour coding is used then the correct orientation is to plug the two connectors in so that the **black** wires on each plug are next to each other.

Make sure that the voltage selector is set correctly for your local electricity supply (in the U.K. and Ireland, 220 or 240 volts). If it is set for 110 volts, you will permanently damage both the power supply and your motherboard.

Finally, check the power lead and remove the existing plug if necessary - many power units come with plugs which are European standard, rather than the British and Irish standard 13 amp. You will need to prepare the leads - don't forget to allow sufficient wire to reach the earth pin. A 3 or 5 amp fuse should be fitted.

One or two importers have been supplying mains leads with incorrect (non EEC) colour coding. The correct colours are blue (neutral), brown (live) and green/yellow (earth) and any other combination is illegal and possibly dangerous. If you can afford one, fit a mains plug with a surge

Installing a co-processor

Locate the socket into which the co-processor will be placed. The 8087 and 80287 will need a socket with two rows of 20 pins - the top or notched end must be identified and the co-processor carefully installed with the notched end facing in this direction. You may need to straighten the legs of the chip - do this in the same way as was suggested for the DIL memory chips. Once it is located correctly, press it in firmly but gently.

The 80387 exists in two forms, the 80387DX which is intended for full specification 80386 machines and the 80387SX which is used only for the 80386SX type of machine. The 80387DX is a square block with about 65 pins and it has a bevelled corner and a white dot for orientation purposes. Look at the socket and identify the corner with a matching bevel and/or white dot. Position the co-processor so that it lines up and then, carefully, press it into position. If you don't get it right, the co-processor may burn out when you switch on.

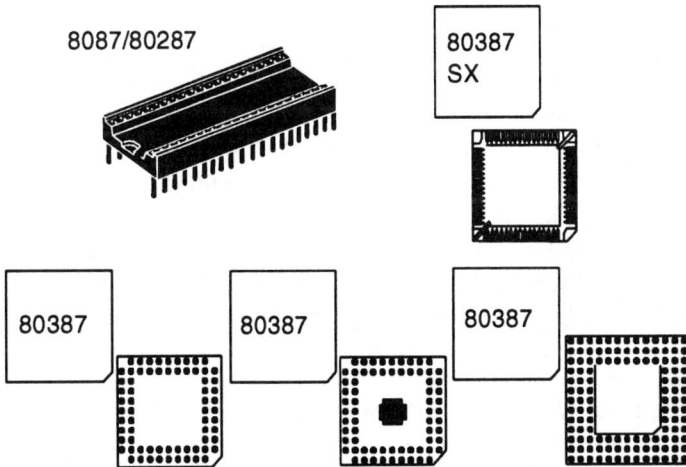

8087/80287

80387
SX

80387

80387

80387

The 80387SX is another square block, with 17 contacts on all four sides. It fits into a square hole socket - one corner of which is bevelled. Line up the pin 1 dot on the chip with the bevel and carefully press the chip into the socket. Again, check that you get it right because mistakes are expensive.

suppression facility. These are more expensive and usually a bit bulkier than normal mains plugs but will cut out much of the electrical noise and spikes on the supply which can cause problems.

A test setup

The next step is to install the motherboard in the case and try it out. The case should have been supplied with a fixing kit as described in Chapter 6 - if not then you should contact the supplier. To decide the positions of the plastic spacers (or stand-offs) in the motherboard, place the motherboard on the bottom of the case, so that the keyboard socket is lined up with the hole in the rear of the case. Locate the holes on the motherboard, generally in the top, middle and bottom into which the plastic spacers would fit and note exactly where they occur on the base of the case.

Remove the board and insert the spacers, leaving one hole which corresponds with an earthing point on the motherboard. An earthing point is an area surrounding a mounting hole which is not covered by protective green lacquer. In the hardware kit you should find a metal mounting nut. Fix the metal spacer in position and clip the rest of the plastic spacers into the appropriate holes on the motherboard. Then slide or clip the free ends of the spacers into the appropriate slots or holes in the base of the case. This sounds difficult, but, with care and a bit of dexterity, it can be done quite easily. When the board is properly in place, check that the keyboard socket is accessible through the corresponding hole in the case. When all is correct, take one of the smaller short bolts and fix it through the board into the threaded metal stand-off. This has the dual effect of securing the board and connecting the case to earth.

At the front of the case, there are a number of wires and connectors which must be joined up to the appropriate pins on the motherboard. You should have already worked out which pair of wires is which. If not you will have to identify each wire now by tracing it back to the indicator or switch that it is connected to. In most cases you should wire up at least: Reset switch, power-on light, turbo indicator light, turbo switch, keyboard lock and loudspeaker. The power light and keyboard lock are sometimes combined on a single socket strip. The reset switch and loudspeaker can be fitted on to the appropriate pins either way round as can the turbo switch if it has two wires. If it has three wires, you may have to experiment - you can't do any harm. The keyboard switch and power light must be put on in a particular orientation - check the user guide for this. The Turbo indicator light can be fitted on either way but it will only work in turbo mode if it is the right way round.

One pair of wires should be left and these are for the hard-disk indicator light. The reason why these are unused at the moment is that they connect to the hard disk controller which we have yet to install!

Finally, attach the power supply leads to the motherboard - with care and ensure that they lock into position. Make sure that they are the correct way round, check and double check this fact because it is the only really critical part of the installation.

In order to test the motherboard to make sure that it is installed correctly and the memory is working, the next step is to fit the video card and monitor. Check the configuration of the video card is suitable for the monitor that you are using and then plug it into any expansion slot. Connect the monitor video cable to the video output socket on the back panel. Connect the keyboard - the plug goes in with the 5 pins at the bottom, near to the motherboard. Tape all of the spare disk drive power supply connectors to keep them out of the way for the moment. It is very important that none of these connectors accidentally touch the metal work of the case or any pins on the motherboard.

Finally, connect the power supply to the machine and the monitor. If the monitor is supplied with a separate power cable and plug then switch it on first so that you can see what is happening. If not then make sure that any mains switches on it are on. Next switch the machine on. You should hear the whirring of the power supply fan. If not then switch off immediately and check that the power connections to the motherboard are correct. If the power supply fan isn't running then it could be a short circuit, caused by an incorrectly placed connector. If you cannot find any problems then disconnect the power supply and try it again. If the fan still doesn't run and the mains cable and the fuses are all OK then you have a faulty power supply. If the fan runs when the power supply isn't connected to the motherboard then the fault lies in the motherboard or the connections to it.

If the power supply is working then you should see something on the screen after only a few seconds. Before this, you should watch the Num Lock, Caps Lock and Scroll Lock lights on the keyboard. If the system is working at all then you will see these flash for a moment. Most machines then go on to test their memory before doing anything else so if you are lucky you should see the memory test count on the monitor. Don't worry too much about any error messages that you might see concerning disk drives or overall configuration at this stage because there are bound to be inconsistencies just caused by the fact that there are no disk drives fitted! You should, however, take any error messages concerning memory faults seriously as this aspect of configuration isn't going to change. If you do encounter a memory error then switch off and check the installation of the chips or memory modules. If you cannot get rid of the fault by examining the installation try moving chips or modules around on the board. If the location of the memory fault moves then you have a faulty chip or module. If not then the problem is likely to be its configuration, the wrong speed of memory chip, or a fault on the the motherboard.

If you don't see anything on the screen at all then there are only two possibilities; either the video card and monitor aren't working or the motherboard has a problem. If the lights on the keyboard flashed just after switching on then the chances are that the motherboard is working and you should investigate the video card and monitor first.

As long as you can see a display on the monitor and you have no reported memory errors then you can switch off and move on to the next stage which is to fit the disk drives and other modules.

Fitting the disk drives

After completing the basic system test the you should switch the machine off, disconnect it from the mains and remove the video card in preparation for fitting the disk drives.

Fix the drives into the drive bays as described in Chapter 7. Before you do this it is a good idea to configure the drives by setting the jumpers to select whether they are drive 0 or drive 1. Notice the floppy and hard disks are treated separately so the first floppy disk in your system should be set up as drive 0 and the first hard disk should also be set up as drive 0. Also recall the complications that using a twisted drive cable introduce - see Chapter 8. If you are fitting more than one drive to the same cable then remember to remove the terminating resistors from all but the last physical drive on the cable. It has to be admitted that it is all too easy to configure drives incorrectly with the result that the one that you thought was going to be drive 0 turns out to be drive 1 when you switch on - so be prepared to take the drives out again to alter their jumpers! Remember that, with most IBM-compatile floppy drive controllers, there is a twist in the cable. This means that both floppy drives, if fitted, should be set to drive 1, rather than 0 and 1.

Warning!
Dropping drives

Disk drives seem to be very robust pieces of metal work but in fact they are very delicate. Try very hard not to drop or bang a hard disk or floppy disk drive while fitting it. If you do there is a good chance that the read/write heads will be damaged. In the case of a hard disk it is possible that the heads bouncing on the surface of the disk will damage it making it impossible to read or write that area. Floppy disk drives usually come with a cardboard dummy disk, which is inserted to keep the heads from hitting together as the drive is moved. Leave this cardboard protector in place until the drive is installed and keep it handy in case you ever have to remove the drive. Remember that dropping disk drives breaks them!

The range of mountings for disk drives is too wide for it to be possible to give a complete account of how it is done in every case. A little thought should reveal the way a drive should be mounted. You should ensure that it is held by two bolts on each side so that it cannot move backwards or forwards or tilt in the bay. It is important that the bottom of one drive cannot make contact with the top of the drive below otherwise this might short out the electronics. Don't tighten the bolts until you have checked that the drives are correctly positioned with their face plates flush with the front of the case. Recall that you might have to remove the front plate from some hard disks to make them fit. Also, do not over tighten the bolts holding the drive.

You should think about how the cables that are going to connect the drive to the power and to the disk controllers will be routed before you choose which drive bay should be used for which drive. Obviously it makes sense to group pairs of floppy disks together but other than this advice it comes down to common sense. In some cases you will only be able to see that there is a better arrangement after you have installed the drives - so once again be prepared to remove the drives and refit them.

After the drives are installed connect the power cables and the ribbon cables. Make sure that all of the cables are connected the correct way round - see Chapter 7.

The final part of the assembly consists of inserting the adapter cards you have purchased into the slots on the motherboard.

Do not use the slot nearest the power connector on an XT motherboard (slot 8) unless this is absolutely necessary. On the original IBM XT, this slot required the card occupying it to provide a signal (-CARD SLCTD) when the card is activated. The slot also has much stricter timing requirements than the remaining 7 slots. Using slot 8 can produce some very strange results both on true IBM XTs and XT clones.

Most cards seem to work quite happily in any other slot and on an AT system your only worry is 8-bit versus 16-bit slot and full length versus half length. Some 386 boards have a special double slot for a proprietary 32-bit memory card. This can be used for 8-bit adapters which will use the part of the double slot nearest the back of the board, but 16-bit adapters should not be used under any circumstances.

If you are installing a hard card in an XT, make sure that you have left enough room and that it has the full length of two slots available. It could be installed in slot 7, where it will only obscure the difficult-to-use slot 8.

When inserting a card, do so carefully, by engaging the edge plug(s) into the appropriate slot(s). Wiggle the board and press down and it should slide in and fit snugly. Secure the mounting bracket onto the rear aperture ledge with a short bolt. Occasionally you might have to bend the metal bracket on the card to make it fit more snugly but this isn't common.

The biggest problem with plugging in cards lies in working out the best arrangement. The obvious rule is never use a 16-bit slot for an 8-bit card if you can avoid it. Although a 16-bit slot will work as with an 8-bit card they might be in short supply! You also obviously have to take into account the length of each adapter card if the case restricts the length of some of the slots. But after these considerations have been taken into account what matters is producing a nice neat cable run rather than a mess. If you want to see how to place the cables neatly then have a look inside a few commercial machines if you can. Ribbon cables should be folded to make right angle bends and routed where they are most out of the way. This is easy to say and it has to be admitted that some people seem to have the knack of making cables neat and others produce rats' nests! There is an argument for leaving cable tidying until you have completed the installation of all of the adapter cards and the disk drives etc. and the testing is over.

If you have a hard drive indicator light on the front of the case, the cable and connector can be plugged onto the controller card. There are 4 pins, close together on the side of the card nearest the front of the computer. The connector attaches so that the red wire is furthest from you. This won't be needed if the activity light on your hard disk is visible at the front of your machine. In this case, keep the wire and connector out of the way.

Other cards should then be inserted in appropriate slots. It is perfectly all right to put an 8-bit card in a 16-bit slot. Some cards will need to have switch or link settings changed, and this should be done before you install them. Before doing anything, make a note of the original settings and then read the manual or instruction sheet carefully.

The machine is now ready for its second test. Connect up the monitor, keyboard and mains cables as before. Switch on at the power plug, then at the computer and monitor. Once again, the power supply fan should start and you should also hear the whirr of the hard disk drive if one is fitted. If either do not start switch off and check everything again. You should still see the keyboard lights flash and the floppy disk drives should seek to track 0 making a clicking sound. You should then see something on the screen. If you performed the first test then the only things that can go wrong are to do with the disk drives. The machine will proceed to self test memory and then the drives, and exactly what happens next depends on the type of machine and what drives you have fitted. One thing that is almost certain, though, is that if you have fitted a hard disk it will not work at this stage because it has yet to be initialised.

Whatever type of machine you are working with at this stagem, you will need a copy of the operating system on a floppy disk of the correct density i.e. one created with:

FORMAT A: /S

where the /S parameter means 'copy the system onto the diskette'. If you are installing MS-DOS 5 then you will first have to use the option to install it to floppies and then go through the procedure to install it to the hard disk later.

On a typical XT-Turbo machine the sequence of events is as follows. If you have no hard disk, the system will prompt you to put in a system disk and press any key. As long as you have a copy of MS-DOS on diskette then inserting the disk and pressing a key should produce the copyright notice and the A-prompt "A:>". If it doesn't, you will get another message about putting a system disk in drive A - in which case, you most likely chose the wrong drive on a two-drive machine! Take the disk out of the first drive, insert it in the second and close the door, type any key and wait for the message to appear. If it doesn't, then you have a fault most likely caused by either the drive or the diskette being the wrong density.

If the XT machine has a hard disk, you will have to wait a while before getting the message to insert a system disk. Preceding this will be a 4-digit error code - probably 1701. This means that there is a problem with the hard disk. This always happens with a brand new disk because it has no information on it and needs to be prepared before the computer will recognise it and it can be properly used.

Insert a system disk as previously described and the system should give you the A-prompt A:>. After this you have to prepare the hard disk for use, by using appropriate software and this is described in the next chapter.

For an AT, the sequence of events is more complex and is dealt with more fully in Chapter 10, but even if an error occurs, pressing function key F1 will enable you to proceed at least part of the way with the checking unless, that is, you have a keyboard error in which case pressing F1 will achieve absolutely nothing!

The usual message on a newly constructed AT is

CMOS CONFIGURATION ERROR, PLEASE RUN SETUP

or something similar. The exact message will, depend upon the BIOS in use and not on MS-DOS. You might also get a

C: DRIVE ERROR

This is not surprising since the hard disk will not have been prepared for use - and possibly a "BATTERY LOW" warning which is also understandable if your board has been in stock for some time so that the on-board battery is almost flat. Leave the machine switched on for a while and the battery charges automatically although it does take several hours of use to be fully re-charged.

Three types of PC-AT (and XT) BIOS (Basic Input/Output System) are commonly found - Phoenix, Award and AMI - and what happens next depends on which type the motherboard has. This should be fully documented in the manual that came with the motherboard but it isn't difficult to get everything working.

» A Phoenix BIOS will ask you to run its Setup program (in older versions, this was supplied on a floppy disk, but newer versions have it incorporated into the BIOS chips. It is usually accessed by pressing F1, the first function key.

» An Award BIOS tells you to press the Ctrl, Alt and Esc keys at the same time and then puts you straight into a Setup screen.

» AMI asks you to press the Del key to run its built-in Setup program.

```
┌─────────────────────────────────────────────────────────────────┐
│   CMOS SETUP                                                      │
└─────────────────────────────────────────────────────────────────┘
┌─────────────────────────────────────────────────────────────────┐
│                                                                   │
│ Date (mm/dd/yy): Wed May 31 1989                                  │
│ Time (hh/mm/ss): 15:20:00                                         │
│ Floppy drive A: 1.2MB, 5.25"                                      │
│ Floppy drive B: 1.44MB, 3.5"                                      │
│                              Cylin   Head   WPcom LZone  Sec Size │
│ Hard disk C: type: 2         615     4      300   615    17  20MB │
│ Hard disk D: type: Not Installed                                  │
│ Primary display: Monochrome                                       │
│ Keyboard: Installed                                               │
│                                                                   │
│ Scratch RAM option: 1                                             │
│                                                                   │
└─────────────────────────────────────────────────────────────────┘
```

Figure 9.1
Typical BIOS Setup screen

In each case, follow the instructions - you should know the types of peripherals (video, hard and floppy disks and amount of normal and extended/expanded memory) and the user manual should be quite helpful. The details supplied with the hard disk should be to hand. At the very least you should know the number of read/write heads and cylinders. There is normally no separate VGA video mode - most BIOSes treat EGA and VGA together.

After you have filled in all of the details using the BIOS setup you can try to start the system again using a floppy disk with a copy of MS-DOS on it. With luck, you won't get any further errors, apart from the C: drive which in most cases still will not be initialised even though the BIOS knows something about it now. Before you can use your machine to it's fullest extent, the hard disk will need to be prepared as explained in Chapter 10.

Configuring adapter cards

Many adapter cards require you to set jumpers or switches to allocate them an area of memory, a particular interrupt number or a DMA channel. It doesn't matter what areas you allocate to what card as long as you don't use the same resources twice! There is a reasonably standard set of addresses, interrupt and DMA assignments for XT and AT systems and if you keep to this you should have no problem. In fact most adapter cards are supplied with these setting as the default. The usual I/O addresses used for XT and AT devices are given in Table 9.1.

Table 9.1

Address	Device
1F0-1F8	Hard disk (AT only)
200-207	Game port
240-26F	Network adapter cards
278-27F	Printer port 2
2B0-2DF	Alternate EGA (usually free)
2E0-2EF	GPIB (IEEE-488) adapter
2F8-2FF	Serial port 2
300-31F	Prototype card (usually free)
320-32F	Hard disk (XT only)
360-36F	Reserved (usually free)
378-37F	Printer port 1
380-38F	Bisync serial 2 (usually free)
390-39F	Cluster adapter (usually free)
3A0-3AF	bi-sync serial 1 (usually free)
3B0-3BF	Mono Display Adaptor (MDA)
3C0-3CF	Reserved - Network adapter cards
3D0-3DF	Colour Graphic Adaptor (CGA)
3F0-3F7	Floppy disk controller
3F8-3FF	Serial port 1

The usual interrupt allocations for an XT and AT are as follows: (note that an XT only has interrupts 0-7):

Interrupt number	Device
0	System timer
1	Keyboard
2	Internal use
3	Serial port 2
4	Serial port 1
5	Printer port 2 (AT) and hard disk (XT)
6	Floppy disk controller
7	Printer port 1
8	Clock/Calendar
9	Internal use
10	spare
11	spare
12	spare
13	Numeric co-processor
14	Hard disk controller
15	spare

The usual allocation of DMA channels for an XT or AT is (note that an XT has only DMA channels 0 - 3:

DMA channel number	Device
0	spare
1	SDLC card
2	Floppy disk controller
3	Hard disk XT only
4	Internal use AT only
5	spare AT only
6	spare AT only
7	spare AT only

You can use the I/O address, interrupt number or DMA channel that is normally allocated to a card that isn't currently in your machine. However, it is better to try to keep to the allocations listed above. It is also a good idea to make a list of the allocations that you have used when you install adapter cards. Notice also that it doesn't matter if you know what a DMA channel or an interrupt is, all that matters is that you don't allocate the same one to more than one adapter card!

Soak testing and cable ties

Even if everything is working, apart from the hard disk initialisation problem, then it is still not a good idea to fix the cover on firmly just yet. It is better to move on to hard disk initialisation and then soak test (i.e. leave it running for a long time) the system in its fully configured state. Most hardware failures happen within the first few hours of use, so leaving the machine on for a while - 8 hours if possible - is a good first test that will also reveal any heat-related faults.

If all this talk of faults and failures is beginning to worry you, I should add that it is quite usual for everything to work first time and if it doesn't then the most likely cause is a mistake in wiring or configuration. Actual hardware failures are rare.

After the soak test the final step is to tidy up the wiring. If the fixing kit didn't include some cable ties, then buy some from your local Tandy or from a mail order electronics company. Make sure that the cables cannot come loose and get in the way of the floppy disk drives or accidentally touch parts of the metal case. This is particularly important for the unused disk drive power connectors. Use cable ties to secure the unused connectors to a convenient part of the case or folded back against the other power supply leads.

After all this work you may be so attached to the inside of your new computer that you are tempted to leave the cover off so that you can admire it! Don't, because the cooling fan is only effective if you run it with the cover in place.

Key points

» To assemble a complete machine you need to work logically in a step-by-step manner.

» Assemble the case, motherboard, memory and video card first. Leave the disk drives and other adapter cards until you have this much tested and working.

» Fit disk drives and adapter cards as a second stage. Do not expect hard disk systems to work at this stage because they have to be initialised before they respond correctly.

» AT systems need the BIOS configuring to let it know the type of display, disk drives and the date and time.

» Have a copy of the operating system that you are going to use installed on a floppy disk and use this to start (boot) the system to check that it is all working. Ignore any error messages concerning the hard disk at this stage - it still needs to be initialised.

» If everything works then soak test the machine by running for a few hours with the cover on.

» If something doesn't work then try to be logical about tracking down the fault to a particular module, see Chapter 11 for more details.

Chapter 10
Preparing a hard disk for use

After everything else is working you have to initialise the hard disk. This chapter describes how it is done.

The process of preparing a hard drive for use can seem very complicated and full of strange procedures and rules. In fact, once you understand the two basic procedures, formatting and partitioning, it's easy enough.

Formatting and partitioning

A new hard disk will have no information recorded on it that can be read directly by MS-DOS, or any other operating system, and in order for it to be usable, its surfaces must be prepared (formatted). Of the five currently available types of hard disks for PCs, two - MFM and RLL- require two separate formatting operations - one low-level or physical format and one high-level or logical format - to prepare them fully, while the remaining three types, SCSI, ESDI and IDE, require only a single high-level format. The physical format lays down a pattern of tracks and sectors but doesn't organise them so that an operating system can use them. This is achieved by the logical format. The logical format is very like formatting a floppy diskette and it even involves the use of the same FORMAT command.

As well as requiring formatting, drives also need partitioning. Versions of MS-DOS earlier than 4.0 had a disadvantage as far as high capacity hard disks are concerned in that they could not correctly handle hard disks with capacities greater than 32MB. Larger disks had to be split into sections (partitions) of this size or smaller. Versions 4.0 and higher do not have the same limitation and very large disks can be handled as one partition. There used to be an advantage in using MS-DOS 3.3 even though it involved partitioning the disk because it used less memory then MS-DOS 4.0 but MS-DOS 5 has overcome this. There were also ways in which earlier versions of MS-DOS could access hard disk partitions greater than 32MB. Typical of these was Ontrack's Disk Manager which worked pretty well, although the large partitions were not directly compatible with MS-DOS. If you can get a copy of DR-DOS 5 or 6 or MS-DOS 5.0 than these are far better choices then earlier versions of MS-DOS.

In most cases, as long as the version of MS-DOS will support it, it is better to create the largest partition that the drive will allow. There are one or two situations where this isn't the case. Another use of partitions is to allow more than one operating system to use the same hard disk. If you partition a hard disk into two equal-sized chunks then you can install MS-DOS in one and Unix, for example, in another. The details of how to do this are beyond the scope of this book but it is useful to know that it is at least possible.

Setting the drive types - XT and AT

Although the basic processes in preparing a drive for use are formatting and partitioning, it is also necessary to let the disk controller know the type of drive that is being used. The drive type tells the controller how many tracks, heads and other characteristics that it can then use during the formatting process. For example, if you set the drive type so that the controller believes that it has 3 heads and 100 tracks then that's exactly how many heads and tracks that are used during the subsequent format operations. If you get the drive type specification wrong then the effects vary from not using all of the available storage to the drive not working at all. You can think of setting the drive type as a step that comes before formatting and partitioning. The methods use to set the drive type differ greatly between XT and AT systems.

In the case of the XT it is up to the drive controller to 'know' what type of drive is in use. Early XT ST-506 controllers often had a collection of jumpers or switches which set the number of heads and cylinders the drive had. In some cases the support for selecting the drive was so limited that there was no choice but to select the nearest drive configuration and sacrifice some storage space. More modern XT controllers can be programmed to accept the drive parameters during low-level formatting. Once the drive has been formatted at low level, followed by partitioning using FDISK and the final high level format and addition of a system, that's all there is to do - simply start off the system and add software as appropriate. You do not need to tell the computer anything more about the hard disk. (Detailed descriptions of these steps are given later in the chapter.)

The situation in the case of ATs is slightly more complex, since the information on system configuration is held in battery backed memory. In addition to the information on monitor and floppy drive types, you have to set the drive type by specifying its number of heads, cylinders and the point at which write precompensation is to be applied. In the case of some modern BIOS setup routines you can specify these details individually but more typically you are required to enter a predefined drive number in the BIOS setup routine which automatically supplies these details.

Originally the IBM AT system allowed for 23 drive types, but since then manufacturers of clones have not only extended the number, but frequently used the numbering system in a different way, with numbers from type 16 onwards often designating entirely different drive types in each case. This is why you **must** have information on your hard drive as described above, so that you can match it with the parameters stored in your clone's drive table.

The original IBM drive table was a good idea when there were relatively few drive types available, and the present situation is nothing if not

Drive parameters

Many users are mystified by the drive parameters that have to be specified to set up a drive. The number of heads and cylinders isn't so bad because this corresponds to something that is obviously important. If you select a smaller number of heads and cylinders than a drive actually has then it will work but you will be wasting some of the drive's capacity. For example, if a drive has six heads and 400 cylinders and you select three heads and 200 cylinders then you will only get a quarter of the storage capacity of the drive.

If you set more heads than a drive has then you will simply get an error message every time the controller tries to use one of the non-existent heads! This of course renders the drive useless and you will have to change the setup and reformat it. If you select more cylinders than the drive has then the everything will go fine during the low-level formatting until the head reaches the final cylinder after which you will hear the noise of the head hitting the end stop! Not a good experience for a drive.

If you have an old ST-506 drive that isn't supported exactly by the controller then it is possible to use its full capacity by setting it up as a drive with the correct number of heads but more cylinders than it actually has. The head will hit the end stops during formatting, but after that you can partition the disk to use the number of cylinders that actually exist and then perform a logical format in the usual way. From this point on the disk never attempts to access the non-existent cylinders because they are in an unallocated partition. Crude but it works!

The remaining drive parameters - start cylinder for reduced write current and start cylinder for write-precompensation - sound a little more technical. These are designed to allow for the fact that the speed of a disk passing under the read/write head is faster at the edge than in the middle of the disk. This means that you have to use different read/write characteristics depending on the cylinder number and this is what these two parameters are determining. Modern disks don't need either because they adjust the way data is written automatically without the controller having to be involved.

inconvenient. Most clone ROM BIOSs (Phoenix, Award and AMI) have a fairly standard range of types, often more than 40. They are accessed in different ways when the system is first switched on: Phoenix asks you to run a set-up program (originally on disk but now in the BIOS); Award asks you to press CTRL and ALT together followed by ESC keys; AMI asks you to press DEL during the initial startup.

For Phoenix and AMI, you can either work through the drive numbers until you come across one which has the right number of heads and the same, or slightly fewer cylinders, or, for drive types which do not match, you can enter the appropriate parameters in the next vacant drive number - usually 46 or 47 - which may be described as 'User supplied'. Unfortunately some early versions of the Award BIOS and some other early BIOSs will not let you set a user-defined drive type at all and so restricts you to the list of predefined types.

What happens if your drive type is not catered for and you cannot enter the exact number of cylinders and heads? You have two choices - either to accept the nearest lower number of cylinders and same number of heads or, if you have access to it, use Ontrack's Disk Manager which allows you to override the BIOS drive table. In the first case, you will lose some disk capacity which is very irritating and in the second case, you can use all of the disk and, as a bonus, have a disk partition greater than 32MB even if you are using MS-DOS 3.3. Drive Manager is a complete disk formatting and partitioning utility and it is worth looking into if you have problems setting up a hard disk exactly as you want it - it will even determine the optimum interleave for any disk. As an alternative you could try the Public Domain disk which contains Western Digital hard disk utilities. I would advise against using the hard disk low-level format program in the IBM Advanced Diagnostics at all.

Notice that IDE drives are special when it comes to setup - see the section on IDE drives later in this chapter.

Initialising ST-506 drives

Before doing anything else, you must find out a few particulars about your hard disk. You need its make and model number, and to find out from the manufacturer's data sheet the number of its cylinders and heads and if it requires any 'write-precompensation'. You should also locate the 'Defect list'. This is normally attached to the top plate of the drive and consists of a list of places on the hard disk platters where the manufacturer's test program has detected faults. If the computer writes data to such faulty areas, the stored data may be corrupted and it may not be possible to retrieve it. All low-level formatting programs will ask for defect information to be entered - with at least the details of the head(s) and cylinder(s) involved. If your drive and controller are MFM types, remember that you with have 17 sectors per track whereas an RLL drive and controller have 26 sectors. This is required as part of the setup procedure for the controller.

Two types of format are necessary, firstly, the low-level (physical) format which prepares the disk by writing a series of tracks and checking the surface of the disk for faults which can later be avoided. This is followed by a high-level (logical) format (identical to that used to prepare floppy disks) to lay down a pattern of sectors on each track for data storage and retrieval.

Low-level format in XT machines

Disks which will be used for XTs can usually be formatted using a built-in routine in the controller card if it is made by Seagate, Adaptec or Western Digital (or uses Western Digital chips). Disks for use in an AT cannot usually be formatted in this way. See the section on formatting AT disks for details.

Seagate controllers are probably easier to use than those made by Western Digital but are less widely available at present. In both cases, the low-level format is carried by starting a machine code program from the DEBUG utility that is provided with MS-DOS. The Seagate version is designed to help the user through the process whereas the Western

Digital process is more complex and less user-friendly. However, both are quite straightforward as long as the drive is a standard type. The procedure is identical for hard cards. Make quite sure that the controller card is suitable for the drive. A controller designed for use with RLL drives will not work correctly with an MFM certified drive.

The system is started up and once the operating system A:> prompt is reached, type DIR to see if a program called DEBUG.COM is available on that disk. If the version of MS-DOS that you are using comes on two disks, it may be on the second, so take out the first and try the second if necessary. Type DEBUG then press the Enter key. After a short while, a "-" prompt appears and you type in the starting address of the built-in formatting routine, as in the example. Comments on what each command does are shown in italics and these are **not** part of the dialogue that appears on the screen:

A:>DEBUG   *loads debug from drive A*
-G=c800:5   *starts the first (low-level) formatting routine*

After this what follows depends on the type of controller.
(Note: some Adaptec controllers use c800:ccc instead of c800:5)

The formatting process for a Western Digital controller identifies if a drive is correctly attached and if so, prompts you to confirm that it is drive C (the default) or select a new drive. As long as you are trying to format drive C simply select the default by pressing Enter.

You will then be asked if you want to use the current interleave of 3 (the usual value) or if you want to select a new value. The idea of interleave was discussed in Chapter 7. Unless you know that the interleave should be set differently then it is simpler to leave the default as it is by pressing Enter.

The system will ask you if you wish to configure your hard disk dynamically. This is a process whereby a non-standard disk can be formatted fully - it is optional with the standard size of 20MB or with a 32MB disk with an RLL controller (this is usually the case with a hard card). If you have a different disk, you will need to provide the following information about the drive:

» Number of cylinders

» Number of heads

» Starting cylinder for reduced write current

» Beginning of section with write-precompensation

» Error burst length

» Option byte

These values have to be obtained from the drive's documentation or manufacturer's data. The correct values are simply typed in sequence.

For example in the case of the Seagate ST-225, a very common 20MB drive, the numbers are:

612 4 0 300 11 05 (the spaces are needed) followed by Enter

The final stage before formatting commences is the response to a question about virtually configuring the drive, to which you should answer 'no' for drives less than 32MB and 'yes' for drives of a greater size than this. If you answer yes, you will be asked to type in the virtual drive split (this is usually half the total number of cylinders) then press Enter.

The system then prompts you to start formatting the disk, and to start it, type 'yes'. The process will then start and the drive light will say on for some time - up to 45 minutes or an hour. When finished, the system will prompt you for information on bad sectors and you should type in the relevant information from the defect list supplied with the disk.

The Seagate ST-11 controller is much easier to use than the Western Digital but it still follows the same general steps. The instructions are clear and unambiguous, unlike those from Western Digital's range. Information is entered when called for and the process is almost foolproof.

Irrespective of the type of controller, once low-level formatting is completed the next stage is partitioning.

Low-level format in AT machines

Low-level format of a hard disk in most AT machines is a little more of a problem in that you need a formatting program. This is because there generally isn't one built into the disk controller as is the case for XT controllers. Recent versions of the AMI BIOS for 386/486 machines actually include a low-level formatter, easily accessible via a menu. Once you have the necessary software or firmware, it is just as easy if not easier than the procedure for the XT. In other words, the problem is in acquiring a suitable formatting program not in using it! You should ask your supplier to provide software which will carry out the low-level format if your hard disk is going to be used in an AT. Don't take excuses - particularly if the dealer says that the disk is already prepared since you may need to carry out a low-level format at a later date to correct errors.

If you find that you have been supplied with a hard disk but no formatting utility then the lowest cost program is the Public Domain version of the Western Digital AT hard disk utilities. You might also have access to a copy of the IBM Advanced Diagnostics but this are very difficult to use and IBM specific. You can also buy disk partitioning software such as Ontrack's Disk Manager. The latter is normally supplied with some manufacturer's disks whose capacity is

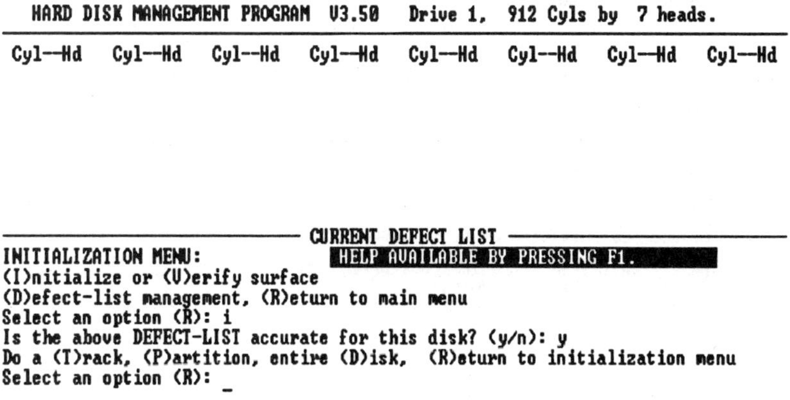

```
HARD DISK MANAGEMENT PROGRAM V3.50   Drive 1,  912 Cyls by  7 heads.

Cyl--Hd    Cyl--Hd    Cyl--Hd    Cyl--Hd    Cyl--Hd    Cyl--Hd    Cyl--Hd    Cyl--Hd




----------------------------- CURRENT DEFECT LIST -----------------------------
INITIALIZATION MENU:          HELP AVAILABLE BY PRESSING F1.
(I)nitialize or (V)erify surface
(D)efect-list management, (R)eturn to main menu
Select an option (R): i
Is the above DEFECT-LIST accurate for this disk? (y/n): y
Do a (T)rack, (P)artition, entire (D)isk,  (R)eturn to initialization menu
Select an option (R): _
```

Figure 10.1
Disk Manager - the low level format menu

greater than 32MBs. You can also now buy Disk Manager directly from Ontrack.

In all cases the low-level formatting program will ask you to supply or at least confirm information about the drive type. You may also have to supply an interleave factor, although DiskManager will test for the best factor, and will prompt you to enter a list of defects. Following this, the low-level format will commence and it will take quite some time - allow over an hour for a reasonably large disk.

After low-level formatting you have to partition and logically format the disk. If you are using Disk Manager then you can perform these operations directly without leaving the program. Otherwise you will need to use FDISK and FORMAT.

Partitioning

Partitioning has to be performed on all types of disk before logical formatting can commence. If you are using ST-506 drives then they have to be low-level formatted first as described earlier.

The MS-DOS command FDISK is the standard way of putting partition information on a hard disk. What it does is to prepare the boot sector of the disk so that the normal FORMAT program can operate correctly. Two types of MS-DOS partitions can exist - the primary and the

```
                    MS-DOS Version 5.00
                   Fixed Disk Setup Program
              (C)Copyright Microsoft Corp. 1983 - 1991

                        FDISK Options

    Current fixed disk drive: 1

    Choose one of the following:

    1. Create DOS partition or Logical DOS Drive
    2. Set active partition
    3. Delete partition or Logical DOS Drive
    4. Display partition information


    Enter choice: [1]



    Press Esc to exit FDISK
```

Figure 10.2
The FDISK dialogue

extended. In MS-DOS version 3.3, the primary partition can be up to 32MB and the extended one as big as you require, up to the limit of space remaining on the disk; but the extended partition must be split up into sections (known as logical DOS volumes) of 32MB or less.

For example, a hard disk of 71MB formatted capacity working with MS-DOS 3.3 might be split up as follows:

Drive C - the primary DOS partition 32MB

Drive D - the first logical drive in the extended partition 32MB

Drive E - the second logical drive in the extended partition 7MB

How exactly you divide up a hard disk is up to you as long as neither the primary partition nor any single logical volume is larger than 32MB.

If you are using MS-DOS 4.0, MS-DOS 5.0 or DR-DOS 5 or 6 then you can forget the limit of 32MB partitions and create a primary DOS partition as big as the full capacity of the drive, if you want to.

To partition the drive you first have to start the machine from a floppy disk containing the operating system. When the A:> prompt appears, type FDISK and you will be guided through a series of questions which will set up the drive for use, prior to the final format. Basically all you really need to know is the type of partition that you want to create and the number of cylinders that you want to allocate to it.

As an alternative to FDISK you can use Disk Manager to establish a partition. However, unless you are trying to do something complicated FDISK is just as easy to use. Notice that partitioning a disk or changing the partition on a disk destroys any data already on the disk.

High-level format

The final stage of hard disk preparation is to use the normal DOS FORMAT command to write the blank file allocation table (FAT) and create the blank directory on the disk, in addition to preparing the sectors for receiving data. If your disk has one partition, the syntax required is as follows:

FORMAT C: /S /V

This will prepare the disk as described above, then transfer the chosen operating system (from a floppy disk) and prompt you for a volume label. It is a good idea to supply a volume label for a hard disk because many formatting programs ask you to supply it as a safeguard against formatting the wrong drive.

If the disk has more than one partition, you will need to repeat the format command for each drive, but without the switch '/S' since you only need to store the operating system in the primary partition.

For example, if the drive has been partitioned into two logical volumes, C and D, then D would be formatted using:

FORMAT D: /V

Once the formatting process has been completed, remove the disk from drive A and try to start the machine from the hard disk. After the system has completed its self test it should start up and display the C:> prompt. Your hard disk is now ready for use.

IDE drives

Although IDE drives do not need low-level formatting they still have to be partitioned and high-level formatted. This is performed in exactly the same way as described for ST-506 disks in an AT machine. However, IDE drives do differ from ST-506 drives in the way that they are set up in the BIOS drive table.

IDE drives usually use more than the standard 17 sectors per track found in ST-506 drives. This can cause a problem if the BIOS drive table doesn't support a user-defined drive type with a variable number of sectors per track. Without this feature it is almost certain that the IDE drive will not be listed in the drive types.

Fortunately, unlike the older ST-506 drives, an IDE drive can emulate (or pretend to be) other drive types. This happens because the drive electronics operate in two modes - Native mode which reflects the real physical configuration of the drive - i.e. number of cylinders, heads and sectors - and Translation mode in which the drive will emulate any traditional 17 sector-based disk geometry as long as the number of heads is less than 17, the number of cylinders is less than 1025 and, most importantly, the resulting total number of sectors **does not exceed** the drive's guaranteed sector count. You can see that the importance of translation mode is that it allows an IDE drive to work in a system that doesn't actually support it in the BIOS drive table as long as it does support a drive of similar capacity.

To install an IDE drive in translation mode you have to discover a drive that is supported in the BIOS table that has almost the same total number of sectors as the IDE drive. This sounds complicated but it is easy to work out:

To find the total number of sectors on any drive simply multiply the number of heads by the number of sectors per track and by the number of cylinders:

Total number of sectors = Heads x Sectors per track x Cylinders

For example, the ST-157A drive in native mode has 560 cylinders, 6 heads and 26 sectors, giving a guaranteed sector count of 6*26*560 or 87360 sectors. You then have to search the drive table for the supported drive that is closest to the IDE drive's capacity without exceeding it. If the BIOS drive table supports a drive with 7 heads, 17 sectors per track and 733 cylinder then this amounts to a total of 87227 sectors. If it also supports a drive with 5 heads, 17 sectors per track and 977 cylinders this gives 83045 sectors in total. In this case, the 733 cylinder translation is nearer but still less than the guaranteed capacity and so it should be used to realise the greatest capacity. With the drive set to emulation mode all you have to do is set the drive type that you have selected in the BIOS setup routine and then re-start the machine. The IDE drive will emulate the type of drive set from then on.

Note that this is an entirely unecessary procedure if the BIOS ROM that you are using supports a user defined drive type with a variable number of sectors per track. In this case simply leave the drive in native mode and set the head, sectors per track and cylinder count to the correct values.

It is important to realise that IDE drives are supplied ready low-level formatted and configured with a 1:1 interleave. You must **not** carry out a low-level format - if you do, the consequences could be serious with older drives. Modern IDE drives will actually ignore any formatting commands that they receive even though they appear to be acting on the instructions.

If you do manage to carry out a low-level format of an IDE drive, it is possible to solve the problem, provided you have access both to the Western Digital AT hard disk formatting program (WDFMT), and the details of the native mode of the drive (this is normally provided as a single sheet document with the drive).

The following tables give details of the Seagate ST-157A drive family native/translation mode geometry:

ST-125A	Translation mode 17 sector/track	Native mode
Read/write heads	4	4
Cylinders	615	404
Sectors/track	17	26
Guaranteed sectors	41280	42016
Capacity (MB)	20.42	20.52

ST-138A	Translation mode 17 sector/track	Native mode
Read/write heads	6	4
Cylinders	615	604
Sectors/track	17	26
Guaranteed sectors	62730	62816
Capacity (MB)	30.63	30.67

ST-157A	Translation mode 17 sector/track	Native mode
Read/write heads	7	4
Cylinders	733	560
Sectors/track	17	26
Guaranteed sectors	87227	87360
Capacity (MB)	40.60	42.66

From these tables you should be able to see that the correct choice of emulation will enable you to format a disk to near maximum capacity. To restore the drive to normal working run the formatting program and enter the required information about the native mode of the drive (cylinders, heads, sectors per track) and the interleave factor (1:1). The drive does not require any Write Precompensation or Reduced Write Current.

Low-level formatting will take place automatically. When this is finished carry out partitioning using FDISK and then do a high- level format in the usual way.

SCSI and ESDI drives

These drive types do not require low-level formatting and, once installed, you merely run FDISK, followed by the standard high-level format, as already described for MFM, RLL and IDE drives. Don't forget to include the '/S' switch in the FORMAT command in order to transfer the operating system - otherwise the computer will not boot up from drive C. If the drive has been partitioned, the partitions will need formatting as well.

Key points

» Before a hard disk drive can be used it has to be partitioned and high-level formatted.

» ST-506 drives also need to be low-level or physically formatted before use.

» In the case of XTs the drive type is set using the controller BIOS or during low-level formatting. In the case of ATs the drive type is part of the BIOS setup.

» If the BIOS drive table doesn't support the drive you are using and there isn't a User-Defined option you either have to use a drive with the same number of heads and fewer cylinders or use a special program to modify the drive table directly.

» A drive has to be partitioned before logical formatting so that the number of cylinders allocated to the operating system is known. By using MS-DOS 4.0 or 5.0, DR-DOS or Disk Manager it is possible to avoid having to have a large number of small partitions. Unless you have a special reason you should aim to use all of the drive as a single partition.

» The final stage in preparing a drive is to logical format it using the command FORMAT C: /S /V. The /S parameter transfers the operating system making the drive capable of starting the machine.

» IDE, ESDI and SCSI drives do not need to be low-level formatted but they still need to be partitioned and logically formatted. (Note: IDE drives can be reduced in capacity and efficiency by low-level formatting.)

» IDE drives support a translation mode which allows them to pretend to be other types of drive which are supported in a BIOS drive table.

Chapter 11
Making it work

Once you have finished assembly there may be problems. Fault finding and preventative maintenance are the twin subjects of this chapter.

If you have just completed putting a machine together or finished an upgrade then you have a serious problem if it doesn't work. Fortunately, the fact that the machine is a modular design allows you to at least track down the problem to the particular module. This is slightly easier in a machine that develops a fault after working reliably for some time because in this case you can reasonably expect the trouble to be a component failure in a single module rather than some incompatibility that may involve one or more parts of the machine. Notice, however, that the same methods that work in finding a problem in a newly constructed or upgraded machine will also work when a machine fails unexpectedly.

Diagnostics

If the machine boots up but behaves in unexpected ways, try to run one of the diagnostic programs. This may give you some clues. The computer will, when first switched on, carry out a series of internal tests to check the functioning of its various components. This is known as POST (Power On Self Test) and the stage which it reaches can be a useful guide to the severity of the problem.

Error codes are almost invariably provided in PC POST operation, both on the screen and as a series of bleeps just in case the screen isn't working. Provided your system has an internal loudspeaker connected, you will hear these as a series of 'beeps' the pattern of which will help you locate the fault. A single short beep means that the machine is functioning correctly and this is what you should hear every time you start your machine. Any other pattern of beeps means that you have a problem:

Beep code	Probable defect
No beep	Power supply or no loudspeaker connected to motherboard
Continuous beep	Power supply
Repeating short beeps	Power supply
1 long, 1 short beep	Motherboard
1 long, 2 short beeps	Video adapter card
1 short beep, poor video quality	Video cable and / or display
1 short beep, system does not boot	Disk drive, cable or adapter

On all IBM machines, the POST also displays the amount of memory being tested, and does not include a test (on ATs) of any extended memory. ROM BIOSs from other manufacturers have other facilities and are able to display the results of tests on other system components; they will also test extended memory. A few have more complex audio signal patterns for the indication of faults and these are detailed in the user handbook which comes with the motherboard.

If an error is found during the POST procedure, a numeric code is written to the screen (if possible). The table which follows gives some fairly standard error codes based on IBM, but these may vary from one manufacturer to another. Check your machine's documentation.

Code	Error Description
01x	Indeterminable problem
02x	Power supply
1xx	Motherboard (system)
2xx	RAM
3xx	Keyboard
4xx	Monochrome display adapter
5xx	CGA
6xx	Floppy drive or adapter
7xx	Maths co-processor
9xx	Parallel printer adapter
10xx	Second parallel printer adapter
11xx	Serial card
12xx	Second serial card
13xx	Games adapter
14xx	Dot matrix printer
17xx	Fixed disk or adapter

This is not a complete listing of all possible error codes but includes most of those you may be confronted when dealing with a typical PC clone which is faulty. The full error codes include extra digits, indicated by 'x' in the examples above. The digit(s) preceding these indicate the part of the PC which is faulty and the 'xx 'digits indicate more precisely what the problem is likely to be.

In a seriously faulty machine, correcting a problem indicated by an error code may apparently give rise to a new and different error code. This is because only one error code is displayed at a time.

Module isolation

The basic principle in finding any fault is to reduce the number of modules fitted to the machine until it starts to work. For example, if you have a completely dead machine in front of you then disconnect the drives and remove all adapter cards except the video. If the machine works in this state start adding cards one by one until the fault occurs. It is even possible for the keyboard to cause a serious fault so it's worth trying the same exercise without it connected - ignore any keyboard errors that might be reported in this state! Always remember to switch the machine off before you plug in or remove any adapter cards.

If you have access to another machine then you can try substituting modules from it into the malfunctioning machine. Indeed if you think that you have isolated the problem down to a particular module you could order a replacement as the final step in testing. In nearly all cases it isn't worth trying to repair a module as replacement is nearly always cheaper. The only exception is the motherboard and even in this case you should consider salvaging the memory and perhaps the processor and co-processor rather than trying to repair it. We seem to be nearing the age of disposable computing.

Some possible faults

» Power supply and power leads.

When you switched on, did you hear the cooling fan in the power supply and did the monitor switch on ? If not, you may have a faulty mains cable (check the fuse) or wall socket. At the very least, you should see an indicator light glowing on the monitor since some power supplies have a low-voltage fan which only works when the power unit is functioning correctly. Are the plugs properly pushed in?

>> Plug trouble?

Are the leads from the keyboard and monitor plugged in properly to the correct places? An apparently dead monitor is usually due to this cause, and will not affect the running of the rest of the machine even though you won't see anything. If the keyboard is switchable between XT and AT, is the switch properly set? Similarly, are any switches on the back of the monitor set correctly (don't worry if you can't find any, some do and some don't have such mode selection switches) - if in doubt, consult the instruction leaflet which came with it.

>> Auto shut down

Did you hear any noises from the disk drives? If not, then the power supply has probably shut down - if a fault develops on the motherboard or adapter cards, this automatically triggers a shut-down to avoid further damage. Disconnect the power supply and see if the fan starts to run when it isn't connected to the motherboard. Some power supplies don't work unless something is connected to them so you might have to connect a floppy to do do this test.

>> Video card configuration

If the power supply is running, the power light is on but you still don't see anything on the monitor or you see something at first but it then vanishes then suspect a video card configuration problem. Check that the motherboard has been set up to work with the correct adapter. Check that the monitor and adapter are configured and are compatible. Make sure that the video card is the only one in the system!

» Adapter card configuration

If the system works most of the time but crashes when you try to use the facilities of a particular adapter card then suspect a configuration error. If they need it adapter cards have to be allocated an area of memory that no other card is using, an interrupt number of their own and a DMA channel of their own. Allocating the same resources to more than one card results in a clash that will make the system unreliable if it works at all! See Chapter 9 for information on configuration.

» Memory faults

Memory faults usually allow the machine to start up as far as the POST which then reports a memory error. If this happens carefully check the memory chips or modules. Are they all correctly inserted, the right way round and with all the pins in their respective sockets? One memory chip with a pin which has bent under as it was inserted can cause the problem. You will need to check very carefully and if you find one, **very carefully** lever the offending unit out with a small flat-bladed screwdriver, straighten the pin carefully with fine-nosed pliers and replace it. This job is a little easier if you have a proper chip insertor or extractor, but the above technique works quite well if you have a steady hand.

Erratic behaviour can be due to chips that are too slow or are working to close to their limits. In this situation a system may work well for a short period after being switched on and then report a parity error and crash. To eliminate the fault replace the chips with ones with a faster speed.

If there really is a faulty chip or module then the best way to locate it is by moving components around. A memory testing program will located the address of the chip or module that is causing the problem but locating this on the motherboard can be very difficult. It is often easier to note the address where the error has occurred and then swap pairs of chips or modules to see which swap makes the address change. This narrows the fault down to a pair of devices, then to find out which of the two is actually the problem swap each in turn with another device. This should pin the fault down to a single chip. If you are using memory in the form of chips then it is worth ordering one more chip than you need to use in a substitution test for faulty chips.

» Co-processor errors

Co-processor errors always nearly always show up as POST error codes but occasionally a co-processor can be so faulty that it stops the entire system. Simply remove the co-processor to check that it isn't the cause of any major problems. Do this with great care - they are quite fragile and expensive!

» Non-responding disk drives

Check the power leads and data/control cables to the drives. The power connectors can only fit one way. The data and control cables should be fitted so that the coloured stripe side goes to pin 1 on both drive and controller card. Did you check that all drives were correctly set - floppies as second drives, hard disk as the first hard drive? If the activity light on a floppy disk remains on permanently, you probably have the data/control cable connected the wrong way round. Correct as necessary and switch on again.

» Incorrect indicator lights

This isn't serious and unlikely to cause any problems with using the machine. Check the way in which indicator lights and switches (turbo, reset etc.) are fixed. The indicator lights will only function if plugged in the right way round, and this is done by trial and error! You can't damage them by putting them on the wrong way round.

Creeping chips

Chips which are mounted in sockets occasionally suffer from the creeping chip problem. The chip appears to become loose in its mounting and may even become so loose as to fall out if the system is moved. Even if it doesn't do this, you will find that the system may be unreliable as a result of poor contacts.

The reason for chip creep is that the inside of a PC becomes warm when it is in operation and thermal expansion takes place. The system cools down when switched off and the thermal cycling which results will ease the majority of socketed chips over a period of several months use.

The cure is simple, but don't attempt it unless the motherboard is firmly supported underneath. Most PC boards are held in place by plastic and metal stand-offs and the best way of dealing with this is to take the board out and place it on a firm bench. Press each socketed chip gently but firmly back into its socket. You will hear a slight scrunch as you do this. If you carry out the operation without supporting the board in some way, you run the risk of bowing or cracking the motherboard since the force required to re-seat some larger chips is quite large, particularly with maths co-processors or the system processor chip. Some of the larger chips are made from a ceramic material which can snap if not treated correctly - with these gentle pressure at each end, applied alternately, is the best method.

Checking the power supply

If you have access to a multimeter then it is worth checking the power supply to make sure that its output voltages are correct. Take out **all** adapter cards and the keyboard lead, disconnect the power plugs from the motherboard and disk drives. Attach the multimeter's common (black) lead to either of the inner two sockets on the 5.25" drive power connector, and the red lead to either of the outer sockets. This will enable you to check at least part of the power supply, provided the meter is switched to a suitable DC voltage range. The yellow wire to the plug carries +12 volts and the red wire, +5 volts; these voltages can vary from 11.4 to 12.6 in the case of the 12 volt supply and from 4.75 to 5.25 for the 5 volt.

Reconnect the power and switch on. Check the voltages on the 5 and 12 volt lines. If they are within the ranges quoted, the power supply is working. Switch off then reconnect the power plugs in the correct order to the motherboard. Switch on again. Some power supplies will not work unless something is plugged into them to act as a load. If your power supply appears to be dead, try plugging in one of the disk drives, or the hard disk, then measuring the voltages.

If the voltage on the disk drive connector is zero, and the test probes haven't fallen out, your memory or motherboard is at fault. An incorrectly inserted chip may be the cause, or there may be a bent-legged chip lurking in the system. Switch off and check again. If a memory or co-processor chip had been put in the wrong way, it may have been permanently damaged. Remove it and, in the case of a memory chip, get hold of another of the same type and speed, and insert it. Switch on again and check the voltages - if they are correct, then your motherboard and memory are probably OK. If not, then you have a faulty motherboard and should contact your supplier.

How to treat a PC

Keeping a PC system in working order is not a particularly difficult job, if you treat it with care and a certain amount of respect. There are a few basic rules by which every PC owner should follow - most of which are common sense but it's surprising how many PC users don't abide by them.

» Make sure that the system is not knocked or bumped by every passing member of the family or office. If you must use a printer on the same table, bear in mind that daisywheel and some dot matrix printers cause a lot of vibration, so get a sheet of foam and hardboard cut to the right size and stand the printer on them to minimise the vibration. The ideal solution is to site the printer on another table. Keep printer cables as short as possible and make sure that trailing wires are kept out of the way. A machine that is regularly pulled off a table by a trailing cable isn't likely to have a long life!

» As far as possible, keep the PC away from radiators, dusty places and people who smoke. Don't drink your tea or coffee while using it - keyboards don't mix with liquids, hot or cold! Use plastic covers for the monitor, system unit and keyboard if dust is a problem, but don't forget to take them off when you're using the PC. Avoid restricting the air intakes or outlets, particularly near the fan since high internal temperatures may result and your system will either shut down or fail through heat stress. Tobacco ash can have disastrous effects on disks and disk drives and it may cause damage to keyboards as well.

» If you are moving the PC, always park the hard disk heads and insert head protection cards into the 5.25" drive(s). If you haven't got them, then use an old floppy disk to avoid damage to the read/write heads; the same advice applies to 3.5" drives. You should take cardboard inserts out of the disk drives before switching on since the POST (Power On Self Test) routines move the heads around and they can be damaged.

» If you are carrying out any work on your machine, always switch it off, and always add or remove cables or cards when it is switched off. It's also sensible to avoid changing plugs too often. If you have a serial mouse and a modem, it's wise to install a second serial port, rather than swap the modem and Mouse plugs when you wish to use one or the other.

» Keep a supply of fuses of the correct types - 3 or 5 amp (never 13 amp) for the computer and printer, and the correct type and capacities for other parts of your system. Temporary expedients like fuse wire or aluminium foil are dangerous and allow a potentially serious fault to persist until something more drastic happens. The purpose of a fuse is to protect the system and if it keeps on failing, then the problem should be investigated. The importance of ensuring that the system is operated with a good electrical earth is also sometimes forgotten. A bad earth connection can cause problems with data processing and may even damage the circuit boards through the build-up of static electricity. Make sure that a 3 pin plug is fitted and correctly wired.

» Use good quality supplies (floppy disks, paper, ribbons etc.) since this will reduce the chances of floppy disk faults or paper jams in the printer. Cheap, old or well-used disks are frequently subject to 'flakiness' in which some of the magnetic oxide becomes detached and may clog up the floppy drive heads or mechanism. Floppy drive cleaners should be used occasionally, rather than regularly, since even the least abrasive may eventually cause damage to the heads if used as frequently as the manufacturers tell you.

» If you have high capacity disk drives, use the correct type of disk. Formatting a standard 360KB floppy disk to 1.2MB may work but you will have lots of bad sectors and data retention will be unreliable. Similarly, you may, after punching another hole in a 3.5" 720KB disk, be able to format it to 1.44MB but data retention is just as unreliable. The disk may be satisfactory for a matter of a few months but eventually, you will get data errors or the dreaded 'General Failure' error message.

» Avoid the tendency to switch the system on and off too many times a day. Most systems fail when they are first switched on, and the same is true for hard disks. A surge-protection plug is a relatively cheap safeguard against mains supply spikes which can cause your system to crash or behave unpredictably. These 'spikes' are usually caused by domestic or similar equipment which cause heavy current surges when operated. Operating a machine on the same power supply as an electric motor, for example, isn't a good idea unless a surge-protection plug is fitted.

A clean machine

There is no doubt that it is worth cleaning your machine every now and again but like all good things - not too often. If the exterior of the machine becomes dirty very quickly then this is a bad sign for the quality of the air in its environment. Implement a 'No Smoking' policy near the machine and fit an ioniser in the same room but well away from the machine.

When you clean your system and monitor cases, bear in mind that not all cleaners are suitable. Some will dissolve plastic parts or at least render them sticky, so check on a part which is not normally visible. Use as little as possible of the cleaner on a dry, soft cloth and pay particular attention to monitor screen and keyboard tops. Do not use abrasives, kitchen cleaners or fluids intended for grease removal on fabrics. A monitor screen cleaned with an abrasive cleaner looks nasty and may well be badly scratched. If you wanted a non- reflective screen, there are less brutal ways of doing it!

Don't forget the tendency of keyboards and mice to accumulate dust and dirt. You'd be surprised what drops out if you turn a well-used keyboard upside down and tap or shake it gently. Unless you do this regularly, keys may have a tendency to stick or to fail to operate, since their action may be impeded by dust, cigarette ash, biscuit crumbs or dandruff! If vacuuming the keyboard doesn't solve the problem of sticky keys then you might have to take it to pieces - see *Cleaning a keyboard* later in this chapter. Remove and clean the rubber-coated ball in your mouse for the same reason.

Around once a year it may be worth cleaning the inside of the machine - particularly the contacts of the adapter boards. This involves a certain amount of dismantling of the system, but if carried out in a logical sequence the re-assembly shouldn't cause problems.

You will need a bottle of iso-propyl alcohol (sometimes known as iso-propanol) and some pieces of foam to act as cleaning swabs - these will not leave behind fibres which are not only messy but can become conductive as they accumulate dirt. Iso-propyl alcohol can be obtained through most chemists but will usually need to be specially ordered. A litre is more than enough and it is also worth knowing that it can be used to clean video and audio tape heads. It is not drinkable!

A vacuum cleaner is very useful for disposing of the dust which can accumulate in a system, particularly if it can be teased out of the more obscure corners with a small paint brush. You can also use canned air - but this is expensive. A small aerosol of Electrolube contact cleaner is invaluable and a few simple tools - cross point screw drivers, tweezers and fine point pliers would be handy.

Open up the case and, after noting where the cables and cards fit, disconnect cables from adapter cards, then remove the cards. Make sure that the environment is airy and that there are no naked flames nearby since the alcohol is inflammable. This also means that you shouldn't smoke!

Use the vacuum and brush to get rid of the major dust and debris on the motherboard and cards, not forgetting the fan aperture on the power supply.

Clean the connectors and slots with a swab soaked in the alcohol, then carefully clean the edge connectors on the adapters - never use a rubber for this since it will remove part of the gold plating and may also generate a static charge. These connectors sometimes get contaminated with greasy or sweaty fingers, as do the connectors of the floppy and hard drives. Use plenty of alcohol for this since it cannot harm the system in any way.

Cleaning a keyboard

Inevitably, the most abused part of any computer system is the keyboard. Cleaning the gunge off the key tops is straightforward if you use iso-propanol, but to cure the other problems requires the keyboard to be dismantled - not a difficult job if you're patient. However, it is possible to damage a keyboard or just not manage to put it back together after the cleaning process so it's best to regard this procedure as a last resort before buying a new one.

Most PC keyboards use either contact switches, which make an electrical contact when pressed, or what are referred to as capacitative switches where the depression of a key alters the electrical state of a circuit without any electrical contact being made.

The dismantling of a keyboard is fairly straightforward - make sure that it is unplugged and lies upside down on a clean sheet of newspaper. Look around for a series of small screws on the base plate and undo these carefully, noting where each screw goes - this is important if the screws are of varying lengths and sizes. If there are no screws, the two halves of the keyboard are usually held together with clips which can usually be loosened with careful use of a screwdriver. Once the screws or clips are removed, the keyboard electronics and keys can be carefully removed on their frame. Be very careful and note exactly how the frame fits when you come to re-assemble it.

Blow away the dust from the keyboard and keys and make sure that any loose grit is removed completely. Check that all keys work properly and if not, loosen them by lubricating with a couple of drops of iso-propanol on the key shaft. Temporarily re-assemble the keyboard and check its operation with the computer. If problems such as stuck or non-active keys persist, then more fundamental cleaning is indicated.

If the keyboard problem involves isolated keys which refuse to work, there are two courses of action which will depend upon the type of keyboard switch.

The conventional switch has a pair of contacts which are soldered in lines on the under-side of the keyboard; in this case, try squirting a very little Electrolube contact cleaner down the key stem into the key switch and pressing the key very vigorously lots of times - this usually works.

Capacitative switches do not have soldered connections, so the easiest way is to dismantle the backplate by taking out all the tiny screws and then to wipe clean the inner surface and all the key 'contacts' with iso-propanol. This is tedious but it does work, and may well save you the cost of a new keyboard.

Carefully re-assemble the unit, taking care not to get your fingerprints all over the board.

Other keyboard problems are more difficult to sort out since they usually involve the integrated circuit which controls the keyboard's activities. If your problem isn't sorted out by cleaning up, you will probably need to buy a new keyboard.

Repairing floppy drives

In addition to the use of a head cleaning disk, which most machines need on an occasional basis, the need may arise for more fundamental attention if the computer is being operated in a dusty environment. Luckily, 3.5" drives rarely need attention but, because of their open construction, 5.25" drives are quite prone to dust problems which may cause mis-alignment of the heads. The cure is simple and involves removing the drive from its mounting and, after blowing off any loose dust, gently swabbing the rails along which the read/write heads move with a sponge dampened with iso-propanol. Gently move the heads along the track and clean the tracks thoroughly. Allow to dry and then apply to each rail the merest trace of very thin (watchmaker's) oil or Electrolube.

Floppy drives can go out of alignment due to being dropped or just because of old age. It is possible to realign them and there is even software that will help you do it but it is a slow and difficult job that takes patience and some skill. In nearly all cases it is cheaper to buy a new drive.

Be prepared

There are a number of things that you can do to prepare for the day that your machine fails.

» Keep a log book for your computer. For example, a ring binder in which keep all the relevant user manuals and guides, together with notes on the settings of switches and links on the motherboard and adapter cards. Include information of the hard disk - make, type, serial number and the numbers of cylinders and heads, together with details of special plugs, leads and adapters.

» If you have access to them, do run diagnostic checks from time to time, and check as much as possible of your system by these means. One of the best is CHECK-IT fromTouchstone Software. The cost (about £100) is well worth it for the facilities it offers; it's infinitely better and more user-friendly than the IBM Advanced Diagnostics. If you have a good diagnostic program it could well pay for itself in time and trouble saved. For example, a diagnostics program reported an increasing number of bad sectors on a hard disk of mine. Prompt action enabled me to back-up the data and send the disk back for replacement under guarantee.

» Keep a couple of copies of a 'boot' disk of a size that will fit your computer's A: drive. For a 5.25" drive, use a 360KB disk and, apart from the DOS system, include any device drivers your system may need. The 3.5" disk should be a 720KB type with the same contents. The reason for this is that, particularly with AT machines, the battery-backed CMOS RAM may very occasionally become corrupted, or the battery voltage may not be sufficient to retain configuration data in the RAM. AT machines will normally boot off a 360KB disk (or a 720KB) even if they cannot boot from the hard disk. The configuration information can then be re-entered via the Setup program and with luck, you should be back in business. Don't forget to make a note on the disk label of the configuration of your system including the system's type number corresponding to your hard disk. Including details of the make and model number and the number of cylinders and heads is a wise precaution. Write-protect these disks and put one away safely.

» Carry out regular backups of your hard disk, just in case it develops a fault and you cannot retrieve your programs and data. Backups can be done on tape system (which is usually fast) or disk - for the latter, you can use the BACKUP facility on the DOS disk but there are many backup utilities that do the job better and faster. Make sure that your chosen program allows you to do partial backups and restores, and, if possible, incremental backups where only files modified since a particular date are selected and backed up. For really important material, carry out regular backups at least once a day and make sure the backup disks are properly labelled and dated. Keep them separate from other disks. Backup disks or tapes can be recycled, and you need at least three sets, labelled so that they can be updated in rotation. The details of how to manage a backup procedure are usually described in the software manuals.

Key points

» You can use your knowledge of the modular structure of the PC to isolate faults.

» In most cases it is cheaper to buy a replacement module than have it repaired.

» A PC has a long life it you treat it correctly.

» Make sure that you prepare for the day that things go wrong. Keep your system documented and back up the hard disk often.

Chapter 12
Upgrading and optimising

Although upgrading a machine has been a recurring topic in earlier chapters, the economics and choices involved in upgrading are discussed in detail in this chapter.

Within a few months of buying or building a machine the moment arrives when it doesn't quite satisfy its user in all respects. One of the advantages of putting a machine together yourself from modules that you have selected is that you have the knowledge, the skill and the confidence to perform an upgrade. You should be able to understand the effect each module has on the machine's performance and how best to go about changing it. Even if you haven't actually put the machine together yourself then reading the earlier chapters should give you the knowledge and confidence to approach the upgrade problem.

What is less easy is to work out is when an upgrade is economically viable. There is a common tendency to treat upgrading as the only path because replacing the machine would be far too expensive. This results in machines that are upgraded far beyond their natural life span at a huge cost spread over a number of years. The problem is that there is an upgrade ladder. Each step up the ladder seems a reasonable cost, perhaps even negligible compared to the purchase price of the machine, and yet each step up the ladder takes you to a higher total cost and a less and less attractive machine. To avoid this trap it is very important to be able to evaluate the upgrade options logically and without too much sentimental attachment to your existing investment! It is also worth remembering that it is nearly always better to put off an upgrade or replacement of a machine until later. The reason is that in the computer industry prices are always falling and performance is always improving. Next month's machine or upgrade is usually cheaper or better and sometimes both! Of course this doesn't mean that you should never buy an upgrade or a new computer - only that you should be sure that you would benefit from it now.

The logical upgrade

If you feel that a machine isn't powerful enough or is failing in some way then you should try to answer the following questions:

» Exactly what has made the machine unsuitable in its current role?

It could be that you want to install Windows or other new software. Or perhaps existing applications are becoming more demanding - for example a database has increased in size of to a critical point.

Knowing why a machine is unsuitable in terms of exactly what is causing the problem can help you to work out the likely impact of performing the upgrade. For example, if your general dissatisfaction with a machine only really stems from its poor performance with a particular program then how much you use this program puts the upgrade question into perspective. To make it even more clear you should make a list of all of the programs that the machine uses and give each a rating from 1 to 10 on their usability. If you discover that there are only isolated trouble spots then this might suggest to you a different way of living with the problem until the day that you decide to change the whole machine for a better one.

» Have you made all of the changes to the software and hardware that you already own to ensure that you are getting the best possible performance?

Before you proceed, check software and hardware manuals for sections called 'performance', 'optimisation' etc.. Many an upgrade is performed simply because no one bothered to read the manual to find out what makes a program go faster. It is always worth exploring optimisation if only to gain an idea of what sort of upgrades would make a difference!

» What aspect of the machine needs to be improved - speed, storage capacity, display resolution etc..?

If you have a simple upgrade requirement such as a high resolution video display or more disk storage then it is very easy to know which module needs upgrading. If you have a vague problem such as lack of speed then actually pinning down what needs to be done is more difficult. A program can run slow because the processor is slow, because it lacks memory, or because the disk drive with which it is being used is too slow. Changing to a faster processor must increase the speed of every program but not necessarily by the theoretical amount. The reason for this could be that the program needs to access memory which is not available, and therefore resorts to writing to the hard disk instead. The clue to this is the constant accessing of the hard disk, as indicated by the hard disk activity light. In this case installing more RAM, if possible, and leaving the processor alone may be the cheapest and most effective option. Of course you then have the problem of which type of RAM - extended or expanded?

» Which possible upgrade path will make the improvement that you deem necessary

For example, if you decide that a processor upgrade is called for then consider an upgrade co-processor card or replacing the motherboard. If a memory upgrade is called for then consider adding memory to the motherboard first, next consider a memory expansion card or replacing the motherboard. It is only by considering each option can you possibly arrive at a sensible decision.

Costing

Having established the areas of your machine which would benefit from upgrading, the next step is to cost the exercise.

You should first work out the cost of each module in your current machine at today's prices - i.e. a replacement rather than its second-hand value. It helps to draw up a table something like the following:

Module	Price
Motherboard with 0KB fitted	£
RAM	£
Floppy disks	£
Floppy disk controller (if separate)	£
Hard disks (minus controller)	£
Hard disk controller	£
Case and power supply	£
Keyboard	£
Serial card	£
Printer card	£
Video card	£
Monitor	£

Of course life is never that simple and it is quite possible that you will be using a multifunction card that has a serial, printer and games port all rolled into one! In this case simply make an entry for 'interfaces'. When you add up the cost of all of the modules you have an estimate of the replacement cost of your machine as it is now. You should also look up the cost of a completely built machine with as near the same specification as you can find. This gives you a second estimate of the replacement cost of your machine.

One way of evaluating the upgrade is to think of your machine as not as a finished working machine but as a box of parts to which you can add to make a finished machine. For example, if you were going to upgrade to a 486 by replacing the motherboard work out how may of the modules that you already have, case, video card etc. will be usable in the 'new' machine. The value of these parts is exactly the value of the old machine that you are carrying over into the new. If this is low then you might as well replace the whole machine either by buying a ready built unit or by buying new modules and building your own. After all, following this course gives you two working machines. The less powerful one can be pensioned off into a less demanding job or sold as second-hand. Notice that a complete machine has a higher second-hand value than a collection of parts.

To summarise:

» Always think in terms of your machine's replacement value rather than how much it actually cost you. When it comes to upgrading it is current value that matters, not historical value.

» Consider your existing machine as a source of parts to build a new machine. If the value of the existing parts that you can actually use is low then an upgrade probably isn't a good idea.

Upgrade dos and don'ts

Although cost is an important consideration, there are a number of situations in which upgrading should be avoided no matter what the cost. Although some of these points have been made in the relevant chapters it is worth gathering them together.

» Any machine that has a plastic or otherwise non-standard case isn't suitable for motherboard upgrades. For example, the Amstrad 1512, 1640 and the 2000 series are unsuitable.

» Integrated motherboards, that is types that have the video or disk controller built in, generally make most upgrades uneconomical because the built-in facilities cannot be re-used in any way.

» Specialised designs, such as games-oriented PCs that do not use a standard motherboard with built-in expansion slots, are also best not upgraded. It is usually cheaper to start again.

» Don't try to upgrade a machine with a 150W power supply to include too many hard disks and adapter cards - change the case and power supply first.

» Adding a hard disk to any machine is a good idea but don't overload a low powered machine, such as an XT, with a high capacity disk drive unless it is part of a longer term upgrade plan. Typical XT hard disk sizes are 20 to 40MB. For 386 and 486 machines 100MB and more is reasonable.

There are also some upgrades that are so obviously valuable that they are almost always worth carrying out.

» It is nearly always worth upgrading conventional memory to 640KB. The only exception is where the motherboard can be replaced for less cost.

» It is always worth upgrading machines with empty chip sockets, for example adding memory to an Amstrad PC1512 to give it a full 640KB. The job is easy but notice that in the case of this machine there are two variations of the model (which are not distinguished in any external way) that need slightly different sets of chips. Inspect the empty sockets before ordering the extra chips.

There are also some general conclusions that can be drawn from costing standard upgrades. Although these are true at the time of writing it would be worth checking them for yourself. They can also be invalidated by the availability of a one-off special offer!

>> A motherboard upgrade is usually cheaper than adding a 386SX accelerator card. It is also produces a faster machine.

>> A motherboard upgrade is often comparable in price to the cost of a memory expansion card and usually preferable in performance terms.

>> It is usually cheaper to fit a second hard disk than to remove the existing drive and replace it by one of a larger capacity.

>> The memory and the hard disk generally represent the most valuable part of any system even though it is the motherboard and box which are thought of as the major part of the machine.

Accelerator cards

Accelerator or co-processor cards (not to be confused with a numeric co-processor) have already been mentioned but without any discussion. These usually consist of a 286 or 386 processor, some fast (cache) memory and a few other chips. The idea is to fit the accelerator card to your existing motherboard where it replaces the existing processor. In theory (and usually in practice), the upgrade will enable the machine to run rather faster than previously and, in the case of 386 accelerators, to run some of the more sophisticated programs that make use of the special attributes of this chip (either the full DX or restricted SX versions).

The advantage of such an upgrade is that existing memory can be retained, but the cost of these cards is quite high for what they do and you would be better advised to think of getting a 386SX board and building a more powerful and versatile machine.

Maths co-processors

Maths co-processors are specialised chips that can be fitted to most motherboards next to the main processor to speed up arithmetic. There is a numeric co-processor for every type of processor except the 486DX which has one built in. Your need for one of these devices will depend upon the type of work your computer does. In general terms, word processing will not be affected by the presence of a co-processor, while programs that involve a lot of mathematics will. Even with applications that do involve a lot of arithmetic, the increase in speed will depend upon how the arithmetic can be dealt with by the numeric co-processor. In most cases, the likely increase in speed of execution will be less than you might at first expect since co-processors do not speed up integer arithmetic. It is important to realise that simply fitting a co-processor will not improve your system's performance unless the software that you are running makes use of it.

The following table may possibly help you to decide if it is worth fitting a numeric co-processor

Application	Need for co-processor
Word processing	none
Database	none
Hypertext	none
Spreadsheet	only when worksheets have lots of formulae
Graphics	few graphics packages make use of one
DTP	only if using a PostScript interpreter
CAD/CAM	often essential
Statistics/Engineering	highly desirable

In most cases, if a co-processor is not fitted, the application will run, but much more slowly. But there are applications, such as AutoCAD that will not run without a co-processor. Most co-processors, with the exception of the Weitek range, are software compatible with the Intel equivalents and thus will recognise 80x87 calls in programs.

Each processor has its corresponding co-processor designated by the same type number but ending in 7. For example, the co-processor for the 386DX is the 387DX. Although some AT 386s can use the 80287, the extra money spent on an 80387 will be worthwhile, since if you opt for the cheaper 80287 you will be slowing the processor by using 16, rather than 32 data bits and you will not have the additional facilities that are only found in the 80387, such as a full range of mathematical functions.

The original manufacturer of co-processors is Intel, who also make the standard microprocessors (the 8088 and 80x86 series). Recently, a number of other firms have devised their own co-processors that give an equivalent or possibly better performance than the Intel versions, often at a lower price. Cyrix's FasMath 83D87 is claimed to be 10 times faster than the Intel 80387 and IIT's IIT-3C87 is advertised as being twice as fast. Among the 80287 look-likes, Advanced Micro Devices' AMD80287 is considerably cheaper than the Intel 80287 and delivers a similar performance.

The exception to all this compatibility is Weitek's Abacus co-processors (3167 and 4167) are not usually compatible with a 386 machine and are best used with a 486 machine. The 3167 may, in some cases be used in a machine that already has an 80387 installed, but in order for it to be of any help, the software would need to be re-written since the majority of languages with co-processor support use only Intel-type instructions. The Abacus chips are still very expensive when compared to the standard x87 co-processors.

Before you buy a co-processor, you should find out the system clock speed of your machine. Co-processors work satisfactorily at (or below) their stated system clock frequencies and if they are used at higher speeds, overheating will occur that may shorten the life of this expensive component. Faster chips are more expensive than slower versions and you may get away with running a co-processor a little above its rated speed since they do have a margin of tolerance, but if you have a premature failure, then it is unlikely that it would be replaced under guarantee.

The 8087 co-processor runs at the same speed as the system, thus for a 10 MHz XT system you will need an 8087-1. If in doubt, ask the supplier what speed of device is recommended. The 80287 is different. It normally runs at two-thirds the system clock frequency and this means that an 80287-2, rated at 8 MHz, will run satisfactorily at 12 MHz if this frequency can be supplied direct to the co-processor. The 80387SX co-processor has to be rated at the same speed as the 80386SX, but many 80386DX boards have an option to allow a co-processor to run at a lower speed than the system clock. This is worth investigating if you wish to economise.

Although co-processors tend to be associated in the buyers mind with Intel, the three other manufacturers - Cyrix, Advanced Micro Devices (AMD) and IIT are worth remembering. It is sensible to check prices, since these alternative sources offer compatibility with the Intel products, but at considerably lower prices.

Motherboard optimisation

An alternative to upgrading is optimisation or modification of the existing hardware.

The speed of the motherboard is governed by the type of processor and the speed of the system clock. A much publicised modification that was very popular was to change the crystal that set the clock rate. For example, a standard XT has a clock speed of 4.77MHz but most will run at twice this speed. Changing the crystal is a very cheap option but full of potential problems. For example, the increased speed will need faster memory chips and if you don't change them then you are bound to see parity errors as the machine warms up. If you do change them then you might as well do the job properly and fit a new motherboard. In short, crystal replacement is fiddly and risky and rarely worth the effort.

You can also upgrade an XT by fitting a replacement processor from the NEC V series - there is one for the 8088 (V20) and one for the 8086 (V30). This is a simple upgrade - remove the old processor and fit the new - but it only produces a 20% or so speed increase at best. Given the current cost and the simple fact that 20% is a small speed increase on a very slow machine such upgrades are only worth it on machines that are difficult to upgrade in any other way, such as the Amstrad PC1512 and 1640.

Another speed improving modification that applies to ATs is to reduce the number of wait states in the hope that the memory devices really can work that much faster than their stated speed. For example, if you have a 12 MHz AT, with memory chips rated at 100ns or better, altering the wait state from 1 to a lower value (usually 0) will improve the overall performance quite significantly. Of course, if the chips cannot work that fast then you will start to see parity errors. The solution in this situation is to set the wait states back to their original values.

If memory interleaving is used on the motherboard then obviously adding memory to make the number of banks in use even will result in a speed increase because of the reduction in wait states.

While on the subject of wait states and memory timing, it is worth mentioning that the BIOS of many ATs allow you to alter many details of memory timing and access. These settings are best left well alone unless you know a great deal about the design of the machine. Altering them can make the motherboard fail to work or to become unpredictable in its behaviour.

Most AT motherboards will allow the use of a 'Shadow RAM' feature if more than 1MB of memory is installed. This allows the ROM BIOS to be moved to a location in the computer memory above the 640KB DOS limit where it can be accessed more rapidly than would otherwise be the case. Video RAM can also be shadowed in this way, with a corresponding speed increase, and your motherboard manual will let you know if this facility is available. If you have only 1MB of RAM then using the extra as shadow RAM is very definitely worth it.

Disk optimisation

There's not a lot you can or need to do about the operational speed of
floppy disks but the performance of hard disks can be improved if you
install disk caching software. This improves performance by taking
over a part of the memory of the computer and storing programs and
data as they are accessed on the disk. When the same material is
required, the information is in memory and is available much more
quickly than via a conventional disk read. Disk caching is particularly
useful for older, slower hard disks, but because it requires some of the
computer's memory, it's not without penalties. Newer drives don't
really need it if their access times are less than 30 ms.

If the interleave factor is not already at the optimum value for the
combination of drive and controller, the performance of the hard disk
will be poor. It can be improved by determining the correct interleave
factor and re-formatting but this can be a long and tedious job and
should not be necessary if you have correctly carried out the initial
formatting procedure.

As a rule of thumb for an AT system, a new hard disk with an access
time of about 25 - 30 ms will, when used with a modern hard disk
controller, work best with an interleave of 1:1, or at worst, 2:1. A typical
XT hard disk controller needs a slightly greater interleave, usually about
3:1 or possibly 4:1. If you suspect that a disk has the wrong interleave
then the easiest solution is to buy a copy of SpinRite which will alter
the interleave without having to reformat the disk. The public domain
program Bracking's HDTEST will do the same but may not work with
all hard disk types.

Another common performance problem is disk fragmentation which
occurs as the disk fills up. Files are stored and then deleted and slowly
but surely the free space on the disk becomes split up. This makes is
necessary to store files physically split or fragmented across the surface
of the disk. Fragmentation slows disk operations because the head has
to move excessively to read each fragment. A de-fragmenter, such as
found in Mace or Norton Utilities, will soon solve the problem by

moving files around so that they are stored in one location in one piece. This can speed up disk operations a great deal.

If you have a disk drive that suddenly becomes slow then fragmentation might be the cause but it could equally well be the first sign that the disk is about to fail. When a disk error has occurred the drive attempts to re-read the data 10 or more times. If it still cannot read the data then an error correction procedure starts which will reconstruct the data unless the fault is very serious. As long as the error correction is successful MS-DOS doesn't bother to tell you that there has been a near error. The only outward sign is that the disk read took longer than usual. You might also hear the disk making a slightly different noise as the head is moved back to track zero before trying to read the data again. If this is repeated on every sector of a large file then the time to load can go from a few seconds to minutes. If this happens it is vital that you back up the data as soon as possible and reformat the drive. Alternatively, SpinRite (and programs supplied in the 386/486 AMI BIOS) will carry out an analysis of the hard disk which may enable you to isolate faulty sectors and mark them as 'bad'.

Key points

» When evaluating an upgrade you should always think in terms of your machine's replacement value rather than how much it actually cost you. When it comes to upgrading it is current value that matters not historical value.

» The best way to think of your existing machine is to consider it as a source of parts to build a new machine. If the value of the existing parts that you can actually use is low then an upgrade probably isn't a good idea

» It is important to evaluate all of the upgrade options - even if they seem to involve replacing more of the machine than you might think reasonable.

» Optimising your existing machine is, in some situations, an alternative to upgrading.

Glossary

Access time The time taken for information to be called for and received. Usually relates to memory chips where the time is measured in nanoseconds or to hard disks where the time is measured in milliseconds.

Adapter A circuit board plus components which acts as an interface between the motherboard and devices (such as monitors or disk drives) attached to it.

Arithmetic co-processor See Numeric co-processor

AT (Advanced Technology) Machines in this class use 16- or 32-bit processors, such as the 286, 386 or 486.

AT host adapter An adapter or system-supplied interface, which provides a 40-pin connector, normally used with IDE hard disks.

AT interface drive (or IDE drive) A type of hard disk which uses the IBM AT interface (40 pin) and 8- or 16-bit data transfer. Up to two drives may be daisy-chained (connected together) on the same host computer bus. See also Translation mode.

Backup The process by which data in the form of files is copied onto another disk or tape.

Bad sector A floppy or hard disk sector which cannot hold data reliably because of damage or a manufacturing defect.

Bad track table A list of cylinder and head numbers attached to a hard disk which indicates which tracks are flawed and cannot be used reliably. Always entered during the low-level format.

Bank A group of memory chips which make up one of the memory blocks in the computer which can be read by the processor in a single bus cycle. It may contain 8, 16 or 32 bits, and a parity bit for each 8 data bits. Blocks may therefore contain 9, 18 or 36 bits for each bank.

Baud rate This is an indication of the rate of data transmission and is roughly equivalent to the number of bits per second.

BIOS (Basic Input/Output System) This is found in one or two EPROMs on the motherboard of the computer, and controls the essential routines for testing the system when it is first switched on and also any other activities which involve the input or output of data, such as disk drive activities, keyboard input or video output. Different BIOS types may be found on some of the adapter cards.

Bit A binary digit which takes a value of 0 or 1.

Boot A start-up sequence which loads the operating system, usually from the bootstrap, or boot sector, of a system disk. The bootstrap is a simple program in one sector of the disk, which reads in the rest of the operating system which is on the system disk.

Buffer A memory segment where data can be stored temporarily while it is being transferred from one device to another. For example, a keyboard buffer stores keystrokes and releases them as required by the system.

Bug A defect or error in a program or operating system.

Bus A pathway over which power, data or other types of electrical signal travel.

Byte A group of 8 bits, enough storage to represent a character.

Cache A portion of the computer's memory which is reserved for special tasks such as holding information on disk accesses so that more commonly used files can be rapidly located. Some 386 and 486 CPUs have between 8 and 256KB of very fast cache memory built in so that they can operate efficiently at high speeds, transferring information out to the conventional memory as required.

Chip An alternative name for an **integrated circuit (IC)**. So called because of the small piece of silicon inside the encapsulation (generally plastic or occasionally ceramic). Pins connect it with the outside world for the transmission of power and data.

Clock The source of the computer's timing signals and usually derived from a quartz-crystal controlled oscillator.

Cluster One or more sectors on a floppy or hard disk.

CMOS (Complementary Metal Oxide Semiconductor) A type of chip which requires very little power to operate. In AT systems, a CMOS memory chip, powered by a battery, is used to store information about the system. This is known as CMOS RAM.

Conventional memory The 640KB of memory directly accessible by all 80x86 or 80x88 microprocessors using DOS.

Co-processor A specialised processor designed to undertake special tasks in association with the main CPU. Common types are numeric co-processors and graphics co-processors.

CPU (Central Processing Unit) The main processor in a system. The computer's microprocessor chip. VLSI (Very Large Scale Integration) methods are used to include many functions into a small piece of silicon. The microprocessor contains resistors, capacitors, diodes and transistors, and the number of individual transistors in a microprocessor can range from 50,000 to over 1,000,000 in the most complex types.

Crash i. A fault which brings the system to a halt, usually caused by a program malfunction. The system will not restart unless it is re-booted. ii. In a hard disk system, the violent contact of the read/write head(s) with the magnetic media which will almost always cause damage to both.

Daisy chaining Connecting together two or more devices (such as hard disk drives) to exchange information with other devices through a common data cable.

Debug i. A utility program contained on the system disk, used for specialised purposes such as minor program amendments or tracing program execution. ii. To detect and cure problems in hardware or software.

Default The assumptions the computer makes about a process if no other parameters are given. Often default parameters are placed into a program or a controller so that it will execute specific actions without user intervention.

Device driver A memory resident program which controls a non-standard device such as a specialised adapter card.

Diagnostics A program used to analyse the operation of a computer system to detect the presence of a malfunction and indicate in what part of the machine it has occurred.

DIL (Dual In-Line package) and **DIP (Dual In-line Package)** Both refer to integrated circuits in which the external connecting pins are placed in rows on opposite sides of the plastic or ceramic encapsulated package.

DIP switch Usually a number of small switches grouped together in one package and about the same size as an integrated circuit. Always mounted on a circuit board.

Disc, disk or diskette i. A flexible plastic circle coated with a mixture of iron and other metal oxides which can be magnetised in such a way as to store data. The disk is enclosed within a protective plastic jacket and the amount of data which can be stored depends partly upon its size and the density with which the information can be stored. See floppy disk. ii. Part of a hard disk and sometimes referred to as a platter. The surfaces of the rigid aluminium disk are coated with a thin layer of magnetisable oxides. A series of such disks are enclosed in a sealed, dust-free environment to form part of the hard disk drive. In both types of disk, the data is recorded onto the disk by a combined read/write head, which moves across the surface on a series of tracks. On a floppy disk, the head touches the medium whereas in a hard disk, it travels a fraction above the surface.

DMA (Direct Memory Access) A process whereby data is moved directly between a device and the main memory without the direct intervention of the CPU. This frees the CPU for other tasks.

DOS (Disk Operating System) For PCs, this is a selection of programs stored on the DOS or system disk which enable the system to manage information provided by the user, and also to manage the various parts of the computer system. It is the first set of programs loaded into the computer before any other programs are started. In the context of this book, DOS refers specifically to the IBM and Microsoft disk operating systems for PCs. PC-DOS is the IBM version and MS-DOS is Microsoft's own version for non-IBM DOS machines. DOS can mean either of these types since they are very similar. (See also DR-DOS).

DRAM (Dynamic Random Access Memory) Computer memory in which information can only be retained if it is refreshed by appropriate signals at regular and short intervals

DR-DOS Digital Research's Disk Operating System. Different from but almost totally compatible with MS-DOS or PC-DOS.

EEPROM (Electrically Erasable and Programmable Read Only Memory) A type of read only device in which data is retained, but can be selectively erased by the use of a small voltage. Sometimes used for the configuration information in AT machines.

EISA (Extended Industry Standard Architecture) A standard for adapter cards devised by manufacturers to compete with IBM's proprietary MCA standard. It is not compatible with MCA.

Emulation A process whereby a device operates in a manner which imitates the activities or performance of another. Emulation is normally carried out by means of software, but occasionally, hardware emulation may be used. Typical examples of emulation can be found in CPUs where software enables a microprocessor to operate in a manner more characteristic of another type, or in certain types of hard disk drives where it is possible for the drive to operate with a number of cylinders, sectors and heads other than the number found in its physical construction.

EPROM (Erasable and Programmable Read Only Memory) Similar to an EEPROM but the data can only be erased by exposing it to short- wave Ultra Violet radiation for a time, and all data is erased by this process. New data is written by applying an appropriate high voltage (between 12.5 and 21 volts) in a programming sequence using an EPROM programmer.

ESDI (Enhanced Small Device Interface) A standard high speed interface for hard disks, which can transmit over 1MB of information per second.

Expanded memory Memory, accessible in 64KB blocks by a 'window' in the computer memory map, and managed according to the LIM standard. It is much slower in use than conventional or extended memory owing to the restriction of the 64KB window but is available for use on XT and AT machines.

Extended memory Memory additional to that used in the conventional memory of the computer and located at and above the 1MB boundary. Not available on XT machines.

Extended partition See Partition

FAT (File Allocation Table) An area on disk where records are kept of how much space is available on the disk and where it is located.

File Information, collected together and held on disk or RAM DISK, but not in the random access memory.

Firmware Instructions for the computer usually found in ROM chips; a pedantic way of differentiating such material from software found on magnetic disks or tapes.

Fixed disk - see Hard disk

Floppy disk A circular piece of plastic, coated with a magnetisable material which can be used to store data. It is contained within a protective sleeve and is intended as a removable storage device, in contrast to a hard disk. Nearly all floppy disks used with PCs have diameters of 5.25" or 3.5". The disk may be capable of storing data on one or both sides, and data may be recorded in either double or high density mode. See also High density (HD) disks.

Format (high-level format) A process whereby a pattern of tracks and sectors, file allocation tables (FAT) and directory tracks are laid down on one or both sides of a magnetic disk. The process also identifies and marks defective parts of the drive media if these are present. See also Low-level format.

Gigabyte (GB) 1000 Megabytes or 1,073,741,824 bytes.

Hard card A combined 3.5" hard disk and controller mounted together on a metal plate and connected to the computer by means of the controller card. Usually encountered in XT systems although modern types are available which will work in AT systems.

Hard disk A non-removable data storage device. Sometimes referred to as fixed disks.

Hardware The circuit boards, chips and other items which make up a computer system.

Head or **read/write head** A movable device inside a floppy or hard disk drive which reads, writes or erases data on the floppy disk or hard disk platter. There is one head per side of the disk or platter.

Hidden file A file which is not displayed by normal DOS listings of directories.

HD or **high density** Floppy disks which can store more data than standard density disks - 1.2 or 1.4MB as opposed to 360 or 720KB.

High-level format See Format

Hi-memory (high memory) The memory located between the 640KB DOS boundary and the 1MB boundary, above which extended memory is located.

IDC (Insulation Displacement Connector) A plug or socket which clamps onto a flat, multiple-wire cable. Electrical contact between the connector and the cable is achieved by an internal arrangement which pierces the insulation around each of the wires during the clamping process.

IDE (Integrated Drive Electronics) A type of hard disk and interface, sometimes known as the AT Interface.

Interface A means of matching the output of one device to the input of another, usually via an adapter or protocol.

Interleave The way in which sectors are marked on each disk track or cylinder so that the next sector to be read from or written to in sequence is ready underneath the read/write head when the system is ready to read it. The **interleave factor** is the ratio of the interleave to 1 - so an interleave of 3 has a interleave factor of 3:1.

ISA (Industry Standard Architecture) The 8- and 16-bit standard for adapter cards used by IBM and most PC clone manufacturers for XT- and AT-based designs, but now superseded for current IBM PS/2 designs by MCA, and, on 386 and 486 machines from some other manufacturers, by the EISA standard.

Jumper A small connector which can be placed over two pins on a circuit board, short circuiting them. It is like a simple switch and linking two pins is the same as connecting them electrically.

KHz (Kilohertz) A frequency measurement of thousands of cycles per second.

Kilobit 1024 (210 i.e 2 to the power of 10) bits.

Kilobyte 1024 bytes; referred to as K or KByte or KB.

Landing zone An unused track on the platters of a hard disk where the **heads** can be parked. This normally occurs when a parking program is run or an automatic parking facility is present. When power is shut off, the heads will come to rest on this track.

LIM The Lotus Intel Microsoft standard for managing expanded memory. LIM 4 is the most commonly occurring version.

Logical drive DOS refers to drives by a letter; for example, drive A is usually a floppy drive. In large hard disks, formatted under DOS 3.3 or earlier, the physical drive was split into several logical drives, usually C, D, E, and so on. See also Partitions.

Low-level format A process which prepares the platters of a hard disk for use by laying down a pattern of tracks and sectors, according to the interleave factor, with identifying information. It also marks defective sectors so that they cannot be used for data storage at a later date.

Master/slave A way of defining which, of two hard disks attached to the same controller card, is drive 1 (the Master) and which is drive 2 (the Slave).

MCA (MicroChannel Architecture) An IBM standard for adapter cards. It is not compatible with the earlier ISA standard or the EISA standard.

Megabyte 1,048,576 bytes, usually abbreviated as MByte or MB.

Memory Part of a computer system which stores information.

Memory resident program A program which, once run, remains in the computer memory for later use. Sometimes known as a TSR - Terminate and Stay Resident program.

MFM (Modified Frequency Modulation) A process by which data is encoded and written to a floppy disk; also used for some hard disks.

MHz (Megahertz) A frequency measurement of millions of cycles per second.

Microprocessor A small silicon chip which acts as a central processing unit of a computer by accepting coded instructions for execution.

Modem (MOdulator/DEModulator) A device which converts electrical signals from a computer into audio-frequencies for transmission over a telephone line, or vice versa.

Motherboard The main circuit board in a computer which contains the microprocessor, memory and expansion slots. Sometimes known as the system board or main board.

Mouse A pointing device, which transmits positional information to the computer when moved over a flat surface. This is converted by the computer into the movement of a character (such as an arrow) around the screen. Pressing one or other of the keys on the mouse may transmit information to the computer.

Multisync (Multiple synchronisation) This term is usually applied to video monitors which can sense the nature of signals which are produced by the video adapter card and are able to switch automatically to an appropriate type of display. In this way, a single monitor can display CGA, EGA, VGA, etc. as required.

Multitasking Running several programs, each in their own section of memory, at one time.

Nanosecond nS A very small time interval, 10^{-9} or one thousand millionth of a second.

Native mode The physical geometry of an AT Interface (IDE) drive (number of cylinders, read/write heads and sectors per track).

Native/translation mode This defines how an IDE drive is actually recognised by the host computer.

Network A system in which a number of independent computers are linked together so that they can share peripherals and software.

Non-volatile RAM A segment of memory which is powered by a battery so that it does not lose information when the main power supply is switched off.

Numeric co-processor A specialised co-processor for performing numerical tasks. In most PC systems, the numeric co-processor is one of the 80x87 types, and corresponds with the processor type. Thus an 80286 based machine needs an 80287 numeric co-processor.

Operating system A collection of programs which enable the computer to operate and which manage memory, data transfer and the acceptance of information from peripherals such as the keyboard or mouse.

OS/2 An IBM operating system for AT and PS/2 computers which enables multi-tasking and avoids the 640KB memory barrier (it can address more than 16MB). It also has the ability to allow a program to split itself into a number of tasks which can run concurrently, known as multi-threading. OS/2 will not work on XT computers.

Overlay A program segment which is only loaded into memory when required.

Parallel A method of data transmission where data is sent down a number of wires to a peripheral device (usually a printer) simultaneously.

Parity i. Communications - A simple error checking procedure where an extra bit of information is transmitted to the receiving device to indicate whether an even or odd number of bits have been sent. ii. Memory - Parity checked memory (8-bit) has an additional parity bit included which allows the system to check the integrity of each 8-bit byte of information in the system.

Parking The act of moving the heads on a hard disk to a safe 'parking' area, to avoid damaging the data area should the heads touch the surface of their platters during an intentional (or unintentional) move.

Partition A method of managing large hard disks by splitting them, potentially with the partitions holding different operating systems. Under DOS 3.3 and more recent versions, a hard disk may have two DOS partitions. The first, from which the system can be booted, is known as the primary partition and the second as the extended partition. This partition can contain as many logical disk volumes as it will hold, each up to 32MB in extent.

PCB Printed circuit board.

PD (Public Domain) software Having been donated by the author, such programs may be copied and used at no cost. The quality of PD software varies, but you may find some real gems such as older but still serviceable versions of commercial applications programs.

Peripheral Anything which is attached to the computer system, such as a printer, disk drive or keyboard.

Physical drive A single floppy or hard disk drive. See Partitions.

Pixel (PIcture ELement) A group of dots which make up part of a picture on screen.

Platter A single disk in a hard disk drive. There is usually more than one, and each surface is coated with a very thin metal film on which data is recorded.

Port i. A logical address where a microprocessor can communicate with a device attached to the computer. ii. A plug or socket which will allow a user to attach a peripheral to an adapter card.

Port address A specific logical address to which an adapter may be configured so that it communicates with a computer.

POST (Power On Self Test) An automatic process which starts when the computer is switched on. It will check many aspects of the computer and report on its findings.

Primary partition In DOS 3.3 or greater, the part of the hard disk which holds the operating system. See also Partitions.

Processor speed The quartz crystal-derived frequency at which the microprocessor handles data. The original IBM XT had a clock speed of 4.77MHz and modern AT 386s use much higher speeds (often in excess of 25MHz.).

Program A set of coded instructions which tell the computer the method by which it should handle data or complete a task.

PROM (Programmable Read Only Memory) A PROM holds data permanently once it has been programmed by a series of electrical pulses, unlike an EPROM where the data can be erased.

PS/2 A range of 8086, 286, 386 and i486 machines made by IBM, most of which have micro-channel architecture (MCA), rather than the older ISA type.

RAM disk A part of memory which is set up so that it can hold data just like a floppy disk. Because it is electronic, access times are very short, but the contents of a RAM disk are lost when power is switched off. Also referred to as a virtual disk.

Random access file A type of file in which items of data may be read or written in any order.

RAM (Random Access Memory) Any memory within the computer which can be accessed at any time by the microprocessor. RAM is divided into two types - DRAM and SRAM.

Read only A file which cannot be over-written until its attribute byte has been changed.

Read-write head Found on floppy and hard disk drives, this reads data from and writes data to tracks on the disk.

Refresh If it is to retain its contents for more than a few milliseconds, dram needs to have the relevant memory cells refreshed on a regular (cyclic) basis. The refresh process is not needed by SRAM.

Resolution Used to describe the size of the picture elements (pixels) used in graphics. The lower the resolution, the larger the pixel size.

RLL (Run Length Limited) A type of encoding used for hard disks which encodes binary data on the platters. More troublesome when used on cheap drives than the MFM type of encoding but can store more information for the same amount of disk space.

ROM (Read Only Memory) A permanently programmed memory chip whose contents cannot be altered. A typical example of this is the ROM BIOS which holds the computer test and start-up routines.

ROM BIOS (Read Only Memory Basic Input/Output System) The start-up sequence for the computer is stored in this memory chip (or chips, in the case of a PC-AT).

RS232 A widely used serial communications convention often used as a synonym for the serial port(s) of the computer.

RWC (Reduced Write Current) A technique used to decrease the intensity of the signal which is transferred to magnetic media.

Scanner An optical device consisting of an array of photo-electric sensors which is moved across a picture or text and, via an interface card and image-processing software, converts the output into a form which may be stored on disk and viewed and edited on screen.

SCSI (Small Computer Systems Interface - 'Scuzzy') A general purpose interface which operates at the system, rather than controller level (unlike ESDI, for example). Usually, but not exclusively, met in connection with hard disks.

Sector Part of one track of a floppy or hard disk which normally contains 512 bytes of data. Standard 360KB and 720KB floppy disks have 9 sectors per track and high density disks (1.2MB and 1.44B) have 18 sectors. MFM encoded hard disks usually employ 17 sectors and RLL encoded, between 25 and 34 sectors per track.

Sequential file One in which records are not of a fixed length but have a delimiter between each record and the next. The data can only be located as a result of a sequential search through the file.

Serial A method by which data is transmitted (or received) through a cable. The originating and receiving equipment must operate at the same speed (Baud rate), parity and with the same number of stop bits. The bits in each transmitted byte are sent in sequence with a start bit preceding them, and followed by a stop bit. Modems, some printers and mice use serial data transfer. In its simplest form a single wire and an earth return wire are needed, but most systems allow two-way communication with a wire devoted to transmission, another to reception of data and the earth return wire. More complex systems may be needed to signal whether the source or destination equipment is ready to send or receive data.

Servo data Coded markings written on one platter of a hard disk which has a Voice Coil Actuator. These enable the read/write heads to locate each track quickly and reliably.

Shareware Software which is available for the user to try out before purchasing a licence for regular use. Just as with PD software, the initial cost is supposed to be no more than the cost of providing and copying the disk, and associated postage and packing.

Shell The name given to software which acts as an interface between the operating system and the user.

SIMM (Single In-line Memory Module) A small circuit board on which are mounted a series of memory chips. The module plugs into a special socket on the motherboard. SIMMs are NOT physically interchangeable with SIPs, but, like them, allow for a much greater amount of memory to be installed on a computer motherboard if it is able to receive them. SIMMs do not have pins, but instead use contact strips on an edge connector.

SIP (Single In-line Package) A small circuit board on which a series of memory chips are mounted. The SIP connects to the computer by means of a series of pins which plug into a socket on the motherboard.

Software The instructions used to direct the computer to carry out a task. Software may be written in a low-level language such as Assembler (specific to the type of microprocessor) or a high level language such as BASIC or Pascal which is subsequently converted into a form which the computer can use directly.

SRAM (Static Random Access Memory) A type of memory chip in which data, once entered, remains until it is replaced by other data or the machine is switched off. The data does not require refreshing as is the case with DRAM. Static memory chips can operate more rapidly than dynamic types and are often used to provide small quantities of high speed cache memory in 386 and 486 computers.

ST-506 or ST-412 The original standard interfaces produced by Seagate and used by computer hard disks. Now being superseded by interfaces such as SCSI II or IDE.

Stepper motor A motor used in floppy and hard drives to move the heads across the surface of a disk by small or large amounts in a series of partial spindle rotations. The amount of rotation can be as little as 1/500 of a revolution.

Surge protector (Surge limiter) A device which limits the effects of fast, transient voltage 'spikes' on power supplies to the computer.

System crash This is usually caused by faulty software and causes the system to stop. It can only be re-started by pressing the Ctrl/Alt/Del keys, or in extreme circumstances by pressing the reset button. It does not cause any permanent damage to the system.

System files The two files in a DOS system (IBMDOS.COM and IBMBIO.COM for PC-DOS and IO.SYS and MSDOS.SYS for MS-DOS) are known as system files and are hidden from a normal directory listing. Another essential file is COMMAND.COM.

Tape streamer A device which attaches via an adapter and allows data to be backed up rapidly from or restored to a hard disk. The storage medium is usually a specially modified cassette tape which can hold between 20 and 60 megabytes, depending on the type of machine and magnetic coating.

TPI Tracks per inch 40 track 5.25" 360KB disks have 48 TPI, 80 track 1.2MB disks have 96 TPI while both types of 3.5" disk have 135 TPI. Hard disks can have track densities of 500 - 1000 TPI.

Track A concentric circle on a disk which holds data. Data is written onto the tracks sector by sector.

Trackball A pointing device, not unlike an upside-down mouse, where direct rotation of the ball with the fingers or palm produces a movement of a pointer on the screen.

Translation mode The mode (number of cylinders, sectors per track and number of read/write heads) in which an IDE (AT Interface) drive will power-up. A default mode is normally specified and can be over-ridden by the user, provided the total number of sectors required is less than the guaranteed number of sectors on the IDE drive.

TSR (Terminate and Stay Resident) A type of program, which, when loaded, remains in the computer's memory.

Unformatted capacity The theoretical number of bytes which could be fitted onto a disk before the pattern of tracks and sectors is applied during the formatting process. Formatting reduces this figure since sector boundaries have to be defined.

UPS (Uninterruptible Power Supply) A device operated by high-capacity rechargeable batteries which automatically comes into effect when the mains power supply fails. It steps up the battery voltage to about 220 volts AC and will allow operation of the system for a time ranging from a few minutes to an hour or so. The batteries are automatically re-charged when power is available.

Update The modification of data already in memory or in a file.

VDISK Virtual Disk This is synonymous with RAM disk.

Virtual memory A method of dealing with programs and data which are larger than the actual memory. The technique is to keep parts of the programs and data on disk and to swap them in and out of memory as required.

Virus A program that is accidentally copied onto a system with other software, which then acts in a destructive manner, destroying legitimate data or programs.

VLSI Very Large Scale Integration A technique whereby extremely large numbers of transistors, capacitors, diodes and resistors can be fabricated on a very small piece of silicon. Usually found in microprocessors and other large chips.

Voice coil actuator Found in hard disk drives, this device positions the read/write heads more rapidly than is the case with stepper motor actuators.

The necessary positioning information is written on a dedicated platter which enables the servo to operate with great speed and accuracy.

Volume A portion of a disk which is designated by a drive specifier letter. Later versions of DOS allow the partitioning of a single hard disk into several volumes, each of which is a logical drive.

Volume label A means of identifying a disk using a name of up to 11 characters.

Volume serial number A unique identifying number written to any disk after it has been formatted under DOS 5.0.

Winchester Historical name for a hard or fixed disk.

Write precompensation A technique designed to vary the timing of signals to the read/write heads to compensate for differences between the inner and outer tracks of a disk. Now usually met with only in connection with hard disks.

ZIP (Zigzag In-line Package) A type of memory chip in which the pins are found along one edge, and are arranged in two staggered rows. This enables more memory chips to be included in a given space than is the case with DIL packages.

Appendix

When buying equipment there are two major points which you should always bear in mind. Shop around for the best prices you can get and, where possible, pay by credit card as this gives you a certain amount of protection. Some firms make a small charge for the use of credit cards, particularly if their prices are keen.

Suppliers

The list of suppliers which follows is based jointly on my own experience and personal recommendations. **Neither the author nor publisher are responsible for any problems you may encounter and this list should be regarded just as an indication of firms which have, in the past, been satisfactory.** Firms whose names are preceded by an asterisk normally operate on a mail-order only basis.

D S Computers, Unit 206, Belgravia Workshops, 157 Marlborough Road, London N19 4NF (071) 281 5096

Matmos Ltd., Unit 11, Lindfield Enterprise Park, Lewes Road, Lindfield, West Sussex (0444) 482091/483830
(Motherboards, hard drives, monitors - new and second-user items)

Swift-Tech, Blackstone Road, Stukeley Mead Industrial Estate, Huntingdon, Cambs. PE18 6EF (0480) 433100

Netcom Systems, High Hall Farm, Nettlestead, Ipswich, Suffolk IP8 4QT (0473) 832679
(New and second-user items, also part-exchange)

*Y and J Enterprises, 106 High Street, Wootton Bassett, Wilts. SN4 7AU (0793) 850470
(New and second-user items of all sorts)

Memory Direct, 33 Grosvenor Road, Aldershot, Hants GU11 3DP (0252) 316060

Morgan Computer Co., 64-72 New Oxford Street, London W1 (071) 255 2155
(Manufacturer's overstocks and ends of ranges plus second-user items)

*Biological Software, 23 Darwin Close, Farnborough, Orpington, Kent BR6 7EP Tel. 0689 858510
(Memory chips - new and second user, also PD software compilations)

Thuna Technologies, 2432-A Palma Drive, Ventura, CA 93003, USA (0101-805) 650 2030 Fax: (0101-805) 650 2030
(AMI and Phoenix ROM BIOS upgrades)

DIY importation

A few adventurous individuals may think about importing their own boards and adapters from Taiwan, Japan or the USA. In general, I would advise against this for a number of reasons. Importation from the Far East can be tricky - you have to get the right address for the firm, establish the 'one-off' price of your requirements and if there is any surcharge on their normal price. If they **will** sell on a one-off basis your next step is to arrange for payment, probably in US dollars - and your board could take several weeks or months to reach you. If it goes wrong within 12 months, you will probably have great difficulty in getting a replacement under guarantee! Who will help you if you cannot understand the manual? In view of all these pitfalls my advice is to do some pretty thorough checking of U.K. prices first and unless you really cannot get the item you require at the right price, leave it to the experts!

If you decide to order from the USA, the prognosis is more hopeful. Most American firms take credit cards (remember that Access is known as Mastercard in many parts of the world). If you can, telephone the firm bearing in mind the different time zones, (better still, fax them) and establish if they will sell outside the USA, the current price of the items you want, the cost of air freight. If you don't have a credit card, Lloyds Bank sell American Express Cheques which are the cheapest way of sending a remittance to the USA.

You should have your order within a couple of weeks of the US firm receiving your instructions (if they require a written order use Air Mail). If you are still waiting for delivery after 3 - 4 weeks, phone or write, and see what the problem is. If you still have problems, and you have paid by credit card you can try talking to the credit card company about it. The odds are that you won't save a lot of money but if you fancy the challenge, go ahead, bearing in mind the problems that you may have if the board is faulty or if you meet with unexpected problems.

Second-hand equipment

If you are building a PC on a tight budget, the use of second-hand or superseded components is a possibility, provided you realise that such components may be nearing the end of their useful life and are more likely to fail than equivalent new components. Items of this sort are usually described as second-user (if they look a bit tatty) or 'as new' if they are presentable. Avoid anything described as 'needing attention' since there is a good chance that it isn't working and you probably won't be able to fix the faults.

There are four main sources:

» Sales columns in computer magazines

» Computer auctions or rallies

» Occasionally from computer shops

» From shops specialising in second-user items, e.g. Morgan

Prices should be considerably lower than that of a comparable item if new - certainly half price or less. If you buy at an auction or rally, you may get a bargain, but you need to keep your wits about you - if the description of the item in the catalogue turns out to be significantly more optimistic than the truth, complain very quickly in order to get your money back. In particular if an item is described as new it should be complete with the original packing, manuals etc..

Many magazines (in particular Micro Computer Mart) have adverts from individuals wanting to sell surplus gear. Some items are priced realistically, others may be over-priced, so be prepared to haggle a bit. Establish that the item will do what you want, and ask about a guarantee. Any seller worth considering should be prepared to give you your money back if the equipment turns out to be unsuitable, or if it goes wrong within a reasonable period - 14 days as a minimum. Try to obtain the manuals and cables where relevant. If the manuals aren't available you could offer a lower price but bear in mind that setting up a card without a manual is a hit and miss affair.

Some computer shops have stocks of equipment taken in part exchange or as a result of upgrades. You should be able to get a written guarantee for 90 days or so without too much fuss. Pay by credit card if you can since this can give you some valuable added protection.

No matter how or where you purchase your second-user items, if you find that any equipment is faulty, then you have a statutory right to receive your money back. This is because the transaction is covered by the 'Sale of Goods' Act and the equipment must be fit for the purpose for which it was intended. It will not cover you if the fault is due to something which you have done by accident.

All items should be examined very carefully and tested as soon as possible after purchase. A bit of dust isn't uncommon, but be a bit careful of any which are scratched or dented - they may have been thrown into a junk box at some time - and this isn't good news for floppy or hard disk drives.

My advice is as follows:

Keyboards Look out particularly for non-standard key layouts and connectors - do the keys stick, and are any key tops missing?

Monitors If possible see these working before you buy. Check carefully that the monitor which you have selected is what you want - there is no point in looking for a VGA colour monitor and buying a CGA by mistake. Avoid monitors with screen burns (usually caused by the continuous display of information at high levels of brilliance) unless you can live with the blemishes. Other points to check are the stability and quality of the display - is the picture properly focused all over, properly centred and of uniform brightness - and that it comes with the appropriate video and power cables.

Motherboards These are usually available for XT and AT 286 machines because of upgrading. They should be quite reliable but do check that the price includes a full set of memory. The on-board battery should be checked with a voltmeter and if low a replacement will be needed. Rechargeable types (usually soldered-in) should have this test repeated when they have been left on charge for a few hours. You must have the instruction manual since without one, it is often difficult to work out what all the links and switches do, and what sort of memory chips are required.

Hard disks and Hard cards These are potentially the most troublesome, particularly as they have a more limited lifetime than other parts of a system. Try to format and verify any such disk and, if possible, use a utility to scan for defects. A good supplier should guarantee a hard disk for at least 90 days. Keep well clear of disks with lots of defects marked on the defect list, or which have several defects on early tracks and avoid those with noisy drive motors. Older, full height drives should be cheaper than their more modern half height equivalents, but if your box can accommodate one, they can be excellent value. As a general rule, second user hard disks should be available at about £2 - £3 per megabyte.

Floppy disk drives Be very wary of drives which will only read disks which have been formatted in them. This fault indicates a bad case of head misalignment and it isn't worth bothering with them. Check that drives are of the advertised capacity and size - early drives for IBM XTs were full height while more modern drives are half height. More recent 3.5" drives are often referred to as slimline, to distinguish them from the earlier half-height types. One or two surplus shops still sell single-sided 3.5" drives (with a maximum capacity of 360KB). Avoid these like the plague!

Cases and power supplies The case is fairly straightforward - either your motherboard will fit or it won't. Make sure that it has the capacity for all the drives you want to use, and that it has all the necessary hardware, including screws and blanking plates. After hard disks, power supplies are potentially the most troublesome components to buy second-hand. I always check them by attaching a 50 watt 1 ohm resistor across the 5 volt supply and measure all the voltages it is supposed to produce. The resistor is necessary (and gets very hot) since some power supplies will not start working until some sort of electrical load has been attached. All voltages should be within 5% either side of the stated voltage. The load resistor must be attached to the 5 volt supply and it should draw at least 2 or 3 amps. from the power supply - the exact value isn't critical. A 2 ohm resistor would do just as well, provided it has a rating of at least 25 watts.

Controller cards A manual of some sort is very important if there are any links or switches which can be set. Adapter cards are quite easily damaged by static electricity and they should be supplied in an anti-static bag. Reject any which look dirty.

Memory chips Second user chips (that is ones that have been pulled out of their original sockets) are usually available for about 40 - 50% of the prices of new chips of the same type and speed. Checking them before installation is difficult but at least ensure that they are exactly the capacity and access speed required. A few unscrupulous firms sell chips described as 'pulls' which, on examination, are sometimes found to have been de-soldered from older boards. The reliability of such chips may have been reduced as a consequence of the de-soldering process and they can also cause problems with sockets since surface roughness will make it difficult to extract them if it proves necessary at a later date.

Superseded software Software is frequently offered for sale at low prices, generally because it has been superseded by a later release. Older versions of well-established programs may lack some of the features of newer versions but they can still be useful. Copies which are still in the original shrink wrapping are fine, but be cautious when considering used and registered versions, since the registration may not be transferable. Insist on the original distribution disks and manuals, since the sale of copies is illegal.

Software on second-hand hard disks Occasionally, you may come across a hard disk which is offered for sale and contains software. In such circumstances, I would recommend caution since you have not purchased the original programs, merely the medium on which copies have been placed. You risk breaking the law if you use non-PD or Shareware programs in this way so the disk should be reformatted, preferably using a low-level format program. Another good reason for reformatting is to eradicate any computer virus that might have infected existing programs. The risk of infection may be small, but it is still worth guarding against.

Useful free or cheap software

If you have a tight budget for software it is well worth investigating what is available as shareware or public domain (PD) software. The idea behind the distribution of these two types of software is that, apart from covering legitimate copying and postal expenses, the agent should not make a profit. PD software is free of charge for anybody to use and distribute while in the case of shareware you try out the program before you pay a registration fee to the author and there is a moral obligation to do this if you decide to continue using the it. In other words, shareware programs are not free - but you try them before you buy. There is an enormous amount of this software about - and many of the programs are as good as, their high-priced commercial counterparts. In particular, if you are just starting out in computing, then it is worth knowing that there are PD or shareware versions of all the applications you are likely to want. The following is just a small selection:

Tutorial - TUTOR.COM, PC-Tutor, PC-Prompt

Word Processors Galaxy, PC-Write or PC-Type II

Databases PC-File Plus, Wampum, PC-File dB

Spreadsheets PC-Calc Plus, As-Easy-As

Languages P-Basic, and various versions of 'C', Prolog and Pascal are available, often with tutorial disks.

A number of commercial shareware retailers advertise in computer magazines but the following organisations offer lower rates to members:

PC Independent Users' Group, 87 High Street, Tonbridge, Kent TN9 1RX

PC-Star, PO Box 164, Cardiff CF5 4SF

The Shareware Library, PO Box 174, Battle, East Sussex TN33 9AQ

If you're feeling adventurous you can order such software direct from the USA using a credit card and often obtain later versions of software than are available in the U.K.

When it comes to utilities there is an abundance of PD and shareware programs such that it can be difficult to know which programs to choose. Biological Software (23 Darwin Close, Farnborough, Orpington, Kent BR6 7EP) can provide you with a compilation of many of the useful shareware and PD programs on eight 5.25" or four 3.5" disks which will help you test your system, and organise your hard disk.

Sources of information

Instruction manuals can be exceedingly frustrating and if you want additional information, your best chance is to contact the firm from whom you purchased the equipment. The chances are that they will have more experience, or have additional information from the manufacturer. Some firms are better at this than others and the best way is to be a little persistent until you find the technical information that you need.

For more general help, you can do a lot worse than join one of the many computer clubs. These are sometimes advertised locally or in computing magazines and membership includes people with a wide range of professional and hobby interests in all aspects of computing.

The IBM PC User Group (PO Box 360, Harrow, Middx. HA1 4LQ (081) 863 1191) is nationally-based and offers a bi-monthly magazine, bulletin board system for members with a modem and a comprehensive disk library. Their attitude is quite commercial with lots of conferences and meetings on various aspects of computing. Membership is reasonably priced and there are local meetings and special interest groups. A couple of pages of each issue of its magazine is devoted to answering readers' problems (computing ones, I hasten to add!).

The PC Independent User Group (87 High Street, Tonbridge, Kent TN9 1RX (0732) 771512) is also nationally-based, produces a bi-monthly magazine, has a bulletin board and an equally extensive disk library. They are significantly cheaper than the IBM PC User Group and more the sort of place where the average computer user would feel at home. There are also a number of local groups. The major benefit is a telephone Helpline and many pages of helpful advice, both from PCIUG staff and other members in the bi-monthly magazine. All members get a copy of the twice-yearly disk catalogue and discounts on the supply costs of Public Domain and Shareware. Both organisations offer trial membership - try them and decide which one suits you.

Books are often useful and for a wide selection of computer titles and first rate impartial advice contact: Just Computer Books, 111 Court Road, Malvern, WR14 3EF Tel/Fax: (0684) 568095

Some computer magazines have a section in which readers' queries are answered, either by magazine staff or by other readers in subsequent issues. Among these are Computer Shopper, PC Plus, PC Today, PC Answers, Practical PC and What Personal Computer. Another good reason for consulting magazines is for the adverts for goods and services. Micro Computer Mart is excellent value if you are looking for new or second-user equipment and it carries a good range of commercial as well as private advertisements. The best advice I can give is to have a look through copies of these publications in your local newsagent and decide which ones suit you best.

Other books of interest

The 386/486 PC: A Power User's Guide (2nd Ed) by Harry Fairhead

If *Inside the Grey Box* has encouraged you to consider a machine based on the 80386/486 then you will find information specific to computers based on these processors in Harry Fairhead's comprehensive guide. This book will answer any remaining questions you may have about extended and expanded memory, LIM, hard disk seek rate, wait states, caching, memory interleave, shadow RAM and other highly technical topics and provides advice about configuring and optimising your system. The revised and expanded second edition also covers Windows 3.1 and OS/2 Version 2. **ISBN 1-871962-22-6**

MS-DOS 5: A Power User's Guide by Harry Fairhead

MS-DOS 5 is the ideal operating system for anybody building or upgrading a PC partly because you can easily purchase it but more importantly because it offers many advantages over earlier versions in terms of its memory management facilities and enhanced commands. The early part of the book concentrates on the basics of commands, files and directories. There follows a section devoted to batch files, explaining their technicalities and what they can be used for. The final chapters cover configuration, customisation and optimisation. **ISBN 1-871962-13-7**

QBasic: The Language of MS-DOS by Mike James

QBasic is a complete, fully structured, and modern version of BASIC that comes free with every copy of MS-DOS 5. If you still think of BASIC as line numbers, games, and GOTO then you might overlook the significance of QBasic. It can be used to create useful utilities or complete systems. In short, it is a natural companion to MS-DOS 5 and the range of applications that run under it. This book will help you learn QBasic and it also makes up for the lack of a QBasic manual in MS-DOS 5. **ISBN 1-871962-20-X**

Foundations of Programming by Mike James

This book could radically change the way that you think about programming. It presents a language independent view of what programming is all about and how best we should go about it. It is packed with new ideas and new ways of looking at old ideas. If you are a practising programmer then this book will change your style. If you are a programming student then it will help you to understand what your lecturers are, or should be, teaching you. If you teach programming then it will help you raise your sights from the details of a particular language or method to a broader view of the principles and philosophy. **ISBN 1-871962-04-8**

For more information on any of these titles or a catalogue contact:
I/O Press, FREEPOST, Leyburn, North Yorkshire DL8 5BR
Tel: (0969) 24402 Fax: (0969) 24375

Index